The author was born in Cyprus in 1944 to a happy but somewhat-unconventional family. John came to England in 1948 and was educated in London. He has been very happily married to Barbara since 1969, having run a business with his wife. John has three children, two boys and one girl, and a football team of grandchildren.

In loving memory of my father, Enver Emin, who played a large part in my life by showing me, by his experiences, what I should not do. For that I am forever grateful.

John Emin

MEAT ON A STICK

AUSTIN MACAULEY PUBLISHERS™

LONDON • CAMBRIDGE • NEW YORK • SHARJAH

A CIP catalogue record for this title is available from the British Library.

ISBN 9781788488013 (Paperback)
ISBN 9781528908115 (Hardback)
ISBN 9781528958806 (ePub e-book)

www.austinmacauley.com

First Published (2019)
Austin Macauley Publishers Ltd
25 Canada Square
Canary Wharf
London
E14 5LQ

I wish to acknowledge the help I had from Matt Tulloch, who helped put the book together. I would also wish to acknowledge the considerable help my wife, Barbara, gave over the months it took to write this book.

Contents

Prologue
Revelation
May 2010

I once asked Mandy, my trusted secretary, whether she knew who her people were and where they came from. Without hesitation, she began to reel off the story of her family. She was the second of two daughters, she said. Her mother worked at the local town hall offices where her mother, in turn, had worked before her, while her father chose the butchering profession rather than following his father who was a docker at Surrey Docks here in London. Her grandfather and several generations before him were all London dockers, Mandy told me, and they had jobs for life, all of them being strong union men who could flex their muscles and keep their employers, if not honest, then at least a close approximation of it. That was until they pushed their luck and went on strike so much that they all eventually lost their jobs as the docks were forced to close down and they had to go elsewhere.

Mandy had done so well, I was impressed. She knew exactly who she was and where she came from. I had thought that I could do that too, but with a little more consideration, I became aware that there were great gaps and riddles in our family history of which I was alarmingly ignorant.

Upon recently becoming the head of the Emin family, on account of my own father's passing, some of these secrets have begun to be relayed to me by those within the family who each treasure a little piece of the puzzle. And my word, what a puzzle it is turning out to be, with religion, betrayal and huge wealth all tangled up together. I confess that I am still getting my own head around it all, so the prospect of explaining everything to you is somewhat daunting. Nevertheless, I shall do my best and perhaps together we will be able to make some sense of the events contained in this book, and furthermore explore through them the fragile notion of who we are, as human beings, and where we have come from.

The true beginnings of my foray into the Emin family history began in the unlikely surroundings of a steam room at the local baths in Lewisham, around 1990 if I remember accurately. I had strained my back at work and my wife Barbara suggested that I went along to the baths to see if the water in its various forms could ease the problem.

There were three saunas there, each with a different level of heat, a steam room and just outside of that a cold plunge pool to take the edge off. It was a pleasant enough arrangement, and after a short time I found myself relaxed and enjoying the amenities, blissfully unaware that my resting mind was about to become busier than it had been in quite some time.

It was whilst in the steam room that I noticed an old man sitting on the bench opposite, watching me with a distinct curiosity in his demeanour. I shook my head clear and thought nothing more about it until all of a sudden the man found his voice.

"Tell me," he said casually, "how is your father?"

"Fine," I replied, covering my surprise, "he's fine." I squinted a little at the man, trying to place him. "Do I know you?" I asked finally, giving up on the task.

"Of course you do," he replied, almost admonishingly.

Still puzzled, I got up and went over to sit next to this strange man who was, clearly, in the most charitable sense possible, nearing the end of his time on this Earth. I tried to imagine him younger, without the wrinkles, but after a moment it was his eyes that gave him away.

"Uncle Devrish?" I asked, "Is that you?"

"I knew you knew who I was!" Devrish smiled. "I knew who you were at once, even though I haven't seen you in… must be going on thirty years now."

The steam was getting to me by now, so I suggested that we adjourn to one of the cooler sauna rooms so that we might talk more comfortably.

The Dervish Hassan family, from which Devrish came, his mother being my great aunt share a history with the Emins.

Here in England, we're used to being able to trace our families back many generations by means of the simple device that is the surname. Muslim families are not nearly so simple, even now I question the given name of my great, great, grandfather, though Abdullah seems to have been prominent in our family. The children of old Muslim families might be given their father's chosen name, sometimes their grandfather's too, there are family names and in some countries tribal names and all kinds of combinations, and it gets, frankly, rather complicated. Sufficed to say that the Hassan's and Emins are first cousins, which made Devrish and my father first cousins too. I had heard some of the stories from when the two of them were growing up together, we all knew within the family that Devrish helped curb some of my father's more outrageous impulses, and on several occasions had reason to give Dad's ears a good boxing. The last time that had happened, followed Dad trying to pull a fast one in regard to a large property deal that he and Devrish were partners in. The two of them had some forty houses between them, all bought and paid for and profitable. It was a good arrangement. Unfortunately, nothing is quite so simple in matters where my father was involved with large sums of cash, as I discovered myself in the sixties when he pulled a similar thing with me.

In Devrish and Dad's case, the fall-out from their disagreement over this business arrangement way back in the fifties was such that they barely spoke again after that. My auntie tried to bring them together once in a while, but Devrish always resisted her overtures. The old man looked me in the eye now, in the comfortable heat of the sauna, and seemed to be at great pains to emphasise that this lengthy estrangement was not due to the holding of a grudge over money, or pride, or any such thing. Blood is thicker than water, he said, and most problems, no matter how acrimonious, can be resolved over time. No, it seemed that there was something else my dad wanted from Devrish. Something important that his cousin didn't want to give up. At least that seemed to be the gist of what he was trying to tell me.

To be honest, I thought that the old man was just rambling. He said a lot of things that I cannot fully recall just now, about how it would all become clear in time, about how he had written a book that would surprise us all regarding the family and the things that he himself had seen and done. He talked of a huge house with high walls, dishing out pots of food to the poor, and something about a black horse.

I was getting tired by now, and sitting on the wooden benches was beginning to do my back more harm than good. Devrish's strange, disjointed story seemed to me to be a fiction conjured by the tired mind of an old man who fancied leaving a few good tales around for after he was gone. But now, having become the head of the family and spoken to several relatives about some of the details Devrish was talking about, it is clear to me that he had been telling the truth, trying to give me little clues. Maybe he meant for me to take the information back to my father, I don't know. What I do know, what I've managed to piece together now from various sources, is that Devrish was sitting on a family secret of epic proportions.

As a young man, Devrish Hassan served in the British Army in World War Two, during which he was felled by shrapnel somewhere in Italy and was captured. But Devrish escaped and rejoined the fight, and helped beat back the enemy all the way into Egypt. When the war was over, he was free to return home to Cyprus, but for whatever reason, he decided to remain in Africa and seek out the family he had never known, in the place where his uncle, my grandfather had told him they might be found.

Devrish travelled a long way until eventually, through word of mouth, he was lead to a big house with high walls and huge gates guarded by burly security men. He approached the gates and stated his business, in broken Arabic, to the guards, who opened up and allowed him into the grounds.

It was an old house, well used and frequently repaired by the looks of it. In fact even as Devrish made his way inside there were painters refreshing the great white walls of the compound. Devrish had stated his business at the gate, which was understood to be of the greatest importance, and a man had appeared to escort him towards the main entrance to the house. He was asked to wait a few paces from the steps leading up to the open door, and after a few moments, a man appeared on the threshold. He looked intently at Devrish for several seconds before disappearing back inside without a word.

Devrish thought this a little odd, but he said nothing and waited patiently for the situation to resolve itself. There were some horses nearby, tied to a long post and rail near the entrance to the house. One, in particular, a black horse with fierce eyes, drew his attention. He wandered over to greet the magnificent animal, but it reared up and became agitated. Remaining perfectly calm, Devrish reached out to stroke the stallion's neck, speaking in his most soothing voice until the animal was peaceful and content, whereupon he adjusted the bridle that looked a little tight, before returning to wait at the foot of the steps. Only now there was yet another man standing there in the doorway, an elderly man this time, watching him with a mixture of curiosity and suspicion.

"What do you want?" asked the man pointedly.

"Only to inquire about my family," replied Devrish simply.

"Ah," said the man thoughtfully, "well that's a problem now, isn't it?" He read the puzzled expression on Devrish's face and continued, "Well, just look at yourself. The family is black, you are not, how do you account for that?"

Devrish replied simply that he was from Cyprus, and that his grandmother and father were white.

"Hmm," mused the man, who turned out to be a clerk of sorts, "who was your grandfather?"

"Abdullah Mehmet," replied Devrish. The clerk hesitated, one eyebrow raised. Clearly, this was not an answer he had been expecting.

"What traits then do you believe that you possess, that would mark you out as a member of this family?" asked the man.

Devrish thought for a moment. Nobody had ever asked him such a question before, as to want to know what sort of character he was, so he had to think on his feet.

"I have a strong will," replied Devrish, "I am tenacious. I always try to do well." The man said nothing and gave nothing away, so Devrish pressed on, "People call me intelligent and honest, and a man of my word. I have proved myself in the battle against the Germans. I am a respectable man, and when I return to Cyprus now that the war is over I intend to start my own business."

"Anything else?" asked the clerk, flatly.

"Horses," said Devrish. "They are my passion and have been for as long as I can remember, I understand them and them, me. I have a horse of my own, who must be missing me as I have been away fighting the war for so long."

Then the clerk did a strange thing. He repeated what Devrish had just said, in a voice loud enough to echo off the tall walls of the compound so that everyone within earshot would be clear as to what kind of man Devrish had claimed to be. Then he looked at Devrish with a cold eye, nodded towards the black stallion, and challenged him to prove his so-called love of horses.

"Be warned," said the clerk, "no one had ever been able to ride Ahmet. He has the most terrible temperament."

By now several people who had been working in and around the yard had stopped what they were doing and formed a small crowd to watch what was going on. The clerk asked a boy nearby to run and fetch a saddle so that Devrish could attempt to ride the horse.

"You people from Cyprus are soft," said the clerk harshly, "so I will give you a soft seat on Ahmet. May God be with you."

Well, Devrish didn't wait for the saddle. He strode right up to the horse whose bridle he had adjusted minutes earlier and began speaking to it softly so that only the animal could hear. He reached out and rubbed Ahmet's nose, and in a flash, he was up and on the stallion's back. It reared up and made quite a racket, but Devrish held on and leant forward to rub the horse's neck until it was calm again, whereupon the two of them trotted off around the compound to the astonishment of the onlookers. As he gained confidence, Devrish encouraged the horse more and more, until it was fair galloping around the large space with him astride it, his arms held out like a bird, beaming triumphantly.

As Ahmet slowed back down to a walk, Devrish spotted another old man standing in the doorway of the house watching him and guessed that this must be a member of the family. Spurred on by the cheers of the crowd, Devrish resolved to give the man a little encore, and he kicked his heels sharply, sending Ahmet the stallion shooting off around the grounds again like a great black bullet.

Glancing across to gauge the new figure's reaction, Devrish noticed that the old man has raised his arm and was gesturing for him to stop, so he pulled up near the post at the front of the house, tied up the horse, and made his way up the steps until he was face to face with the stranger, who he now noticed had tears in his kindly eyes. He took a long, hard look at Devrish, so long that he might have been searching for his very soul, before finally finding his voice.

"Go wash and refresh yourself," said the man. "This boy will look after you," he said, gesturing to the same boy who had been sent to fetch a saddle, "I will send refreshment for you, and see you again later."

Devrish was shown in through the front door, then right along a corridor and through a green door, beyond which was a large, comfortable bed and some fabulous furniture, silk carpets and tapestries, and intricate Ishnik pottery with the most delicate patterns, treasured artefacts and stunning examples of the craftsmanship of the Turks. Off of the bedroom was a beautifully tiled blue and white bathroom, the most interesting feature of which was that it contained modern taps and a European-style toilet, plumbing and everything, which was very unusual in this part of the world and surely a sign that this was the house of a very rich man.

Devrish washed up, and then took a nap as many people do out there in the middle of the day until the sun's strength has waned a little. Then at about four o'clock, there came a sharp knock at the door. It was the boy who had shown him around earlier, whose name was shared with the stallion Ahmet.

"You will be more comfortable in this," said the boy in broken English, handing Devrish a traditional Arab robe. Devrish did his best to wear the unfamiliar outfit correctly, but he couldn't wrap the turban properly and as much as he played with it still it looked a little ridiculous next to those of the clerks.

"Oh well," muttered Devrish, taking one last glance in the mirror, "when in Rome…" He made to follow the boy out of the room but then checked himself at the last moment and returned to the bed to retrieve his army trousers. He just didn't feel right without them under the robe.

15

The boy Ahmet had instructions to show Devrish the whole compound, then the land and lastly the house, so they set off on what turned out to be a thorough tour. The outer buildings within the courtyard were full of goods, ranging from tinned foods to sacks of salt and sugar, and even furniture, carpets and so forth. He guessed how the family must make their money, surely they were wholesalers of some sort.

Then there were garages housing several large, luxury cars, alongside which the stables at the far end of the complex were chock full of the most beautiful horses he had ever seen, bred for racing he was told and they must have been successful he thought, judging by the look of them. Devrish spotted the stallion Ahmet, being tended to by a couple of nervous-looking servants who were struggling to put a saddle on him, and he wandered over to help them out.

"As you are the only one to have ridden him safely," said the boy, "you have the honour to ride him again while I show you the rest of the grounds. But wait," he interrupted as Devrish made to mount the horse again, "come with me first."

Devrish followed the boy the entire length of the courtyard towards the house. There was one last building situated to the right of the steps joined to the main structure, more of a fascia really protruding from the main house. Devrish took it in curiously, wondering what might be inside such a structure that was locked with two large and very visible padlocks.

"No one goes in there," said the boy simply. For a moment Devrish wondered why he had been brought to see it if no one was to enter, but he realised that it had been done on purpose, a little theatre for their unusual guest. At any rate, the point was made, so the two of them returned to where the horses were tied up and headed out through the huge open doors of the compound.

There were great fields being tended by yet more servants, and a pump house with a slow diesel engine driving a huge flywheel, which powered the pump that carried water up from the Nile into a huge concrete tank and from there sent it off along a series of pipes in all directions. Devrish didn't tell me what was being grown, but it was clearly food and lots of it. Out in the fields, there were also many more horses grazing, along with cows, sheep and goats. The family certainly seemed to have their fingers in a fair few pies, Devrish thought.

Finally, the boy led Devrish back towards the house. Just outside the walls, they came upon a small building with servants buzzing busily around. There was a huge metal pot perched atop a fire, so big it must have held at least ten gallons, with beans and other ingredients being constantly added to what looked like a vast stew.

"What's going on here?" asked Devrish.

"Preparations are being made for tonight's meal," replied the boy. "We feed the poor every day with fresh bread and nourishing food. Once a day, every day." He noted the slight surprise on Devrish's face and finished simply, "It is only right."

Inside the courtyard in front of the house, there was quite a feast now getting underway. A huge mangal was blazing away, like a barbecue as we would think of it only much larger. This one had a whole sheep above it, rotating slowly on a large spit. Devrish noted fruit of all kinds on display and soft drinks in large buckets full of ice, and there were men playing traditional music nearby. The old man whom Devrish had met earlier sat outside in a high armchair, at the head of a long table, with two women who appeared to be tending to his every need, and a group of people gathered around him. Devrish approached the group, but it seemed that they were in the midst of an important discussion and with a polite smile he was simply waved away to go and explore the house, as that was the only place he had yet to be shown.

Well, the house itself was even more astonishing than his tour around the grounds had been. A veritable Aladdin's cave of priceless artefacts spread over four floors with, Devrish noted, a substantial Turkish influence rather than Egyptian as one might expect. It must have taken someone with a huge passion to collect so many beautiful things, he thought.

"They were all left by Emin," said Ahmet simply off of Devrish's questioning look.

At one point, Devrish and his guide came upon a huge oil painting depicting a bloody battle. The brass plaque underneath described it as showing a man named Mohammet Ahmed brandishing a sword at the vanquished General Gordon. A carpet of corpses littered the scene, and a clearly bloodied and trampled British flag lay on the ground. In front of the painting, in a glass case, there was a beautiful sword and a folded British flag, old and stained, and tattered. It didn't take a genius to put two and two together and surmise that these were probably the artefacts pictured in the painting itself, but the boy would not answer yes or no, preferring to tease Devrish with the possibility.

Devrish wondered, as they pressed on with the tour, who this Mohammet Ahmed had been. Was he a relative? And did he really have some involvement in the bloodbath surrounding the last stand of General Gordon? These were uncomfortable questions for him, especially as he was wearing the King's uniform at the time, albeit only the trousers under his Arab robes.

Up on the large, flat roof, several great chimney type air vents sprouted up taller than a man, tiled in beautiful colours. The parapet was a safe height so that one couldn't accidentally fall, and beyond it the fields stretched away to the winding river Nile, the sun glinting off of it as it hung low in the sky.

Returning to the party finally, Devrish was waved over to join the old man and his companions at the head of the table. "I am Abdullah Mehmet," began the man in perfect English. "We have arranged this feast in your honour and everything is ready to begin. But first I must say that you have presented me with quite a problem."

Devrish didn't understand what the old man meant, so he kept quiet and just listened respectfully.

"I nearly sent you away," Abdullah went on, "and I hope that you and God will forgive me. It is well known around these parts that Suleiman, the son of Abdullah Mehmet Emin, was taken as a boy. We have had one visitor before who dared to claim that he was a direct descendant, but he turned out to be nothing but a liar and we had to teach him a lesson in honesty. He crawled away, in the end, to heal up."

Devrish shifted uncomfortably in his seat.

"As for you," said Abdullah, "you are not black. Also, you have failed to give your grandfather's true name and you didn't give the families most important trait that was asked of you. Can you blame me for being cautious? We are no fools here." He touched his nose knowingly.

"I believe everything you say," replied Devrish carefully. "But why, that being so, did you decide that I was who I said I was? Why am I not crawling away right now to lick my own wounds?"

"That's easy," said Abdullah, cracking a broad smile. "There were two remarkable things that occurred on your arrival. Firstly, the horse. Nobody else could ride that horse the way I saw you ride him earlier, with such absolute confidence, with total disregard for your safety. 'The Angry One', we call him, as he throws every man who tries to tame him, every last one. He has a strong sense of freedom, as you see, and we do not beat our animals here in order to subdue them. That is in the hands of God."

"The point is," Abdullah finished, "no one other than Suleiman himself at seventeen could have done what I watched you do with my own eyes. He was one of the best horsemen there has ever been, as everyone knows. He could talk to the animals, they say and had the skill to calm even the wildest beast. I saw you do that today with Ahmet. You have the spirit of Suleiman, your grandfather within you, right down to the way he used to ride around the grounds with his arms outstretched like a bird, just as you did. There is no doubt in my mind that Suleiman's blood flows in your veins."

Devrish didn't speak for a moment, his mind reeling from what he was being told. Finally, he asked, "What happened to Suleiman that last day here, as all he would say was he was following God's will?" Devrish explained that his grandfather was reluctant to talk of his family and took his demise as a rebuke from God himself, a punishment that he was willing to endure. But no one ever understood what it all meant. "He was always known as Abdullah, never as Suleiman"

"Ah," replied Abdullah sadly, "his father searched high and low when the boy did not return home, but all he ever found was the horse that Suleiman and his little sister had been riding on the day they disappeared. It was clear to everyone that they must have been taken by Egyptian slave traders. Mehmet Emin tracked down several of the traders, threatened and bribed and did everything in his power to find his lost son, without letting on the boy's true identity of course for fear he and his sister would be killed on the spot, but it was to no avail."

Devrish did some quick calculations in his head even as he tried to absorb all of this information. Given the timeline of events that he was aware of, he guessed the man sitting across from him now was not that old. It occurred to Devrish that Abdullah may well be the eldest son of Suleiman's brother, the second son of Mehmet Emin.

Now Devrish saw clearly the problem of which Abdullah had spoken earlier. If he, Devrish, was indeed as everyone seemed to think now the descendant of the lost boy Suleiman, he would be the rightful heir to his father's inheritance according to strict Muslim law. The eldest brother took everything, always, and a son of Suleiman, eldest son of Mehmet Emin, would be by rights the head of the family.

As Devrish considered these possibilities, two burly young men around the same age as him arrived in the courtyard in an open-backed lorry. Clearly, they had been running an errand of some kind when they had been informed of their visitor's presence and come as speedily as they could. The sight of a party in full swing and a freshly slaughtered sheep roasting over the mangal was confirmation to these boys that their birthright was in jeopardy, and they were not best pleased. It was left to their father Abdullah to calm them with a stern look and a firm word, which he did, before turning his attention back to Devrish.

"And now I have a few questions for you," said Abdullah. "Please tell me, if you can, why Suleiman never returned here to claim what was rightfully his?"

"Well," replied Devrish, "I will tell you what I know. My grandfather was only released from servitude when he was fifty years old. He was married with young children and not in the best of health, and he realised by that time that his own father was most likely dead. I think he decided that it must be God's will that he shouldn't return home, and chose instead to live out his life in Cyprus, keeping the name Abdullah and never revealing even to his children his true identity."

"Still," Devrish went on as the crowd of people now listening to the story looked on fascinated, "there were several things that marked him out as special. When in the company of sophisticated people he was able to speak Arabic, Turkish and English eloquently. He read poetry and was regarded as an absolute treasure by his master. He was bright and articulate, a voracious reader who consumed as much knowledge as he could get his hands on and generally regarded by all who knew him as a remarkable man. When his master finally passed away, Suleiman was granted his freedom."

"By the time of my grandfather's death," finished Devrish, "he had six children, five boys and one girl. I am the only son of that one girl."

By now the atmosphere around the table was pure electricity. While the party carried on all around them, with speeches being given to toast the return of the lost one and everyone giving thanks to Allah for this blessed day, the old man Abdullah held serious conversations with his sons and most trusted advisors as to what to do about the dilemma that had arisen. The Imam from the local mosque was sent for, but it was late and that might take some time.

Finally, the Imam arrived with another important-looking man, who may have been a clerk, Devrish wasn't sure. They went inside the house, along with Devrish, Abdullah and his eldest son, to discuss this most serious business away from the others. Abdullah and the Imam spoke to each other in Arabic for a while, before Abdullah finally turned to Devrish and asked if he understood everything that was being said. Devrish replied honestly that he had not understood very much, Arabic not being his native tongue.

"Forgive us," said Abdullah, "we have been rude to our cousin. Please, everyone, speak so that he can understand, in English as much as possible."

The Imam recited some religious verses, and mentioned something about 'Hazreti Muhammed' before saying a little prayer and asking for God's guidance.

"Choose your words well," he warned Devrish simply.

The men began to question Devrish, asking him about his grandfather and again why he had never come home to claim his inheritance, to which Devrish repeated what he had already said about Suleiman having a young family and deciding that it must be God's will for him to stay away and make do with what he had. Besides, he was old and unwell, and too weak to travel such a long way. What he didn't realise was that the small gathering in that room was more than a simple family meeting, it was a religious court that had been convened by Abdullah in order to determine the right course of action in the name of Allah.

Finally, the questioning seemed to be over, and the Imam turned to Abdullah and his eldest son, who both solemnly nodded their agreement.

"It will be written, therefore," said the Imam, "unless there is some objection." Then he turned to Devrish and went on, "It will be noted that Suleiman, your grandfather, could likely not return to claim his birthright due to old age and illness. There is some confusion as to what is now your right, given that you are not the eldest of the eldest son, but rather the eldest of all the cousins. But then, God works in mysterious ways. We shall see."

At this point, Abdullah took Devrish aside and cautioned him to say nothing more for the time being, as his inheritance was hanging in the balance. But Devrish already knew what the situation was, and he had made up his mind as to what he wanted to do.

"Please," he said to all assembled in the room, "let me make this perfectly clear. Whilst I am deeply touched by your hospitality and generosity, and I appreciate everything that you have said and done since my arrival, my sole aim in coming here was to meet my family. I ask nothing more of you, and would never consider taking something that has already been passed on generations ago." He continued, "Besides the eldest son of the eldest son is my cousin Abdullah. Who I knew was my father's elder brother."

At these words, Abdullah's eldest son bowed his head and said a little prayer, clearly moved by what was happening. The old man himself looked rather sad.

"Our laws regarding this matter are clear and strict," he said. "You are entitled to what is rightfully yours, but if you choose to knowingly abandon it, then your will must be recognised. Either way, you must sleep on it. We will carry on with the festivities and reconvene in the morning to settle the matter once and for all."

After the Imam and his clerk had departed, Abdullah took Devrish aside again.

"My heart is heavy," he said, emotion clearly evident in the lines of his wise face, "with the events that have transpired today. You have behaved just as Suleiman himself would have according to all the stories we know about him. Did you know that after he disappeared, his father would often sing and tell stories about his lost son's generosity? He would take gold and silver and give it to the poor, whom he pitied, and yet his father never questioned or chastised him for his actions. After Suleiman disappeared, Mehmet Emin took it upon himself to make sure his son's spirit persisted and decreed that every day they would feed anyone who came to the house with fresh bread and the same food that he himself ate. Indeed he often sat with them himself, sharing a story or two over a good bean dinner."

"Suleiman was an extraordinary boy," said Abdullah, "and the apple of his father's eye. And you are just like him."

The next morning Devrish dressed in his army uniform rather than the Arabic dress he had worn the previous night and made his way back to the dining room for breakfast. There was nothing so ceremonial about this meal as he had experienced at the feast, the breakfast table lined as it was with toast, jam, boiled eggs and other things to which he was accustomed, so quintessentially English, he thought, he could almost have been back home.

He tucked in heartily, being served by women he learnt were the wives of Abdullah and his eldest son and the mother of the boy. Then after a while, Abdullah himself made an appearance, wearing a suit so smart he wouldn't have looked at all out of place on the streets of London. Noticing Devrish's surprised look, he explained that it was often useful in his line of business to dress as the Europeans did and that he regularly travelled to Germany, France and Belgium to do deals before the war started, and those places were beginning to be open again.

"Tell me," asked Devrish, who was still hugely curious about the family, "how all of this started. How did we begin?"

Abdullah considered this question for a moment before replying simply, "Mehmet Emin."

Well, it had to start somewhere. There was a few seconds' silence before the old man continued in hushed tones.

"Mehmet Emin was a special man. Yes, he owned land that had been passed on to him through generations, so he was never poor. He grew crops and raised sheep and lived a dignified life, and God always provided for him. Yet there was something within him that wanted more, wanted to better himself, wanted the fine things and the big house that you have seen here. From an early age, he read voraciously and learnt everything he could, absorbing the knowledge with the good brain that God had given him. He had a will of iron and went as far as his conscience allowed while paying lip service to the law and to religion but always on the edge of both. He always said that he was going to be rich someday, and as you can see he was not mistaken."

"What did he do then to earn all that money?" asked Devrish. The old man hesitated. He looked uncomfortable, as though he didn't want to answer the question, but Devrish had come a long way to get these answers and his look was one of steely resolve like his great-grandfather's might have been.

"Well," sighed Abdullah finally, "as you may have guessed we were much more than we are now, traders of all things. As you heard from the Imam last night we are from Hazreti Muhammed, so we must always set a good example, it is in our blood, it is our family trait. But sometimes this has not been so."

Devrish shocked at this news, nevertheless remained quiet and allowed the old man to finish in his own time, for telling the story was clearly causing him some distress.

"You have a right to know," whispered Abdullah, "yet know too that we are all shamed by what has happened. You see, Mehmet Emin…" he hesitated, then the words came gushing out as though from a split keg. "He went against the blood," gasped Abdullah, "he bought and sold whole villages of people. The tribal people of the South are not Muslim, and Mehmet Emin considered them less than, unworthy of respect and dignity. Unworthy of their freedom. But he forgot that Muslim or not, we are all of us God's children. That is surely why God punished him by taking away his eldest son. Mehmet Emin knew no shame, he grew rich on the blood of this land and bought all of these priceless artefacts with the money he got from buying and selling people…"

"He bought and sold people," Devrish repeated back in the sauna, with the hint of a giggle that made me slightly uneasy. "He knew no shame, no conscience, and was completely self-centred." He looked at me pointedly. "Do you know of anyone like that?"

I said nothing, but the description fitted my dad down to a tee. There weren't many people on this Earth like dear old Dad, that's for sure, and it sounded like he was a real chip off the old block if what Devrish said was true. I am not exaggerating at all when I say I'm sure that if Dad had been allowed to buy and sell people the way his great-grandfather had, he would have done it in a heartbeat, without hesitation. The two black sheep of our family, Mehmet and Enver Emin.

And now the broken relationship between Devrish and my father became clearer. Devrish had held on to the secrets of the family's past most of his life because he knew that if Dad found out he would be on the first plane to Sudan and knocking on poor Abdullah's door demanding the inheritance.

"Well," said Abdullah over the breakfast table, "now you know. You have had a good night's sleep and a good breakfast, and a chance to reconsider your position with regard to what is rightfully yours. Just say the word."

But Devrish said nothing, and Abdullah sensed that he was struggling with the decision.

"But first," said Abdullah, breaking the silence, "let me show you something else that might convince you to stay."

He led Devrish out to the small building sealed with two heavy padlocks, of which the boy Ahmet had said nobody was to enter. Taking a second look at it now, Devrish noted that it really was like a jail, with great iron bars riveted to the door and great clunking locks. Inside and down ten steps there came another thick metal door with two more locks, and beyond that, a small, dark room that Devrish guessed must have been actually underneath the main house.

Abdullah flicked a switch and the room was illuminated, revealing beautiful tiles from floor to ceiling, and several large, strong boxes, each set atop its own stout wooden table in the centre of the room. Abdullah's eldest son must have followed them down there because he appeared now holding a bunch of keys and proceeded with a smile to open the largest box, then the next largest, and the next, and so on until all of the boxes on the tables lay open for Devrish to inspect. What he saw fair took his breath away.

There were bundles of bank notes and chunky gold coins, more money certainly than most people would ever see in their lifetimes. Devrish knew by now that the family was rich by anybody's standards, but there in Sudan with this kind of wealth they were surely princes.

Abdullah and his son stood back, and it struck Devrish at that moment how much they were behaving not as wealthy men themselves but as guardians or caretakers of the wealth, and he realised why they had brought him down here. It was a test. If he decided to change his mind and pursue his inheritance, all of this could be his. For a few long moments, the temptation overtook him and he felt nothing else. He closed his eyes and opened his mouth, every inch of him dying to say yes. But he couldn't utter the word. Something deep inside of him knew that it would be wrong. These riches were not his to take. Even by their own strict laws, this inheritance could only be claimed by the eldest son of the eldest son, while Devrish was the eldest son of the daughter. And besides, they had been passed on generations ago.

I felt a pang of something as I listened to Devrish's story. Tracing the family tree in my head as I knew it, the eldest son of the eldest son would have been my uncle Abdullah Mehmet Emin (so named after his grandfather and great-grandfather), but he was now dead. Surely that would have left my own father as the possible heir, not Devrish. And I knew that given the same opportunity, Dad would have said yes in a heartbeat and fought tooth and nail for those riches. These are the moments that whole futures turn upon, but Devrish was stronger than that. Besides, warning bells in the back of his mind were ringing, telling him that something about the offer wasn't quite right. It didn't make sense to him.

"I came here for one thing and one thing only," he said, as the moment of temptation passed. "I said that all I wanted was to see my family and learn about them, and I have done that. I am a man of my word and I have no desire to take your home, your money, or anything else from you." And with those words, he turned and left the room.

Later that day, Abdullah joined Devrish sitting in the shade and watching the sunset.

"I am sorry," he began in a philosophical tone of voice, "that you do not see yourself as the true inheritor of the family wealth. But you have demonstrated true honesty and spirit that has tested us all. We will look after all of this, in case such a time comes when the rightful heir returns to claim it for themselves."

Devrish nodded appreciatively. He was grateful for the old man's words and the sentiment behind them, and he had made peace with the decision that he had taken. Yet there was just one thing still troubling him.

"You said when we first met," said Devrish, "that there were two things which convinced you to accept me as a legitimate descendant of Suleiman. You told me one, the horse. What was the other?"

Abdullah paused for a moment as though gathering himself.

"Did you notice the grandfather clock to the left of the front door when you arrived?" he asked hoarsely.

"Of course," replied Devrish, "it is a beautiful clock with a nice deep sound, how could anyone miss that? But what is so special about it?"

"Well," said Abdullah quietly, as though he himself could not quite believe the story that he was telling, "that clock was brought back here by Mehmet Emin. It was his favourite possession, his pride and joy, and he took great pleasure in winding it and hearing it tick away. It was the heart of the house, he used to say, and no one was allowed to touch it. Then on the day he died, the clock stopped ticking."

Devrish blinked at the old man, convinced that he was having his leg pulled now and looking for some sign of it, but Abdullah's words were completely genuine.

"We have had experts come and look at it, but they always told us they could find nothing wrong, and it was a mystery to them why the clock just would not work. Well, when the boy ran to fetch me out to watch you ride that horse yesterday, I passed by the clock and felt something very strange. I stopped in my tracks, and then took a step backwards and turned towards it. It was working. I couldn't believe my eyes and ears, but there it was after so many years, tick-tock, tick-tock. I took it as a sign that the grandson of Suleiman must indeed have returned to us."

By this point, the old man had tears in his eyes. He turned and spoke to his eldest son who had arrived on the scene, and he, in turn, barked an order that caused all of the people nearby to clear out of the compound. A few moments later a groom appeared at the far end of the compound and left the black stallion Ahmet all alone there.

"Call him," said Abdullah quietly, "let's see what happens."

Devrish walked down the steps that they had been sitting on, raised his arm and called the horse's name. Ahmet reared up and began to move, not directly towards Devrish but in a sort of zig-zag pattern that took him past Devrish and off around the inside perimeter of the compound, his great hooves striking the ground with power and echoing all around. Then suddenly the stallion turned and ran full-tilt straight at Devrish, pulling up just short of him and rearing up, towering over him and making such loud, exuberant noises that people started coming out of nearby buildings to see what was going on.

Devrish was not afraid at all. He stepped under the horse as it reared up, as though putting on a show for the crowd. He could easily have been crushed, but somehow everyone knew that that wasn't about to happen. Abdullah stood up and clapped his hands wildly, his face full of happiness, and all of the other bystanders joined in the applause. They had never before seen someone who possessed such a magical gift with horses as Devrish clearly did with this stallion.

Once the show was over, Devrish thanked Abdullah for his kindness and wise counsel and prepared to head back home. But even as he said his final goodbyes, there was one question left to be answered.

"Abdullah, you have been very patient and answered everything that I have asked," said Devrish, "but there is still one point about which I am confused. You mentioned earlier, as the Imam did last night, that our family is from 'Hazreti Mohammed'. Is that so? Please tell me because if I do not learn about it now I will probably never know."

Abdullah looked at him in amazement.

"But surely," he said at last, "surely Suleiman passed this information down to his children."

Devrish shook his head.

"All he said about his past was that his downfall was the will of God and likely punishment for the sins of his father. But that he had a good life and a good master, and it could have been worse."

"Sadly, that is probably true about his father," said Abdullah. "Nevertheless, he should have told you that you are a descendant of the family of Mohammed. A clear bloodline has always been known and recorded through the generations."

"You don't mean to say Mohammed, surely," said Devrish, shocked.

"No," replied the old man quickly, "of course not, no one can ever say that, it would be blasphemous. We must say that we are descended from the family. At any rate, that is your birthright and you should have been told. You have a duty now to go back and let your family know, and your children too when they are old enough. And you must always behave according to your stature, which you now know. Though there is no doubt in my mind that you possess the right kind of traits to carry such a noble heritage."

Abdullah finished speaking, and it was clear from his body language that this was all he was prepared to say on the matter. The revelation of his birthright left Devrish reeling for weeks, as it did me when I heard it from my auntie following my father's death in 2010, as I had not appreciated what Devrish had told me years before.

Having spoken to Devrish at length over the course of those two days, Abdullah had determined that whilst he was not exactly poor, neither was he rich, so as his nephew prepared to leave the old man handed him a large roll of English bank notes and a bag of gold coins. This was his seed money, Abdullah said, so that he could start a business and secure his family's future. He must not refuse it, they would not allow him to this time, so Devrish accepted the generous gift with humility and went on his way.

Two or three months had passed after the events in Sudan, when a note arrived for Devrish to let him know that a ship would soon be arriving and bringing with it something that he would like. The consignment note bore two numbers, which he assumed must correspond to shipping containers, so he made his way down to the docks at the appointed time and waited for his mysterious packages to arrive.

There was a great deal to be unloaded, and the dockers were typically less than helpful, so Devrish waited around for several hours watching the containers being moved. Then he spotted, dangling over the ocean in a harness and obviously not happy about it, a great black stallion. Devrish recognised the horse at once and rushed over to calm him as he was lowered back down to earth, removing his blinders, soothing him and making him safe. Upon hearing Devrish's voice, the stallion became calm almost at once. He knew that he was safe now and in good hands.

The second box that arrived for him contained a beautiful saddle and some other bits and pieces, along with a second note which explained that no one else had been able to ride Ahmet since Devrish left. His minders feared him and nobody knew what to do about it, so it had been decided that the most suitable thing would be to send him over to Devrish. The note also stated that for as long as Abdullah lived, Devrish was to receive the sum of £100 every month to help the family grow. This was a huge sum at the time, and especially for someone living in Cyprus.

So Devrish did as he had promised, at least to some extent. He told both my father and my aunt, during one of the moments that she had tried to bring the two cousins together to heal old wounds, that they were from Hazreti Muhammed and should always behave as such. He kept the part about the inheritance quiet, for obvious reasons, but distributed some of the money to those in the family who needed it.

I suspect that my father knew some of this story, though not all of it because as I said, he would have been at Abdullah's door in no time demanding his riches. But thinking back on it now I do remember him telling me something about the family lineage. I wonder if Devrish chose to pass along that information to his own children, or whether he decided it was more trouble than it was worth and just let the matter drop.

So it is said that the sins of the father fall upon their children. Mehmet Emin took away the sons and daughters of others and sold them in order to become monstrously rich, then, in turn, he found out what it was like to have his own son taken away from him in the same manner. Suleiman had meant the world to him, and it was said that after his disappearance, Mehmet spent every waking hour in a kind of tortured dream, tormented by his loss and speaking of the day when his son would return and ride around the courtyard as he once did, atop the finest black stallion and with his arms outstretched as though flying on the very wind. But then he would be gone again, as no inducement would be able to keep him. It seems to me that Abdullah was playing out the whole story with Devrish exactly as it had been foretold and entered into family lore.

There are still many questions left unanswered. Who was the Mohammet Ahmed of the painting in Abdullah's house, who was said to have vanquished General Gordon? Was he a relative? Did he know Mehmet Emin? Perhaps

Mehmet Emin funded the campaign even, a holy war to purge his guilty conscience? I do not know. What is certain is that Mehmet Emin was a character taken from a unique mould. Blessed with great intellect and memory, he would stop at nothing in pursuit of personal pleasure. The incredible collection of priceless artefacts at the house in Sudan are testament enough to that. He loved the women too, taking many wives and leaving behind him, at the best guess, some twenty-two children. Still, the only one that really mattered to him was taken, and he was never the same after that. Some say that Mehmet Emin changed that day, realising the error of his ways and resolving to give back to the poor and make sure that his family would always do likewise in payment for the terrible blood-debt he had created.

Sitting in the Turkish baths in Lewisham all those years ago, my Uncle Devrish held my arm tightly and shook it in earnest as he spoke words that I will never forget.

"There are many secrets," he said in a whisper, "I am writing them all down and they will surprise you all. Tell your father that the time is not right as far as he is concerned."

At the time, I took it as the ranting of an old man. What else could I have done? Me being a staunch pragmatist, I had never seen nor heard any proof of the things Devrish was saying, and they seemed to have no relevance to me whatsoever. The twinkle in his eye only made me think that he was having a little fun with me, so I played along in the name of humouring an old man. But in retrospect, that was the day I should have begun to learn the importance of listening and appreciating the words of one's elders. I only wish that I had listened harder at the time, and asked more questions, maybe it would have been easier piecing this whole story together. I know that there is truth at the heart of everything that is written here, because I've always wondered how my father and Devrish were able to buy 42 houses between them in the fifties, yet every family member I speak to seems to have a slightly different story to tell. Most seem to know as far back as the story of Suleiman (known as Abdullah) and not much else, which may make me, after the death of Devrish, the holder of all that is currently known about the events in Sudan. I'm sure that one day the truth will be revealed and we will all know for sure where we stand.

For now though, all of us in the family are content to wax lyrically upon the story of Devrish Hassan, how he became a legend in Cyprus due to the bond that he shared with a horse that none other could ride. Ahmet, the black stallion, and Devrish Hassan, eldest son of Zulihya, the only daughter of Suleiman the slave.

Introduction

Assassinations, recriminations, a near-death experience with a suicidal flying examiner, love at first sight, a ghost or two, or three, a famous half-sister, visiting Heaven and Hell, inventing the hydrofoil and getting caned for it, a naked plumber, a TV wrestler's trouble in the bedroom, cleaning out a casino and then throwing it all away, helping John Major fight the Kuwait oil fires, dowsing for dead people, patents and planning decisions, lies, truths and uncertainties.

Following a fairly serious motor accident in 2005 which damaged a disc in my neck. I then had, along with the pain of a trapped nerve which kept me awake at night, the luxury of time that I never previously enjoyed to reassess some of the more curious things that have happened to me during my time on this Earth. Some of these things are only now beginning to make sense to me. Others perhaps never will. Taken as a whole, all of them lead me inexorably to believe that mankind is far greater than the simple reflection we see of ourselves in the mirror.

I believe that we all possess as yet untapped greatness, and that reason and common sense, while in their own right excellent tools for plotting a path through life's many mysteries, are nevertheless insufficient to deal adequately with the sheer wonder and strangeness that we all encounter on a daily basis.

How many of us believe that we have seen a ghost, for example? Or experienced déjà vu so strong that it makes us seriously doubt for a moment the truths that we cling to about the world in which we live? How does a genius like Einstein pluck a kernel of hitherto undiscovered knowledge seemingly out of thin air, without even being able to explain how he did it? How is a mother able to perform superhuman feats of strength when her child is in danger? An honest recollection of our own lives would, I believe, find that such phenomena are far from exceptional. They are commonplace, and a crucial part of what makes us who we are.

This book contains the story of my life. A story that I am sure will appear strange at first glance, but one that I think, if you are honest, you will find is not so different from your own experience of the world. If that is the case, please let me assure you that you are not, in fact, crazy. Merely human.

And what is human? Now that, my friends, that really is the question.

Chapter One
Christos
1947–1956

The truth is, hardly any of us have ethical energy enough for more than one really inflexible point of honour.

~ George Bernard Shaw

I was twelve years old the first time I saved my father's life. The second time involved an airliner shot down by the Russians over Moscow. The third concerned a psychotic member of the Turkish 'Grey Wolf' terrorist group. There may well have been more that he just never got around to telling me about, Dad being the consummate charmer, though also the kind of man who tended to bring out the murderous intent in people. But this first time is all about an old friend, a newborn baby, and a matter of honour.

My father was a policeman, as well as a driver, interpreter and general help to the deputy commissioner of police in Cyprus, a man we knew only as Sir Humphrey. When not helping his boss in some way or another Dad sat in the passport office doing police checks on applicants. We lived in an annexe house next door to the deputy commissioner of police so that Dad would be available at any time, day or night, to drive the commissioner about his business.

Now, the commissioner had a large garden that required quite some tending, and one of Dad's jobs was to go along to the local jail and pick out trustworthy-looking prisoners to come and do the work. As you might imagine, working in a nice big garden out in the fresh air was a treat for those men, so Dad held a certain degree of power over them. Power to grant pleasure or inflict pain. Power to grant favours. It was the kind of position that suited him just nicely.

Cyprus, while governed by the British at the time, still very much operated a 'you scratch my back, I'll scratch yours' system with regard to most things, and so it came to be that a certain notorious terrorist leader came to my father with a special request. He had been in jail for a long time and was looking at many years still ahead of him, all of which he appeared to have made his peace with, except that he had a strong desire to start a family. Conjugal visits weren't on the agenda, but this man, let's call him Christos, suggested to Dad that if it could be arranged for him to meet up with his wife in the potting shed of the commissioner's splendid garden twice a month, it could prove a beneficial arrangement for all parties concerned. He had no desire to escape, he assured Dad, and swore on his honour, following such a kindness he would happily return to his cell afterwards without complaint.

Never one to let an opportunity pass him by, Dad agreed to this modest request, and for a few months, Christos and his wife were able to spend what I'm sure was extremely quality time together, while Dad enjoyed a few bottles of wine and other goodies that were periodically delivered to our house by way of thanks for greasing the wheels. On reflection, knowing Dad as I do now, I'm quite certain that Christos wasn't the only prisoner to have struck some sort of deal with him. Neither, as it turned out, were wine and sundry luxuries the only forms of payment that he'd been accepting.

Cyprus being Cyprus, there were always plenty of rumours buzzing around, and sure enough one day the word went around that at last Christos was to become a father. There was much jubilation to be had, and parties were thrown as was tradition where Dad was the honoured guest and had all manner of Christos' extended family patting him on the back and thanking him for being such a grand chap and helping bring about this joyous turn of events.

Under normal circumstances, consorting with villains would have been frowned upon. More than frowned upon. Christos was a dangerous prisoner and granting him favours like that could have landed my father in jail, no doubt a whole lot of back scratching occurred at the prison even before my father was involved. But then, the villainy in question here was for shooting at the English police and soldiers that many of the locals wanted off the island, so it was okay.

Some months later, as Dad tells the story, he was driving Sir Humphrey as usual from one engagement to another when shots rang out in quick succession, thudding into the front and side of the car. Miraculously, no one was hurt and the gunman slipped away, but there was an almighty fuss kicked up about the terrorists becoming more active again, and after that Sir Humphrey's guard was increased several times over. It proved to be of little deterrent. Barely a few days had passed when the same thing happened again, shots were fired at the car and again nobody was hurt, but this time the police were on their toes and they caught the shooter.

A hanging offence, one of the officers explained to him gleefully, if he'd killed the commissioner. But the deputy commissioner apparently wasn't the target, but rather 'that bastard driver of his' spat the man. He said he didn't mind going to the gallows if it meant that Dad would get what was coming to him.

This was the brother of Christos. He had been at the hospital a week earlier, with the whole family, to welcome a new arrival into their ranks. 'It's a boy!' the cry went up as the little chap struggled, screaming into the world. And then the crying baby was all that could be heard, as every other soul in the room had fallen silent.

The baby was wrapped up straight away so that only his little face could be seen, but as the shocked grown-ups gathered round it was perfectly obvious that something had gone very wrong. Outside in the hallway, oblivious relatives were still celebrating, making toasts to the happy couple Christos and Jana, and to my father who had made the whole affair possible. The trouble was, Christos and Jana were about as pale white as it is possible to be, while the little baby now being looked down upon by half a dozen very troubled faces, had the same unmistakable milk chocolate colouring as Dad.

Well, there was nothing else for it, honour had to be satisfied. Dad would have to die.

Sir Humphrey was reluctant to lose such a useful employee, but he had to be honest and explain to Dad that he would not be able to protect him, or his family. Furthermore, there was new trouble for Dad as the CID had amassed details of Dad's 'helping hand' in some of the passport applications he had dealt with. "Resign or be sacked and possibly face charges," said Sir Humphrey. So it was suggested that he should take his wife, me, and my little sister, on a trip to England where we might keep our heads down for a while until this all blew over. If it ever blew over.

So it was that in October 1948 we came by sea to England to stay with my uncle in a Guinness trust building in South East London. I know it must have been October because I remember seeing that date, every time I went to the bathroom in the first house we lived in, a big sea chest there that had carried our possessions over with us, and it was clearly marked in black paint across one side with the date and destination address.

Initially, Dad became a cook, that having been his first trade in the British Army before joining the police, but his sharp eyes were always on the lookout for opportunities, and he found a cracking one in the property business, buying up war-damaged buildings on the cheap, fixing them up and selling them on for a hefty profit. At one point he had a whopping twenty-one houses that he actually owned, deeds and all. After the first couple were sold, we finally moved out of the Guinness trust building into a house of our own, and never looked back.

Despite being shot at twice and having to move his family to another country, Dad, it seemed, had not learnt his lesson. He loved women, and whisky, and had no compunction in messing with other people's wives if he saw something he wanted. He was an entrepreneur but also a reckless gambler who made mountains of money and then let it all slip away again. I have known him as a postman and a delivery driver in a crockery firm, and for a time he worked in a sweet factory too. All of these jobs were beneath a man of such fierce intelligence, but then it was the drink that always brought him so low rather than any lack of ability. Anyone could tell that the man had a sharp mind and a propensity for lateral thinking, at least when he wasn't pickled to the gills.

Eventually, things in that area came to a head, and in 1961, Dad had part of his cirrhosis-riddled liver removed in an attempt to save his life. The shock of the process finally did the trick, and after that, I never knew him to touch a drop to his dying day.

At any rate, Dad pottered around buying houses and doing them up, and we all lived quite comfortably in a large corner house with a shop underneath it and a garage to one side. Though Dad being Dad did have a tendency to spend more than he earned, so problems did arise with predictable regularity. His biggest problem, however, had rather less to do with money or drink, and rather more to do with his wandering eye and discretions half-forgotten.

I must have been about twelve years old when I came home from school one day to find both my mother and grandmother in tears. 'What will become of us now?' they were saying over and over, though neither would explain what was the matter. Mother told me to go to my uncle's until she called for me to come back, and when I asked her why I should she replied in anguish with tears running down her face that I ought to just do as I was told before going back inside and closing the front door behind her.

I just stood there for several long moments in shock wondering what all the fuss was about when I noticed a man standing on the corner of the pavement nearby smoking a cigarette. He looked Turkish, so I thought, but I didn't recognise him at all and supposing he might be looking to buy one of Dad's houses I went over and spoke to him in Turkish.

"Are you waiting for my father?" I asked.

"Yes," he replied in English. "I am Christos."

The name meant nothing to me, but this man had an easy smile and a way about him that made me like him immediately.

"I would invite you in," I said, "but Mum and Nan are having a crying session for some reason so I think it's better if we both just wait for Dad out here. He ought to be back soon."

I sat on a nearby wall and he did likewise, and we talked a little. He had come all the way from Cyprus, he said, where he had a son just like me except a little younger. His boy was inquisitive too, he explained with a smile, and like me, he was not shy to talk to people. He told me how proud he was of his son, and how he was already looking forward to getting back home and checking in on the family business that he ran.

"So you don't want to buy one of my dad's houses?" I asked. Christos shook his head. Little did I know that his intentions were far more sinister than that. This man had a gun in his pocket and every intention to use it. He must have known that he would almost certainly be caught with so many witnesses around, but it was a matter of honour to him and something that had to be done. Christos and I hit it off famously. He told me stories about life back in Cyprus and about his son, and I told him how we'd all been getting on since we moved to England, which he seemed very interested in. We laughed and joked, and then at one point it got to the stage where Christos was giving me serious fatherly advice on how best to negotiate a business deal, and telling me sternly that I must pay attention at school, and learn, and cherish knowledge which was worth more than money. He could see me as a lawyer or a doctor, he said. Something well paid and respected.

Christos came across as a real thoughtful family man, and I liked what he said. One of the things he said to me that day has always stuck with me and I happily pass it along whenever I can, which is to always do your job well and never worry about money, as money will always follow. I've always found that advice to ring true and possibly the best advice I have ever been given.

Well, all good things come to an end they say, and my conversation with Christos was cut abruptly short when Dad finally rolled up, a little worse for wear, and sidled over to greet Christos like a long-lost brother, not having any idea that the following moments were to be possibly the most dangerous of his life.

"Come in Christos, come in!" insisted Dad cheerfully, and into the house, we went to find Mum and Nan now sitting quietly with pale faces at the table. The adults began talking about adult things and I soon lost interest, so I went off down the road to visit a friend for a while, and when I returned I found Dad and Christos sharing a drink together. They were laughing and joking, and reminiscing, and genuinely enjoying each other's company. It couldn't help but make you smile, as Mum and Nan both were, whatever it was they had been fretting about earlier now obviously forgotten.

The delicious smell of roasting meat filled the house, and we all took our places around the table as my sister, a year younger than me, asked where her pet chicken Lizzie had gotten to. We had some five chickens at the time, mostly because it was just hard to break the habits of a Mediterranean family, but also because it was handy to have your own supplies in the years following the end of rationing when fresh eggs and real chicken were still quite the luxury. It wasn't until we were most of the way through our meal that the news was broken and my little sister was distraught. It had to be Lizzie, Nan tried to explain kindly, because she wasn't laying any eggs, but that if my sister wanted she could pick another of the chickens and call that one Lizzie. But it wasn't the same, as you can imagine, for a little girl who had just eaten most of the meat on her plate, only to be told that it was her beloved pet that used to come when she called.

Even her tears, however, couldn't dampen the spirits around the table, as though the adults were sympathetic to the little girl's pain, at the same time they all understood that death was a part of life and that these things happen. And also, there was another reason why Lizzie's passing was not an occasion to be mourned, as I was to find out.

Dad and Christos were telling jokes in Greek across the table, and I remember thinking what great friends they must have been back in Cyprus. Even Nan was wiping away tears of laughter that seemed tinged with relief, and again I found myself wondering what on earth it was all about. Then suddenly, Christos stopped laughing and became solemn in a moment. He reached inside his coat pocket, took out an automatic handgun and, nodding his head, took out the clip containing the bullets, separated the weapon into two parts on the table, and offered the clip to Dad. Dad waved his hand and told Christos to put the gun away, which he did, and nothing more was said of it.

I had absolutely no idea what had just happened, until many years later whilst flying to Cyprus with Dad on business, when I remembered the incident and quietly asked him what it had all been about. He was quite cagey, but as I understand it something had changed Christos' mind at the last moment, and he'd decided that actually, he'd rather not put a bullet in dear old Dad. And the untimely end of my little sister's pet chicken had offered him a tenuous but acceptable opportunity to satisfy the blood debt owed for Dad's transgression. Lizzie had, after all, been practically a member of the family.

I believe, however, that my little chat with Christos on the wall across the road to our house was what really prompted him to think again about what he would be giving up should he have gone through with his initial plan; or a life with his family, and his son, and his business back in Cyprus.

Many years have passed now and still, I have never met my half-brother, the only child of Christos and Jana, who apparently grew up to be a top lawyer in Cyprus, renowned for his razor-sharp mind.

Which I suppose is little surprise, given the stock he came from.

Chapter Two
The School Bullies
1955–1958

Courage is fire, and bullying is smoke.

~ Benjamin Disraeli

So much of what makes a man tick is coalesced during the learning years. Between school and home life, we're taught different variations on how to behave, which is different from simply being taught 'right from wrong' as both concepts are undeniably subjective.

I'm a firm believer that the presence of both mother and father is so important for the upbringing of the brood, the boys gaining a more sensitive touch with mum's guidance and perhaps a more determined 'go get that meat' instinct from dad's influence. My father, as you will find out, was a truly larger-than-life character and as a child, I was proud to be a chip off the old block, my father's son. I listened intently to his advice which he dispensed keenly from as early as I can remember.

"You must be prepared, son," I remember him saying to me, "for the time when you go out into the world and there will be no one there to help or protect you. So you must learn as much, as much as you're able, while you're able, make your decisions and most importantly stick to them. Never allow anyone to beat you into submission, and you will survive well."

I wrongly saw him as an uncompromising man, and therefore so was I from the youngest age, a scrapper who wouldn't take nonsense from anyone. That caused me a few problems growing up, but it also allowed me to learn some valuable lessons.

I remember attending Coburg Junior School in South East London, a few hundred yards from the Old Kent Road where we lived at 211 Neat Street, our first home that Dad bought in 1949 was very nice indeed, four bedrooms and a garden, the sort that sell today in the Camberwell area for a good half-million pounds. Of course, the government had them all pulled down to create a grassy space, which is nice enough I suppose but they destroyed some of the nicest houses in the city in order to make it, and things like that can never be replaced.

Anyway, I remember attending school there, after the summer break, when I was around ten years of age. My new classroom was up several flights of stone stairs, and half-way up there was some kind of contraption hanging on the wall with a knocker, the like of which you'd find on a front door but inclined at a curious angle. Naturally, being an inquisitive child and not fully understanding the notion of actions having consequences, feeling helpful and thinking I was doing the right thing, I put my hand on the strange device in order to return it to a down position and pushed it downwards. It didn't want to go, and I had to give it quite a heave, but after a few moments the mechanism gave way with a heavy clunk and all hell let loose. The little hose that had been dangling limply next to the strange knocker (and which should, on reflection, have given even my ten-year-old self a decent idea of what might be about to happen) sprung to life and soaked everything in sight with what looked and felt like fizzy water. I panicked and tried to get the rogue fire extinguisher under control with the help of a few other children when a thundering voice behind me boomed out.

"Got that, lad?" roared the headmaster. "Everyone stand still!"

We froze like statues.

"Did you set this off, boy?" he boomed, glaring hard at me.

"Me, sir?" I stammered, "No, sir."

"Are you sure?" his eyes narrowed.

"Yes, sir."

"Did you see who it was?" he asked.

"Yes, sir."

I don't really know why I said yes. I suppose I was so afraid of getting into trouble that my survival instinct kicked in. Even as a small boy, I didn't feel comfortable telling a lie but I'd been given the cane before for scrapping in the playground and I wasn't keen to repeat the experience. So if I could get out of it by telling a little lie, why not? Dad always said to make your decision and stick to it no matter what. I did not realise at the time that the point really was to make good decisions.

The headmaster instructed me to follow him, and we went from classroom to classroom looking for the culprit who I was to identify.

"You will recognise him, won't you?" he asked.

"Yes, sir," I replied, feeling sick. I was running out of time, and more importantly running out of children fast.

"Well, Emin," said the headmaster as we arrived at the final classroom, "we have eliminated every class but this one. What does that tell you?"

"I suppose he must be in there, sir." I lied.

"That's right, boy," he replied, "and I suspect I know who it is."

In we went. These were boys my own age and I knew them all. One of them, a big lad, I recognised as a bit of a bully, having pushed and shoved me around a few times in a typical childish attempt to assert a little dominance. I always shoved back harder of course, and I made a point of never giving an inch to him and his little gang, I remembered it was because of him I had been caned by the headmaster last term.

"It's him," I said, pointing to the boy.

"Cousins!" barked the headmaster at the stunned boy. "I thought it would be you. Go to my room and ask my secretary for the cane and book. I shall wait here for you."

While Cousins was gone the headmaster gave the class a lecture on not messing with fire extinguishers, and he mentioned my bravery in trying to bring the wild hose under control. I was a good lad, he said, and ought to be commended. Looking back on it now all I feel is shame.

The cane and book arrived finally, and poor Will Cousins was instructed to offer up his hands.

Thwack.

"Thank you, sir."

Then the other hand.

Thwack.

"Thank you, sir." Strangely, he never complained it was not him, so maybe he did pull that knocker up and set a trap for some hapless lad to set the thing off.

"Now sit down, Cousins," the headmaster barked at the confused and humiliated boy, "I hope you've learnt your lesson."

I knew of course that Cousins would find me in the playground but so what? I could handle him. Come playtime the inevitable happened and Cousins faced me down, but his main problem seemed to be why I had picked him out when we both knew he hadn't set the thing off. The injustice was what burnt most fiercely, not the punishment itself. He even offered me a way out, offering to accept that I'd got one over on him if I would come clean and admit to him that he wasn't really guilty. Still, I didn't budge. I'd made my decision, and I was going to stick with it.

I did not realise at the time, but this would become a defining moment in my life. I hadn't learnt about compromise yet, all I knew was what my dad had told me about sticking to your guns, so that's what I did. I was about to find out how being unwilling to admit to your mistakes can dig you deeper into a hole faster than your mind can make sense of what is happening.

"It was you, Cousins," I kept lying, justifying my actions in my mind that he deserved all that he got for being such a bully, "you did it so stop complaining."

He walked away from me, muttering and punching his hand, getting more and more wound up and looking for all the world like a bull preparing to charge. It didn't take clairvoyance to see what was coming next. Cousins flew at me suddenly, his fists flying, yelling in a blood rage. I stood my ground and then at the last moment stepped out of the way and tripped him up. He planted face down in the dirt and stayed there in pain, he hurt his wrist in the fall and I remember all the kids in the playground laughing loudly at the spectacle and now him sitting up and crying in pain. Already I was making things worse.

Another thing that I had not taken into account when I made my very rash decision was the rest of the Cousins family. The Cousins were like a proper dynasty with brothers and cousins and uncles and whatnot all over town, and suddenly all of them seemed to know my face and all of them wanted a word. I met quite a few of them over the following weeks and each time they asked me to just admit that I'd been wrong. There wasn't really any practical reason why I shouldn't, the punishment had long since been dished out, it would certainly have made my life easier to just say, "Yes, okay, I might have been mistaken. Sorry." But Dad had said never to give any ground, so I wasn't about to. No doubt if I'd actually talked to Dad about it he would have told me I'd done wrong and sent me right round to the Cousins' house to apologise but I was scared that Dad might think I couldn't handle the situation, and I didn't want him to know, so I didn't say anything.

For a long time after that, the Cousins children would corner me and a little roughing up would take place. Usually, one of them would sit on me, spread-eagled on the pavement, while the rest took it in turns to take up the interrogation.

"Admit that Will didn't do it!" they would demand.

"He did!" I always insisted, which earned me more punches. More often than not, some grown-up would have to intervene to save my skin, and as soon as I was up off the ground I would be out of there. I could run pretty quickly and you'd better believe I did plenty of running from the Cousins. My new name on the streets became 'Getthebastard', which they'd all yell as soon as I was spotted. Sometimes they'd think strategically and have three or four people wait for me around a corner while the rest of them chased me that way so that I ran smack bang into their wide smiles. Even the girls got involved, and some of them were just as aggressive as the boys.

One little act of mischief and then one of cowardice caused all this trouble, and it could have been ended at any time if only I admitted that I'd done wrong. But I thought I was being brave, and mature, and like Dad. I thought that sticking to my guns was the right thing to do. What I didn't understand was that true honesty and generosity of spirit are the components of real bravery, not lies and deceit. I thought that telling a little white lie to get Cousins caned instead of me was perfectly acceptable. I didn't like him anyway, and he probably deserved the punishment, if not for that particular incident then certainly for any number of times he didn't get caught roughing up other children. But I was too young to appreciate all the different consequences of my actions. The whole thing must have played havoc with the poor boy's mind, being the subject of all that ruckus, his whole family involved and goodness knows what was going on at his home. Why couldn't they all just let it go? I suppose it was a matter of pride.

Even after all these years I still feel sick with shame looking back on all of it. I was only young, but I could and should have done the right thing and I didn't. I only hope that he can forgive me for it now, and hope that it didn't scar him for life the way it has me.

I was chastened (and pretty well bruised) after the whole Cousins incident, but my big lesson in compromise didn't come until three years later, courtesy of another bully by the name of Elliot.

I suppose that being bullied at school has a marked effect on a young sapling that serves to colour their behaviour in adulthood. It's easy to see how being called names, or even beaten senseless can and does leave you wondering what you've done to deserve such cruelty. For me, being bullied was a little strange in so far as it felt almost fake. Which is not to say that I wasn't punched at every opportunity by the class bully, but rather that it didn't reflect the classic predator/victim paradigm.

There were four boys in our class who were of fairly equal stature and physical presence. Elliot (who joined our class near the end of the third year) was the bully, top dog as it were, I suppose every class has one. Then there was his friend Collins, a nice enough lad on his own and usually pretty sensible, but in the company of Elliot he would pick his side and join in with the punching. It's always sad when good people get dragged down by those around them, but such is our nature I suppose.

The third boy was Young, a big strong lad who would eye me with a certain vigilant respect and me likewise. I certainly never wished to have to test myself against him. Young and I were fairly mature for our ages, though we had markedly different ways of dealing with the threat of confrontation. He would simply laugh it off with a "not with me, mate" or suchlike, and walk away. That never worked for me though. I would always warn the other guy that fighting was the last thing I was looking for, but I could never resist adding a rebuke as well, telling them not to be so childish or something along those lines. Well, that had its consequences of course and I found myself fighting often for one reason or another, not just boys from my own year but sometimes older lads as well. Mind you, I came a real cropper when I took on one boy two years older and with a significant weight advantage. I remember he punched me in both eyes, and it really did hurt which blinded me for several seconds when he could have punched hells bells out of me, but he didn't, he just stood there wondering why this young squirt even tried taking him on.

The trouble with me was that I could never take an insult without punching that person out, or at least attempt to. I became a fighter, always prepared to stand up for myself, and this had a dramatic effect on my character and temperament that, looking back now, shaped my adult self in unmistakable ways. I considered myself a grown-up, still young as I was, and yet while Young was avoiding all the trouble and living a pretty charmed life, I was the one always getting into scrapes, knocking seven bells out of whichever silly lad wanted to take his chances with me that week.

Even from the tender age of eleven, when I went into a fight it was far from a childish affair. It was knuckles to the face and no messing about, and there was blood nearly every time. It was the blood that always gave me away in fact, when one of the masters would spot it and ask the lads nearby where it had come from. It never took long to find me at the other end of the bother, and so I became a fairly regular entry into what was called the 'cane book', and I was given constant warnings that my expulsion was just an incident or two away.

Now, Mr Starkey was the Arts master who wore a handlebar moustache and bore a striking resemblance to the famous comedy actor Jimmy Edwards. He called me into his empty classroom one day and sat me down for a 'quiet word', trying to find out why I was always fighting as he and the other teachers (as far as I knew) always felt that I was a sensible lad on the whole and couldn't understand it.

"Talk to me, Emin," he said. "Tell me why you fight, what causes you to go berserk."

"Berserk, sir?" I replied, shaken. "Never, sir."

"Really?" he said, with the merest hint of a raised eyebrow. "What do you call it then when there's blood all over the place?"

I had no answer to that.

"Just stop and think, boy," he went on, "stop and think about what possesses you to do these things."

I tried to explain that I never ever bullied anyone, that I only reacted when someone kept on pestering me after I'd warned them to back off. That was the first time it dawned on me that my sharp tongue was probably the cause of many of my problems. Young never took a verbal swipe at the bullies, he just walked away and they didn't follow. But I knew I could handle myself and so I was never afraid to toss an insult or two, well aimed so that they would strike the bullies' most vulnerable spots. It was the easiest way to ensure a confrontation, and I knew I could win those.

"There you are then, Emin," said Mr Starkey solemnly. "You're causing the problem yourself with these insults."

"Only after they've wound me up though, sir," I protested.

"Grown-ups don't allow themselves to be wound up, Emin," he replied. "Restraint is mature. What you're doing is childish."

That was hard to hear. I was only thirteen, but I'd always thought of myself as mature, always felt like I handled myself like an adult like my dad might do. To be told now that I was the childish one and at fault for my own troubles was a kick in the teeth and no mistake. Mr Starkey must have noticed my disappointment, and apparently deciding that his words had been stick enough, he then offered up the carrot. If I could go the rest of the year without getting into another fight, he said, he would recommend me to become a prefect.

Well, that sounded pretty good to me, so I promised that from now on I would keep a tight rein on what I said to the other lads. Diplomacy would be my middle name, I resolved, and the tenacity of spirit that had me facing off with the big boys would be redirected towards honouring the promise that I'd given to Mr Starkey. When the bullies took aim at me, I would shrug them off rather than, say, casually suggesting where I'd seen their mother or sisters the previous night (which always provoked an excellent response.) With any luck, that would put an end to my presence being demanded outside the school gates at lunchtime.

It worked, too. A week went by, then two, then a month without so much as a hint of trouble. I felt like I had full control of the situation and things were going to be easier than I could have imagined. That prefect badge was as good as pinned to my chest already. But of course, life isn't as simple as that, is it?

Then Elliot appeared. Elliot was a true bullyboy of the old school, over-large and muscular for his age, with the ability to lay flat just about anyone else in our year. His father was in the army based at Woolwich Arsenal and Elliot had apparently been a young boxing champion somewhere or other. He would go around the class sizing up the other lads to see which were ripe for the picking, easy victims for him and his cowardly friends to bolster their own egos. I don't know whether he knew about my agreement with Mr Starkey or not, but it was impossible not to notice that I was avoiding confrontation nowadays and Elliot decided that wouldn't do at all. I remember him squaring up to Young the way he always did when he was spoiling for a rumble, and Young, as usual, brushing him off with a laugh and a joke. Then Elliot turned in my direction.

"Emin won't hit you back," I remember Collins saying to his friend, "he's gone soft."

"I'll be interested to see how you get out of this one," Young whispered as the two of them sidled over. *Me too*, I thought.

"Elliot, I don't want any trouble," I said seriously, standing my ground. "Have your fun elsewhere today, I've got better things to do."

Smack. He punched me in the arm.

"What's that, Emin?" he jeered. "You've gone soft, so I've heard."

"Think what you like," I replied, trying my best to look nonchalant.

Smack. The other arm this time. Every inch of me wanted to hit him, but I summoned all of my will and walked away instead. I consoled myself that I was thirteen going on eighteen while Elliot and his crony were thirteen going on ten. I was better than them. That thought gave me the strength to walk away.

The trouble is, sometimes you can't walk away no matter how much you want to. Every other day the punches would come to my arms or stomach. At first, it was only Elliot but then emboldened I suppose by my lack of reaction Collins, who knew me very well started joining in the action. My friends were asking me why I let them get away with it. Surely I could knock them both down if I wanted to, God knows I'd done it before with others. Other boys in the class warned the two of them that they were playing a dangerous game and that it was only a matter of time before I fought back. Even the teachers, I learnt, had a sweepstake going as to when I would lash out and leave Elliot's blood dashed across the floor. I suspect Starkey himself was keeping the book on that one, though I never found out for sure.

So the end of the year came around finally and the summer recess provided a much-needed break from the daily gauntlet. When we arrived back on the first day of the next term, I found that Mr Starkey had honoured his side of the bargain and I was to be made a prefect, along with Young and Collins. Elliot wasn't at school that day, I forget why, but I do remember that he returned on the day that the three of us were due to receive our badges during assembly. Young was great at avoiding trouble, as I said, but he loved to stir it up a bit too, so he told Elliot that I had only just edged him out for the prefect's badge by one point and that his inability to provoke me must have sealed the deal. Elliot wasn't happy, to say the least. That morning during registration, he waited until our form master for that year Mr Shelton had stepped out of the room for a moment, and then snuck up behind me from his skiving spot at the back of the room and smacked the back of my head so hard it felt like my eyes would pop.

I knew I shouldn't react, but I also knew that if he kept up this level of hostility a confrontation would be inevitable and my shiny prefect's badge, which I hadn't even got yet, would be in jeopardy one way or the other. I stood up calmly and explained in a patient tone that he must be mistaken, that Young was having a bit of fun with him and that perhaps the reason he hadn't been made a prefect was because everyone knew he was a bully. I said that I wouldn't tolerate being biffed up anymore and that he ought to choose his next action very carefully.

The room broke out into murmurs of encouragement, the other lads who had warned Elliot last term that he was treading dangerous ground now appealing for him to listen to me else he'd be in big trouble. I remember one piping up about how there'd be blood all over the place again while Young leant back in his seat sniggering and obviously loving the chaos he'd started.

One of the smaller boys, a chap named Curry whom I had protected from the bullies before, stood up between us, which must have taken a fair deal of courage.

"Look, Elliot," he said, "we all know what Emin will do to you if you push him too far. He's not soft. Nobody knows why he's let you get away with it for so long but that won't last forever, so you'd better just stop now."

Well, being lectured by this little boy was the final straw for Elliot. He shoved Curry clear across the room and squared up to me.

"I really don't want to do this," I said calmly, taking off my coat and rolling up my shirtsleeves. "But if you insist, I'll let you have the first swing. You'd better knock me out or you're in big trouble."

I stuck out my chin, expecting him to give it everything he had. What came instead was a soft bump from his fist and a nasty grin. He wanted me to land the first proper punch, and by extension be the one to get in the most trouble. Well, that was his mistake. I'd clearly stated that if he didn't take advantage of my generous offer, he would be in trouble. And I am nothing if not a man of my word.

I think I landed six or seven good punches to Elliot's nose and the side of his head. I'd never seen so much blood before in my life, it was everywhere; up the walls, all over the floor, the desks, chairs, sprayed across the uniforms of our classmates who hadn't backed up enough. When Elliot fell to the ground I simply dusted myself off and then, with the calm of a grown-up, picked him up and marched him out of the classroom. He was barely conscious and staggering, blood still dripping from his nose as we passed Mr Shelton in the corridor.

"Elliot fell over and hurt himself, sir," I said. "I'm helping him to the toilets to get cleaned up."

"Good, lad," said Mr Shelton, completely deadpan. "Assembly in five minutes, don't forget," he added and carried on back to the classroom.

As I cleaned the boy up by splashing water on his face, Elliot was still spitting threats about wanting to see me 'in the ring', where he would no doubt have the advantage. Our metalwork master a Mr Compton was a keen boxing enthusiast, and the school had a sort of unofficial rule that boys could work out their differences under controlled conditions by donning a pair of boxing gloves, more akin to pillows really than the real thing, and having it out in the gym under his supervision. This was what we called 'the ring'. Well, I was a bit bored of it all by now, but I couldn't really turn down the challenge either and maybe it would put an end to the whole thing.

The second round was arranged for a week later. I was to enter Elliot's world, where he had the skill and I was out of my comfort zone. I just remember wondering how I could fell him quickly, as I had absolutely no boxing skill whatsoever, and looking at the huge, soft boxing gloves on my fists gave me serious misgivings about what I was about to do. Would I embarrass myself? This was the fight of the year and the gymnasium was filled to bursting point with boys and teachers filling every available space, all expecting a great fight.

The first thirty seconds of the boxing match saw me on the back foot. Elliot was good, he landed two good punches and I spotted a third coming, so I leant back, hoping to dodge it and counter with a blow of my own. Unfortunately, the well-worn plimsolls I'd borrowed for the occasion lost their grip on the smooth gymnasium floor and I fell, the back of my head hitting the floor with a sickening crack. I don't know how long I was out, but I came around to find the metalwork master Mr Compton asking how I felt and seemed quite relieved.

I'd lost the fight but won the war. Honour being satisfied, Elliot didn't bother me again, or indeed any of the other boys while I was around. And I got to keep my prefect badge. Finally, standing up for myself had proved to be worth it, though I remember having a truly shocking headache for days afterwards.

Bullying affects different people in different ways, and though it's never a pleasant experience to be on the end of, sometimes it's possible to take something good from the unpleasantness. What this might be and how to go about it vary depending on the situation, and sometimes you're going to have to rely on those around you to be on the same wavelength, as it were. Clearly, our form master knew exactly what had happened after I dragged Elliot out of there covered in blood, but he let it slide and things worked out for the best.

There were quite a few dangerous boys at our school, or boys with dangerous families at any rate. The Richardson lads in the year below me were apparently related to the notorious gang who nailed their victims to the floor with six-inch nails. These were the kind of people you were dealing with, and it wasn't easy by any means, yet we all managed to live and let live in the end.

In my adult life I have been bullied by all kinds of people, but thanks to my experiences at school I've been able to sit quietly back and bend with the flow of the situation. Not capitulating to the bullies, but not overreacting either and making things worse. If I hadn't learnt to do that when I was young, I dare say my life would have turned out rather differently.

There's nothing so cruel as children, so they say. There will always be bullies at school, the best you can hope is that the victims aren't too badly scarred from the experience and that everyone learns something useful from it. You can't teach children right from wrong like teaching them how to spell words or multiply numbers, life doesn't work that way. They have to experience both right and wrong for themselves in order to properly understand it.

Adults, however, really ought to know better. The last big lesson I learnt from my time at school was that grown-ups don't always know best. And that whilst knowledge is most assuredly a powerful thing, if it is only repeated rather than understood and blindly accepted rather than questioned, it can be more dangerous than ignorance.

Chapter Three
The Eureka Moment

All truths are easy to understand once they are discovered. The point is to discover them.

~ Galileo Galilei

Life is full of inexplicable things, and a recurring puzzle for me is what many call the 'eureka moment' when your brain suddenly solves a problem that's been troubling you with such clarity and precision that it is akin to a religious experience.

This 'eureka effect' or epiphany is a well-documented phenomenon whereby people claim to have suddenly solved a problem that previously appeared impossible. Scientists investigating the eureka effect have noted four key features:

- The person reaches a deadlock in their thinking, where no matter how long or hard they try, they cannot make any further progress towards a solution.
- The person is unable to describe how the solution came to them, and usually report that it happened while they were thinking about something completely different.
- The solution comes to the person suddenly, and at a time when they felt as far away from finding that solution than at any point in the process.
- Creative thinking has a strong correlation with performance in insight-based problem-solving tests.

Einstein himself reports that it was such a moment that led to his Special Theory of Relativity, one of the greatest singular achievements in scientific history. He tells the story thus:

I started the conversation with him in the following way: "Recently, I have been working on a difficult problem, today I come here to do battle against that problem with you." We discussed every aspect of this problem. Then suddenly I understood where the key to this problem lay. Next day, I came back to him again and said to him without even saying hello, "Thank you. I've completely solved the problem."

So it seems to me inarguable that such a phenomenon exists, and what's more that it is responsible for some of the greatest scientific breakthroughs in human history. Yet, nobody can explain satisfactorily how or why it happens. There are many theories, of course, linked to brain function, sleep, dreaming etc., but none that can stand up to any kind of scrutiny.

I have a theory of my own that I will put to you, but first I would like to explore a little more the achievements of some of these inventors, and why the eureka effect may well be more a stroke of luck that randomly blesses people, rather than an indication of some genius-level super intellect.

Einstein is reported to have said that when thinking about relativity, he imagined himself travelling along a beam of light out in space. To me, this indicates a genuine touch of genius and touches on characterisation number four of the eureka effect above, in that it represents a high degree of creative thinking. This is how Einstein visualised his concepts, allowing his mind to shoot off in all kinds of directions, seemingly oblivious to the established rules, as understood, written in books and cast in stone by the learned. Einstein ventures where the average professor of physics could never have imagined or dared to go for fear of their own status being questioned. Indeed, Einstein himself said that he believed inventiveness was what set the real clever people apart from their peers.

Einstein was obviously talking about himself, but while his creative thinking allowed him to achieve the eureka effect and thereby write his name into the history books forever, what is less remembered is that he got far more wrong than he did right. Even now the theories of Einstein that we hold as sacred truths are being cast in doubt by a handful of contemporary thinkers who dare challenge them, which isn't many. As the American author Studs Terkel said, "I always love to quote Albert Einstein because nobody dares contradict him."

This idea that some 'truths' are unchallengeable has always sat uncomfortably with me. But I accept that the premise of, for example, the speed of light in open space, is sound and have no concrete means, personally, of challenging Einstein's theory. Other people, however, do.

Dr Gunter Nimtz and Dr Alfons Stahlhofen of the University of Koblenz announced in 2007 that they may have slaughtered one of physics' sacred cows by firing microwave protons, tiny energetic packets of light, instantaneously between two prisms around three feet apart. This experiment is, at the time of writing, the only violation of Special Relativity currently known, and relies on quantum physics, a discipline that even the brightest minds would admit is very strange indeed. Nevertheless, it suggests that there are yet aspects of our understanding of the physical world around us that are open to question, including those truths held as unbreakable, passed down to us by those whose moments of genius have rendered their whole body of work unchallengeable.

The first time that I experienced the 'eureka effect' was when I was about thirteen, attending science class with the science master, Mr Baxter, who was at the time far more interested in liaising with the gym mistress from the girl's school upstairs than he was in teaching us about science. Everyone knew what was going on, and we would joke about the way he straightened his tie and combed his hair as he left the classroom to 'attend' to other business.

Each time he took his leave of us, he would pick a boy from the class to sit in his chair and write down the names of anyone who misbehaved while we did whatever work he had set for us. Usually, it would be writing about what we'd learnt from last week's experiment, whatever that was. If there hadn't been an experiment the previous week, or we'd already done our write-ups, he'd set us the task of inventing something that might be of use to mankind in the future. Recalling it now it seems quite comedic and farcical, but I promise you every word of it is true.

If you're wondering why a classroom of teenage boys without a teacher didn't up and make one hell of a racket, that would be because Mr Baxter was also the caning master and we were all afraid of this deeply sadistic man who just loved to cane little boys for the slightest indiscretion. So we all got on with our work while the science master got on with the gym mistress, and everyone was more or less happy.

Until, that is, the day I had my eureka moment whilst trying to 'invent' something for one of his time-killing exercises. 'Invent what?' I remember thinking over and over as I sat for ages with my mind muddled and unhelpful. Then I closed my eyes for a moment and there it was, clear as a picture, a machine I'd never seen or heard of before, but somehow I knew everything about it and how it would work. It just came to me.

It was a ski boat, a hydrofoil as we know it today. I could see it perfectly in my mind's eye. Somehow I knew that it could weigh 120 tons and still travel at around 75 miles per hour with a large enough engine to lift it up out of the water where resistance would be less and allow it to just skim along, easy as anything. I knew it would need some sort of small wing just below the water to cause it to lift like an aeroplane, and that the craft would be more efficient out of the water propelling people at speed from one place to another. I knew this all in a moment, without any indication how or why.

I put it all down on paper, sketches, descriptions, numbers, everything, and handed it in at the end of class. The following week Mr Baxter went through all the different ideas and gave each one a mark out of 20 depending on how creative, useful and viable he found them to be. Everyone received between ten (for the worst) and eighteen (for the best.) Everyone, that is, except me. My work was far worse than the others, 'The work of a complete imbecile, a fantasist's' we were told, and deserved a much lower score. He had given me a five-out-of-twenty initially but then reduced that to four because the handwriting was barely legible.

Well, I was bloody annoyed and had to bite my lip to stop myself asking what kind of marks out of twenty he should get for teaching while he was off with the gym mistress half the time. But Mr Baxter wasn't finished with me yet. He spent the whole lesson making a laughing stock out of me and my idea. He explained that this had been tried in the twenties, but "on little boats", "and do we see them now Mr Emin, they were a bad idea and you insist 120 tons". He even drew a boat on the blackboard with a little ski in each corner skimming across the water and wrote up mathematical equations none of us could understand, which he said proved that my 'invention' would take an engine so large that no hull could carry it. For all I know, the equations might have been complete nonsense, but he was the teacher after all and I was just some thirteen-year-old 'squirt', what did I know? He went on about displacement and how I had no idea about it at all, and how my idea for this fast 'ski boat' was complete nonsense from start to finish.

Here was a crossroads in the life of this little squirt and no mistake. Should I just say 'yes, sir, you're right' or 'sorry, sir, I think you're wrong'? Remember that Mr Baxter was also the caning master, so we were all extra-specially scared of him.

"Well, boy?" he barked.

What could I dare say? I'd never experienced such a 'eureka moment' before, so I was confused and unsure of everything I'd written down. Here was a grown man, a science teacher no less, telling me that it was all rubbish and of course he must be right. But still, I knew something that Mr Baxter didn't. Even at my tender age, I knew what I felt, and I felt like everything that had popped into my head that day was somehow old knowledge, like I'd known it since I was born and something in my mind had just triggered that day to make it available to me. Some part of me deep down knew that the ski boat would work, and I said so. I pointed out that it was less of a ski boat and more of an aeroplane I then picked up a chalk and drew an airfoil section that I said would fly through the water.

Mr Baxter blinked at me for an incredulous moment before turning to the blackboard, pointing to the nonsensical equations on it and asking which part of his calculations I wished to correct. Obviously, he had made a mistake, he insisted theatrically, and would the boy genius Emin be so kind as to correct his work for him as I obviously knew best. Each sentence sent the room into gales of laughter until suddenly the science master's demeanour changed and we all sensed it in an instant.

"You're here to learn, Emin," he snapped angrily, "that's what you're here for and that's what I'm here for, and you'll be on a very sticky wicket indeed if you wish to buck the system. We can't have boys trying to teach the masters their jobs, it's pompous and rude and ridiculous. So I'll ask you again, will this invention work? Choose your words well, Emin."

Gulp.

"Well, sir," I began shakily, "I can't argue with you about the maths, and I'm sure you're telling us the truth and that you mean well, but there must be a mistake somewhere because I know for sure that a 120 ton boat can go 75 miles per hour if you build it the way I said."

"Right!" barked Mr Baxter with a mixture of disbelief and fury. "Go to the headmaster and fetch the cane and book, Emin, and tell him it's for arguing with Mr Baxter."

I did as I was told and received a couple of whacks on each hand for my insolence, the obligatory 'thank you, sir' accompanying each stroke of the cane.

The following week Mr Baxter decided to make sure I'd learnt my lesson. He wanted to hear from my own mouth that the invention wouldn't work, else there would be further punishment.

"I think it will work, sir," I said stubbornly. "In fact, I know it will."

Back up to the headmaster I went and back down came the cane. This time the headmaster had a little chat with me, for my own good, of course, insisting that I ought to climb down off my perch and stop challenging the masters as that simply wouldn't do at all. I tried to explain that I wasn't being arrogant or causing trouble for the sake of it, but that I was genuinely convinced that I was in the right on this and that I wasn't about to back down and lie about it. I even suggested that if it was a problem, Mr Baxter could simply stop asking me the question and I wouldn't have to say the things that obviously angered him. Again, the headmaster repeated that I was there to learn and that it would be best for everyone if I considered his advice very seriously, and then he sent me on my way.

The next week, exactly the same thing happened in Mr Baxter's class for the third time now. This time when I was sent up for the cane the headmaster came back down with me and had a little word with Mr Baxter, and after that everything seemed to carry on quite well. But that was not to be the end of the matter.

Mr Shelton was the maths master, and all of the boys liked him to an extent that rather bordered on hero-worship. He was a blonde, six-foot-something superman who loved cricket and made lessons interesting and fun. At any rate, the headmaster was obviously concerned about my rebellious streak, as he saw it, exhibited in Mr Baxter's class, and he thought that maybe Mr Shelton, a man I liked and respected, would be able to get through to me. So it came to pass that one of our maths lessons a short time later became all about my ski boat invention, and Mr Shelton showed with calculations that even a thirteen-year-old could understand how Mr Baxter was right and I was most certainly wrong. The whole class was put to work to see if Emin's boat could float, and though it was a fun lesson I had a sick feeling in my stomach that a car crash was headed my way. *Please*, I thought to myself over and over, *please, oh please, don't ask me if I agree that it won't work.*

He did.

Out came the cane, and the headmaster gave me another lecture on knowing my place before the whole matter was dropped and 'Emin's boat' was never mentioned again.

Until, that is, some three years later when I was walking to school and heard quickening footsteps approaching me from behind. It was the headmaster. He caught up with me and thrust an open newspaper in front of me.

"Have you seen today's newspaper, Emin?" he asked with clear excitement in his voice.

"No, sir," I replied, confused, "but where is your car?"

"In for repairs," he replied dismissively, "but never mind that, Emin, look at this!"

The newspaper story had a picture of a huge military speedboat that looked like it was on skis, and the article claimed that it weighed over 120 tons and had been clocked at some 75 miles per hour over Lake Volga in the USSR.

Well, the headmaster seemed even more excited about this subject than I was, and he asked me now, standing at the gates of the school, what I thought about it all. I said that the speed and weight certainly seemed right to me, and wondered how efficiently the craft would travel at sea as opposed to a calm lake. Oh and by the way, I said casually, would the headmaster be so kind as to pass along this information to Mr Baxter and Mr Shelton, as I didn't wish to embarrass them.

I certainly added a couple of feathers to my cap in the eyes of the headmaster that day. It was a nice feeling and a welcome psychological boost as I was staying for two extra years at school in order to catch up and finish my O-levels. But the questions remains, how did a thirteen-year-old boy apparently know better than two masters? The truth is, I honestly have no idea. I couldn't prove what I thought I knew, I didn't have the mathematical skill or the scientific background to explain it, all I had was this raw knowledge in my brain and an instinct that somehow it was all just true. It felt like a door in my mind had opened and let me in on a secret, complete and perfect.

What would you have done in a similar situation? What would anybody do? Stand up for their instincts, or just accept the judgement of the authority figure and forget the whole idea?

Forgive me now for taking a potshot at the Holy Grail of physics, but $E=mc^2$ has never made much sense to me. We take the speed of light, which is obviously a huge number, square it to make it even larger, then multiply mass to find energy. But how on earth can we be accurate when dealing with such huge numbers and such a tricky little blighter as the atom. We can be sure that manipulating certain atoms can release a huge amount of energy locked up in their structure, but why not use 1.2 times the speed of light or 1.75 times? The speed of light, after all, is only reached by photons forcing their way forward under their own steam, and it makes little sense to me how this can have such a bearing on the behaviour of mass when converted to energy. We're dealing with carrots and apples here, trying to pretend they are one and the same just because it suits the recipe we're currently working to. I believe this calculation needs to be looked at very carefully, especially in light of this new evidence from Germany with regards to the speed of light perhaps not being absolute at all. But then people are so loathe to take on the heroes of science, it may be a long time before we see any movement in this direction.

Whether there is any merit to my tired speculations or not, the speed of light seems to be yet another example of scientists throughout history using their sacred cows as roadblocks to discovery, with a vehemence no different from our forefathers not so long ago when they insisted that the Earth was flat or that atoms could not exist. Even though the Greeks knew that the world was round thousands of years ago. We are all of us slaves to our time and place in history, each generation believing it is wiser than the last while making the same complacent mistakes over and over. For me, I suspect that breaking the 'light barrier' will prove in the end much easier energy-wise than breaking the sound barrier, due to the lack of resistance involved. In order to break the sound barrier, we had to force our way through compressed air akin to a brick wall. The barrier between ourselves and light-speed travel is but a mental one.

Theories are certainly lurking out there that would alter time itself as we understand it, spurred on by the results of experiments where a fraction of a second has been gained or lost, the results fed into computers and strange new conclusions are drawn about what kind of things may happen if we actually did travel at the speed of light. We need to investigate these theories, bizarre as they sound to us at this moment in time, but the will it seems is not there so long as we cling to what we have already discovered and patted ourselves on the back for understanding. I see Einstein as a real barrier to the progress of mankind, and until someone puts their head above the parapet and calls time on this comfortable arrangement, we will simply continue banging our collective heads against a brick wall to any real progress.

We should be thinking for ourselves, not blindly accepting when we're told not to bother. What chance do we have when the greatest brains of our time feel no need to challenge the theories of a man who was born when manned flight was string and canvas wings? We are afraid to voice our ideas for fear that without definitive proof they will be laughed off and we will be thought crazy. Antoine Lavoisier posited the existence of atoms in the middle of the eighteenth century, but it was over a century before physicists accepted them as credible. Einstein bravely picked up the torch in 1902, trying to demonstrate that atoms existed and had a finite, non-zero size. Again, without irrefutable proof, his papers were largely ignored. To be ridiculed by one's peers seems to be the fate of all true inventors and innovators.

Our unwillingness to challenge accepted scientific wisdom is holding us back. In order to explore the universe, we need to be thinking much bigger than current space shuttle technology. I would invest money in any company with a mind to develop a constant thrust engine based on nuclear power, and the proposed ion engine that theoretically at the moment produces too little thrust but at least research seems to be headed in the right direction. The Russians at one time had an idea for a large, strong air vessel that propelled itself forward by means of small, controlled explosions that caused compression and release in a perpetual cycle which could theoretically replenish itself and therefore accelerate possibly forever, but what became of it is a mystery. We are dragging our heels on these ideas, as people seem unwilling or unable to believe in what may be possible.

I am beginning to believe that space travel will one day be accomplished by a means that is only now being considered with the emergence of quantum physics where distance might not be all that relative in the overall scheme of things, where a craft will theoretically at least, slip in and out of realities to emerge in the blink of an eye to wherever they wish to be, a billion times the speed of light yet no speed at all between two points.

We have abandoned our dreams, which are often the most powerful tools that we have.

***

Theories are fine so long as you can prove them, which for me being a pragmatist means actually physically witnessing and experiencing the phenomena being described rather than sitting at a desk juggling numbers until they appear to fit. We are beginning to find now, especially with advances in quantum physics, that many of the 'absolute truths' we hold dear (even though most of us don't understand the theories behind them) are somewhat less than absolute. Conventional wisdom says that a teaspoon of a collapsed star could weigh hundreds of tons or more, but this too sounds suspect on the face of things. When you compress normal matter, energy is used and energy is released. Matter cannot be compressed beyond its true nature, though it may seem possible at first glance. Coal compressed to diamond is still carbon-based and will eventually burn to nothing if you keep squeezing it, just as iron or rock if taken past a certain point. It is the only theory that makes sense to me, far more so than matter compressing more than a million fold to make a hundred ton teaspoon full of super heavy matter at any rate.

Perhaps I am wrong. In fact, the likelihood is that we are all woefully ignorant in these matters and possess only the illusion of knowledge, common knowledge that we accept and pass on without ever really understanding it, it passes in through our ears and out through our mouths without ever coming into contact with our minds and our critical faculties.

But what, you're probably wondering, does any of this have to do with the 'eureka moment'?

The history of ideas suggests that every true innovator has one great invention in them, and that's it. While there are a few outlying cases, this statement broadly holds true. So what is the limitation? If these are people of truly superior intellect, why are they unable to maintain a constant level of 'genius' level thinking and take us forward in more great technological leaps and bounds? Does it not strike you as odd that even the great Einstein blundered many times following his truly great discovery, and spent many long years living off of his reputation. We make celebrities out of our great thinkers, almost to the point that they are deified in a sense, especially after they are dead and gone, and their theories no matter how shaky remain largely unchallenged.

It is my contention that great leaps forward in human understanding are not merely the product of random occurrences of genius level intelligence but of something even more amazing. A secret locked away in our genetic code that speaks to the nature of man and our place in the grand scheme of things.

Let us not get ahead of ourselves just yet, however. We will return to the mysteries of genetics later on, but for now, a more familiar, if no less wondrous phenomenon demands our attention.

Chapter Four
Love at First Sight
1961–1966

If you have it, you don't need to have anything else, and if you don't have it, it doesn't matter much what else you have.

~ Sir James M. Barrie

I met the first love of my life a few days after obtaining my driving license, which was less than two weeks after my seventeenth birthday. I was looking for my friend at a night school where he was learning something electrical, I forget exactly what it was when I passed a girl in the long corridor between the classrooms who got my attention. She wasn't strikingly beautiful in the conventional sense, but she had this bright smile that just attracted me immediately.

A few minutes later I passed her again, at which point, on an impulse, I turned around and asked her her name. The girl blushed red and her eyes fell to the ground as she muttered 'Rose', then she looked back up at me with that smile again and it was clear young love was in the making. Rose had bouncy, bubbly hair set into curls, thin, delicate features and that natural wiggle of a woman that attracts men.

I was driving my dad's car at the time, which was mine whenever I wanted due to Dad having lost his license through drink driving. When I picked up Rose for our first date she seemed so unsteady on her high heels that I thought she must have rushed out to buy them especially for the occasion.

I thought she was the love of my life. No, she was the love of my life, at the time. Seventeen-year-olds with no experience and no real knowledge of the world tend to feel that way about their first time, that it's love and they will be together forever. There's nothing wrong with that of course, dealing with all those strange new feelings is a wonderful thing that we all should experience. But life goes on relentlessly, and in the two years I was with Rose it became clear that while she and her mother were contemplating marriage and everything that went with it, my mind was not so eager.

Rose lived in Eltham, and I in Bermondsey, at least before we moved to a big house in Shooters Hill. I was working for my dad at the time, learning the trade of a plumber under the wing of an experienced pro who was on Dad's books. Dad was a shrewd man, he knew exactly what the Greater London Council wanted from a house to ensure that a mortgage could be issued on it, and he instructed me to follow strict rules in organising the building works so that our properties were brought up to that standard. I became adept at making hard decisions managing the building sites and taking care of the buying side of the property business while Dad found mortgages and sold the houses. We always had people queuing up, so we were never short of work and we always turned a healthy profit.

I was thrown into the deep end as a young lad looking after sixteen or so grown men, but I soon settled into the job and managed to cope with it. When I went home at night though I felt a different kind of pressure, Rose wanted to settle down and I felt increasingly like I wanted more of an arms-length relationship, help things cool down a bit. Which isn't to say that I didn't think the world of her, because I absolutely did. That bond you form with your first love is a strong one, and even to this day, I remain firm friends with Rose, her husband Frank and their two boys.

But at the time, I was young and foolish and didn't know how to deal with the situation, so I dabbled with other girls, mainly one-night stands since I had no intention of settling down just yet. Rose had her suspicions of course, and it threw our relationship into troubled waters. I would never admit to my indiscretions, which led inevitably to lies that held for a time until finally I was caught red-handed.

Carmel was a brassy blonde girl with a wiggle and giggle that was fun and infectious. When I met her she was getting over an engagement to a man who drank too much, and I remember thinking at once that his loss was my gain. At any rate, we were out shopping in C&A one Saturday afternoon, Carmel and me, and her little four-year-old nephew. I lost sight of her in the crowd as she flitted between racks of clothing, me being a man and not paying much attention to that sort of thing, so I lifted the little boy up on my shoulder to help me look for her.

It was at that point that I turned around and came face to face with Rose and her mother. The thunder in the old woman's face said it all, even before Carmel compounded the misery.

"Here I am, lover," she purred, sidling up and draping her arm over me. "Who are your friends?"

"I will see you later," I said quietly to Rose, but she had already turned away. In a moment, she and her mother were gone.

I had done wrong, so I thought I ought to go and face the music. Within a few hours, I was at Rose's front door, but her mum barred the way in and wouldn't budge. I was not welcome in that day. Ho-hum. Well, another tiff, they were becoming a way of life for us and I thought, foolishly, that it would all be forgotten in a day or so as they usually were.

It wasn't.

I didn't put up much of a fight. Even as young as I was, I was aware that teenage marriages usually ended up on the scrap heap, and curiously I knew deep down that she wasn't going to be the mother of my children. Still, our time together will always be precious to me, and I think it was important for both of us to learn a lot about the world. Nevertheless, it was a painful situation. Poor Rose was still really just a child with nothing else to call her own in the world, and me with no money and no home to call my own. I really did care for her, though at the time I'm sure she didn't appreciate the way things turned out.

I learnt a huge lesson then that has served me well over the years, which is never to lie to the one you care about. Treat them as you would wish to be treated yourself, and you will both be better off for it.

Anyway, I got on with my life, in the back of my mind wondering who would be the next girl to steal my heart the way Rose had done years before, wondering what she was doing at that moment in time, unaware that our paths would meet sometime in the future. Sometime. But when?

I continued buying houses with Dad, as a partner in the firm and doing them up until the huge credit crunch in the sixties when all loans on houses simply stopped and we only had one left to work on, which I intended to move into as my own having earned more than enough by now to claim it. Unfortunately, Dad had other plans. Having seen the housing crash put a dent in our short-term prospects, he had taken all of the firm's proceeds and 'invested' them in a row of large properties facing the sea at Margate, which he intended to convert in to one and run as a hotel with his latest lady friend (whom he managed to pass off to most as nothing more than his 'manager', though that didn't wash with me and no doubt Mum took it as yet another assault on their marriage.) I say hotels, actually they were an established bed and breakfast facility, but then Dad always did have a knack for embellishment.

This wasn't the first time Dad had decided to throw our money away after hare-brained schemes. He once tried opening a cheese factory which promptly failed, before importing bath towels from Turkey which I implored him not to do but, of course, he thought he knew best.

He had forgotten to mention, of course, that my half of the business fund, which I had worked hard for over several years, was now tied up in these 'buildings' that I knew nothing about until the deal was done. I had always put my earnings back into the firm so that we could continue to grow, on paper I was a rich young man, though I kept only five or six hundred pounds in cash at the bank, which wasn't a bad sum for emergencies at the time, but now it was literally all I had in the world.

I was livid at Dad's decision and told him so in no uncertain terms, demanding that he handed over our last unsold house along with a few thousand pounds which I would use to keep the business ticking over until such time as the finances of the country took a turn for the better. 'Nope' was his answer. He wanted me down in Margate to help organise the alterations to the properties, and I'm sure he assumed that if I was left penniless and without a job, I would do as I was told and move down there with him. His attitude was that he was the boss and I shouldn't forget that.

"But you've spent my money without my permission," I seethed.

"So what?" he replied arrogantly. "Sue me."

Well, that wasn't going to happen. But neither was I about to be blackmailed and move in with him, his girlfriend, and the twins, Paul and Tracey. I wasn't going to sleep under the same roof as them while Mum sat back in London wondering what the hell was going on. Dad may not have any scruples left, but I did, so I left him to get on with it. I had trusted him with a large sum of money and he had taken advantage. But then, I wouldn't have had it any other way, as the path that I chose in the aftermath of that bitter experience led to a pot of gold not only in cash but far, far more valuable things besides. Of course, I wasn't to know that yet.

Being short of any real cash was a big change for me. Previously, I would never think twice about buying up several houses at once if the price was right. My share of the profits that I'd been accruing all this time would easily have bought a whole bundle of properties, but that was all gone now and I was stuck with no job, no plan and no funds to work with. So I kicked my heels for a few days wondering what to do. I couldn't stay idle, had to keep moving and start building something new for the future.

I'd never worked for anyone outside of the family before, but I thought it might be a good experience now. Besides, being a plumber and property developer with no funds and no mortgages available, what choice did I really have? I had to get my bearings.

Working for Hall, Beddle and Sons Builders kept me busy at the age of twenty-one, and it was around this time that Mum decided I should start looking for a wife to settle down with. She was old fashioned and she didn't think that indulging a string of casual girlfriends, which to be fair was pretty much the norm for men of my age during the sixties, was quite appropriate. I had to be fresh up on Saturdays and work through until twelve-thirty, after which the weekend was mine to do as I pleased and by that point, I just wanted to unwind. Usually, it would be off to Southend for a spot of fishing off the pier for mackerel or garfish. Then in the evenings, there were girls, one after the other, who drifted in and out of my life as I drifted through the weeks and months without much of an idea as to what to do next.

I managed to negotiate a deal to sell the family house in Bermondsey, which consisted of a shop and three floors above where we had been living, and buy a large house in Shooters Hill, where Mum became the queen of her castle. Though typically over the years Dad still managed to take out loans secured on the place to prop up his failing hotels. My mother began badgering me to look for a wife, oh and by the way, she might know of a girl who would suit me down to the ground. I should have seen that coming.

The tradition in Cyprus was one of arranged marriages, but by the time the sixties rolled around it had evolved more towards couples who had already met, usually socially or at wedding parties, going through the formalities of asking to be introduced to the other's parents in order to pay respects to the old traditions whilst still giving people freedom to choose their own partners. Still, there was something to be said for the following tradition, though in my case it was an introduction to a prospective partner, it spoke to the quality of the families involved and I knew it would please my mother, so I agreed to do things the hard way and to meet this girl, about whom I knew next to nothing except for her name.

Meral worked at a hairdressing college where she had just graduated in Lewisham, and where Mum had her hair done. It was a sort of shop where they trained girls by letting them work on paying customers and evidently Meral had got chatting to Mum while she snipped away. Mum showed her a picture of me, and Meral thought I was handsome enough to take the next step, so she asked her parents to invite us round for lunch one Sunday.

"Mum," I began, standing with her and Nan on Meral's doorstep that day, "when you said that all sorts of things could still go wrong, what did you mean?"

She didn't answer. She just smiled and said nothing. Fully ten seconds passed after we rang the bell before, a middle-aged woman opened the door just enough to get a good look at us all.

"We have an invitation to have lunch with the family," said Mum, and she introduced us all in some detail, even going into which village in Cyprus she and Nan originally came from before turning the conversation around to me. When she was finished, the woman smiled.

"Yes, please do come in," she said, opening the door wide for us. We were led through to a large dining room with a big table in the middle and chairs all around the edge of the room where various family members and others were sat to act as witnesses to the proceedings. One was a man I recognised as having been employed by a group of decorators we'd used while we were doing up the houses. He spoke up to the effect that he knew and worked for me for several years, and vouched for my character.

If any of them knew of any reason why I shouldn't marry this girl, any evidence of wrongdoing in the family that they felt was sufficiently important, they would have said so at that time. It occurred to me that what Mum had been really worried about was whether these people might have heard about Dad and his shenanigans with taking most of the family's money and settling himself in with another woman. As it turned out, they had heard a kind version of events and didn't seem the least perturbed by it all. Word gets around in communities like that, and these were very astute people, but evidently, they had decided to give me the benefit of the doubt and nobody said a word.

Meral herself was nowhere to be seen and neither was her father. The fathers were typically kept out of such negotiations, presumably for the good of all involved. So the chattering began, and it soon became clear that our families had lots of friends in common and the women had plenty to gossip about. It was going well, at least. We explained that I worked in property and that the family was now in the hotel business, and we were quite clear about where our money was, which was obviously of interest. As it turned out, of course, they knew all of this already and the questions were really more by way of getting to know more about me personally.

What they didn't know was that Dad had been up to his old tricks behind the scenes, seeing my potential match with Meral as a prime opportunity to drag me back into his mess. He'd had a quiet word with me regarding my intentions, suggesting that if we were both 'compatible' he would let us have the last house and some cash as a wedding present. On the condition, naturally, that I went down to Margate and took my proper place at his side, managing the works that he was having such difficulty seeing through. Typical Dad, thought he would get his own way as usual. Everything was always about him. Well, not this time. "Nope" was the simple answer he got from me. If the meeting with Meral did go well, I was going to do things my own way.

With all this still fresh in my mind, I interrupted the women at one point, which I shouldn't have done really, to explain that I was on my own now and that I would be getting back into the property business just as soon as I had some funds built up and mortgages were available again. This family were shop owners themselves back in Cyprus until the civil war came and one of their shops was put to the torch while Meral's father had been horribly beaten. That's when they sold up and moved over to England. Both families had had their problems, transient we all hoped, but I was speaking their language now and they appreciated that.

At that point, we were offered drinks. Mum and Nan plumped for coffee (medium Turkish) whilst I requested a cold drink. Asking for anything alcoholic would have been a big no-no as it might signify a drinking problem, though this wasn't a problem for me as I was tee-total until the age of thirty-five and even then not much of a drinker. Perhaps because I'd seen what alcohol had done to Dad with his shrivelled-up liver, part of which had to be removed by the surgeons.

We took a breather from negotiations, Mum obviously pleased that several hurdles had been cleared already and things were looking good. It was at that point that a young woman entered the room carrying a tray full of drinks. I knew immediately that this was Meral, but I had been warned by my mother not to give any reaction until she gave me the nod. If Meral or anyone else didn't approve for whatever reason, I was to stay calm and do nothing. Well, staying calm was more of a challenge that one might have thought, as my mouth suddenly went dryer than an Arabian desert.

Meral was absolutely drop dead gorgeous, with long, dark brown hair that sparkled as though she were infused with some kind of magic. I remember thinking that she bore a resemblance to Raquel Welch, but even more beautiful now standing in front of me. I tried not to look too obviously as she went around the room serving drinks to everyone, but I noticed her glance at me before looking away and nodding her head a few times in approval. Mum beamed at me from around Meral, who was now standing between us, and she gave me the nod. I'm sure the look on my face said it all. *Yes, please*, I thought, *she will do magnificently*. Who said arranged marriages were a waste of time? Sometimes Mum really does know best.

"Naturally, you will be staying for lunch," said Meral's mother as an excited murmur rippled around the room, "so that we can talk over the details of the engagement between my daughter and your son."

Well, not only did they fix a date for an engagement party where both sides of the family would come together in a large venue to celebrate, they even went so far as to suggest possible dates for the wedding, all of which were in the near future. But I put a slight dampener on those plans, stating that I was still working for other people and wasn't quite ready to settle down just yet. Maybe we should take things gently at first and just learn to understand each other better. They couldn't understand this hesitance at all, but I was very conscious that I had hardly had a chance to hold this girl's hand, let alone hop into bed and start to make children.

In any event, they were understanding and agreed to leave Meral and me to our own devices for a while. We began our courtship with a series of evenings out, but I soon found that as beautiful as Meral was, the spark was somehow missing. She seemed to be of that attitude that, since we were to be married, whatever I thought was right was okay by her. Ho-hum. Fear began to creep in. Having those doubts in the back of my mind, I was reluctant to take the relationship further. Most Mediterranean girls at the time kept themselves for their husbands, and for a man to take something from a girl and then not marry her, well that would be a disaster for everyone concerned. Both families would be shamed dreadfully.

So I kept to kisses and cuddles, all the while feeling that there was something just not quite right here. It wasn't that I had no real money at the time as I knew that would change. No, something inside of me just said that this wasn't her, not the person I would spend the rest of my life with.

"Isn't she beautiful?" Mum would say, and I had to agree. Whenever I looked at Meral I was filled with such pride that she was so loving and beautiful and mine. We made a great couple and no doubt could have lived a happy life together. And yet. And yet.

"Will I ever love her, do you think?" I asked my mother.

"You're very well-suited," she replied encouragingly, "Everyone said so at the engagement party. Keep at it." She pressed on, noting the look of uncertainty on my face, "It will take time, but she's a very caring girl and she thinks the world of you. You're very lucky."

If you say so, Mum.

Meanwhile, I had been working very hard to get two office buildings completed for Hall, Beddle and Sons just outside London. I suspected that they had sent me out there to get me away from the other plumbers, who were beginning to resent the speed at which I worked. It was near the end of this job when Rube, the plumbing foreman, came down to inspect my work.

He looked at the first job, then the second then had a little chuckle to himself and asked how I was doing.

"Another hard day," I said, "I think six weeks might have been a bit tight to get both buildings finished, but it will be done."

"Young man," he replied, repressing another chuckle, "if you had listened to me properly you would have heard that I gave you six weeks each to complete them."

It was all I could do not to collapse on the floor in a heap. I looked over at George, the only plumber's mate who could keep up with me as he had the uncanny ability to cut the pipe to whatever length without even measuring it, and his face said it all. Well, at least I was in for a decent bonus said Rube, and with that, he was gone.

That was April 1966, on the penultimate day we would be working in Horley, and there was still slush in the streets from the late winter we'd had. I remember going across the road to buy five President Cigars and the *Daily Mail*, but they were closed due to a funeral that day. So I went over to the nearby café-come-restaurant, where a lovely lady named Kitty looked after George and I every day and cooked us our meals, and asked her where there might be another newspaper shop. "The end of the high street," she said, "then through the underpass to the railway where there was a newsagent called Mallinsons." This was a moment in time that I have often pondered. Had I gone back to work and worked on and sent George and not gone myself, I would have most certainly missed out on finding a fantastic treasure, more desirable than mere gold.

George offered to go, but I noticed that he had a tear in his left shoe and it was a decent distance to walk. *No way, mate*, I thought, *I'll go*. So off I went in my Wellington boots, woollen bobble hat, scarf, bib and brace overalls and donkey jacket and a few days stubble, looking as scruffy as you like. I sludged through the slush, eventually reaching the shop not realising I had found the end of a rainbow and within a dozen breaths my life would change forever I picked up the newspaper, dropping it on the counter without looking up and asking if they had five President cigars.

"Yes, sir," replied a soft voice.

"Thank goodness," I replied, "I've come a long way for these."

"How far?" asked the voice.

I looked up at the girl for the first time, and at that moment felt like I had been struck by a bolt of lightning.

"Turkey. No, Cyprus." I said absent-mindedly, tripping over my words. A little voice in my head was telling me that I had found the woman I was going to marry, the mother of my children, here she was at last!

"I mean, just down the road."

My brain wasn't in gear at all. I paid for my items and left, then just as I passed the big shop window I took a step backwards and peeked at the girl who had just served me. *Hmm*, I thought and headed back to work. I was puzzled. No, tormented, and it showed. I went back to work, though all I could do was squat on the floor of the last room we had to finish. George later said he'd never in all his time working with me seen me stay still for such a long time, even when we were eating. Well, this lasted an hour or so before I decided to ask the site foreman for a pair of size 9 Wellington boots from the storeroom.

"George," I said, "can you do me a favour? Put these on and go down to Mallinsons, have a good look at the girl there and let me know what you think. See if you can get her name and find out how old she is. I don't want to make a complete fool of myself. For all I know, she might be twenty-two with three kids, or worse. You're a man of the world, see what you can do, mate."

George went off with a chuckle, returning some time later with the job no further progressed in his absence.

"Well," he said, "she doesn't seem to be wearing a wedding ring or an engagement one for that matter. She could be fourteen but she could be twenty-two like you say, it's hard to tell, sorry. She does seem grown-up to me though."

"What about her name, George, did you get it?"

"Oh yeah, the owner of the shop Mr Mallinson told me her name was Agitha," replied George.

"What a beautiful name," I replied.

"Well, that does it," grinned George, "I may not be the man of the world you think I am, and maybe I can't judge a girl's age, but I do know that you're smitten and no mistake." Then he quietly chuckled himself red with laughter.

What I hadn't told him was that the second I lifted my eyes and saw this girl, I knew in an instant who she was and what she would mean to me. Honestly, I didn't even have long enough to properly look at her face as it felt like a mist had come down over me and I was in a state of shock. I was already engaged to a wonderful, beautiful girl and our families were busily getting ready for us to be married. What was going on? I wondered what lunacy had invaded my mind.

I am a practical man, and love at first sight? Was that possible? Maybe, maybe not. Maybe this was something even more profound, something that happens to some of us without anyone understanding how or why. All I know is that none of this was making any sense to me whatsoever.

On my last day in Horley, I picked up my tools and got in my car, stopping at the newsagent one last time to pick up a newspaper and say goodbye to this strange situation. I remember she told me her name was Barbara, not Agitha. Mr Mallinson was obviously just being protective of her. I could understand that.

Well, I had a few sleepless nights after that, and after struggling with myself a bit, resolved to send a card with a bunch of red roses to the shop where she worked. The girl later told me that I'd spelt Barbara incorrectly, but the gesture nevertheless had the effect that I was after. On Sunday 24th April 1966, at one-thirty in the afternoon, I picked her up from the end of her road and we went to Brighton. I remember saying as we turned to walk onto the pier that I had something to tell her. We both stopped and looked at each other.

"I'm engaged to be married," I said heavily. Barbara didn't say anything. "Not only that," I went on, "but I'm a bit of a bastard too. In fact, I'm still messing around with another girl as well. I wanted to tell you all this so that you'd know exactly what you're dealing with here."

She looked deep into my eyes, almost right through into my soul, and said simply, "Do you want to marry me?"

That's a trick question, I thought. But I turned things over in my mind and reasoned that I had promised to tell the truth no matter what, and now here this girl was standing in front of me.

She was probably going to give me the elbow anyway after this silly confession, so what was there to lose? "Yes," I said, with some misgivings. "I feel the same," she replied, smiling. Maybe I was in shock, but we walked a few steps more and then a pier photographer came seemingly from nowhere and took our picture. Still stunned, I paid him half a crown and left an address, and a few days later received an envelope containing two pictures of my future wife and I, taken less than a minute after she 'proposed' to me. How strange, less than one hundred minutes from picking her up for this first date, without even exchanging a kiss, not even held her hand, not even so much as a simple touch, she seemed to know something.

"Why did you do that?" I asked her in the car on our way home.

"I really don't know," she said. "I'm usually very shy, but I feel like I've known you all my life. I feel like I've been waiting for you and wondering what you would look like. Then when I first saw you in the shop I knew it was you. I had sleepless nights lying awake wondering if you would come back, and you did."

Now there's a thing.

Mallinsons closed half-day on Wednesdays every week, so Barbara would get on a train to Victoria Station and find her way to the job I was working on at the time. Then we would drive back to Shooters Hill where I left her to have a soft drink at the local pub while I washed off the grime of a day's work before taking her out for the night. Around nine-thirty pm I'd take her to New Cross station and she'd catch a train back to Horley. We had to do things this way, keeping it a secret, and all the while I was torn up wondering how I was going to find the right words to break off the engagement. On the other hand, maybe I was waiting for me to wise up from this ridiculous situation. Meral was stunningly beautiful, our lifestyle was compatible, Meral and I would make a formidable business couple for our respective parents to be proud of. Common sense and practicality dictated that I should be sensible and just get over Barbara and my silly notion of a future with her. If I did not take care. I knew it would hurt Meral terribly, and both our families too. But that decision was about to be taken out of my hands.

After one such Wednesday evening, I returned home to find Meral and her mother, and my mother sitting in the front room, a distinct gloom settled over the place. I had been rumbled. Meral herself had seen me with a young woman in my car as I passed the bus that was taking her home.

"That was the nice disabled girl down the road," I said, without missing a beat. "I saw her at the bus stop and couldn't go by without giving her a lift home." Neither of them looked as though they believed me. "Let's go now and I'll introduce you to her and her family," I pressed on, throwing myself completely into the lie, "I've told them all about you and they really want to meet you."

Mum never lied, but she gave me the benefit of the doubt, and bless her when Meral's mother asked if there was such a girl. She had to agree or else lose face, so she confirmed my story. I took Meral and her mother home, and they apologised over and over for jumping to the wrong conclusions. I felt terrible involving my mother that way, especially as all she would say afterwards was, "I hope you're not behaving like your father."

It was about to get worse.

After the scare she'd just had, Meral resolved to get me somewhere she could keep an eye on me, and about a month later, she asked me to take a slightly different route back to her home. I followed her directions until we came to a corner shop, a hairdresser's with a covered yard off to the side. An estate agent's 'sold' sign was clearly displayed.

"Do you think you could get back into the property business from here?" she asked, adding that my problems with my father could be forgotten as her father would be more than happy to invest heavily into the property business, me supplying the knowledge and know-how and him the cash. I looked at this building her father had bought for us. It was a three-floor pile and quite capable of being a good base for the things I was planning. "Well, that's ours now," she said. "Now take me home."

But we weren't quite done yet.

"No wait, that way," said Meral, and again I followed her directions to the Old Kent Road this time. "Stop!" she exclaimed suddenly, jumping out of the car and waving excitedly for me to follow. We stood outside the Ford showroom looking at this huge executive car, the like of which I'd seen while I was working on a job and commented that I would own such a vehicle someday.

"That's my wedding present to you," said Meral, grinning. "It will be delivered on our wedding day."

She was so happy, but a gloom was settling over me, which I just could not shake. I need time, time to consider the future. Two paths before me, one paved with light and riches and the beautiful Meral, the other not so clear, virtually no cash and a shop girl that I hardly knew and a silly notion in my head. What should I do? I knew I couldn't put it off any longer, the house was bought, plans were made and everyone was looking forward to a marriage within thirty days. Funny this, it was easy really. I simply listened to my conscience and decided there and then. There was no way to be gentle about what I was about to do, but she didn't deserve any more of this.

"Things have a way of coming around in time," said Meral. "I've taken you at your word and made things come around, and now look! Aren't you pleased? We can marry within a month!"

"I'm not sure we can," I said sadly. "I appreciate everything you've done and I know that this is the done thing in Cyprus, doting parents giving such gifts as a dowry for the bride. But I wouldn't be a man if I took your generous gifts without having in my possession money or property at least equal to their value."

I genuinely felt as though I was being bought, though I didn't say it like that. So what would be my excuse? I had laid out carefully how we ought to proceed through the engagement, telling her over and over that things would work out well, and who knows maybe I would have got Barbara out of my system by then and for her to be patient. But all that was undone now. I took off the ring she'd given me and handed it back to her. After that, we went our separate ways.

Meral was young and beautiful, I knew she would be okay in the end even though it was no doubt painful for a while. I regret what I did to her as she didn't deserve any of it, but I feel at least that it was better to end it then rather than go on living a lie. The genuine justification about my not having enough money to bring to the table was at least something her family could understand. It allowed everyone to save face and retain their dignity. And really, what else could I have done? I knew deep down that I would spend the rest of my life with Barbara, even though she was still an enigma to me and I couldn't understand the powerful feelings that enveloped us both. It didn't make any sense in my head, and yet somehow it did, deep inside me.

What still confuses me now though when I think back on it, was that the first time we met in that little newsagents I barely got a look at her. No long, lingering look, no taking in her form, or the way she moved, we hardly said two words to each other. Surely, this isn't a situation you'd normally associate with the idea of 'love at first sight'. It was more like something clicked in us both, instantly, in a single moment, and for me at least it was the last thing I had ever expected.

Sometimes I try to rationalise that it was simply a case of naïve mutual infatuation. But then I know what that feels like, I would describe myself as something of a rampant youth after all, but this wasn't the same thing. Even after we got married and started a family, I would still appreciate other girls aesthetically, comparing them to my wife and mostly to her favour, even telling her as much. For me, dishonesty would be to take a sly look at a beautiful girl and pretend not to have seen her. Barbara never got jealous when I'd make these remarks, we've always been able to talk completely honestly on any subject without holding back, we just seem to understand each other naturally like two people who've spent a dozen lifetimes together rather than just the one. I think that's the true mark of finding someone to love, and I wish everyone could experience the happiness and contentment we have, but sadly many seem to settle for less, or for convenience.

Maybe I should believe in reincarnation. That would at least explain the shock of laying eyes on someone for the first time and feeling like you've known them forever. Though it wouldn't explain how we found each other, how her mother was that same Kitty who looked after George and I in the café, sneaking us extra food now and again. Or how I would never have set foot in that newsagents at all if George hadn't had a hole in his shoe. It makes you wonder whether some things are just meant to be.

Sometimes I wonder if it's all just a game we play for puppet masters.

Chapter Five
X Marks the Spot
1988–1996

If there is magic on this planet, it is contained in water.

~ Loren Eiseley, *The Immense Journey*

If you want to learn a little something about human nature, try presenting people with events and situations outside of their customary understanding of the world. Things that make them uncomfortable, deep down in that indefinable place within us all, which conducts our most base instincts. Their reactions will speak volumes.

The following stories illustrate exactly that, putting under the microscope not only myself but also the many people I met along the way, attempting to determine why events unfolded the way they did, and what our responses to them might tell us about who we really are.

Dowsing, simply put, is the process of trying to find something that cannot be seen. Some call it divination or doodlebugging, while others speak in hushed tones of dark magic and witchcraft. Dowsers can use twigs, or metal rods, pendants, or even nothing at all to assist them in their search for ore, or gems, oil, or any manner of trouble.

I have been for many years now a professional dowser. Finding water was my speciality, and I became rather known for it back in my home country of Cyprus. We have a holiday residence there, built into the side of a mountain overlooking the sea, and whenever we would visit we would always find several letters and telephone messages waiting for us from people wanting me to go and dowse their land and find just the right spot to start digging down.

Benjamin Franklin once said that when the well is dry, we know the value of water. Most of us take it for granted, hooked up to the mains supply all we have to do is turn the tap and out it pours. But without the benefit of that infrastructure, for the entrepreneurs building things from scratch as many were on the Island back then, tapping their own supply was like striking oil and it was a business fraught with uncertainty.

That's where I would come in. When I had the time, I was happy to work for free, dowsing being something I enjoyed anyway and the satisfaction of seeing a beautiful piece of land fulfil its potential was reward enough for my efforts. Two notable situations, however, virtually put a stop on my doing any further work without a fee for strangers, and at the same time gave me a peek of insight into what makes mankind tick.

At the time of the first incident, we had just moved into the new house and I was having much of my furniture made at a local carpenter's shop. The craftsman in question was a small, genteel man with a delicate touch on wood the like of which could transform any set of drawings into fantastic-looking furniture. His workshop was situated on the main road, behind which another road trailed off lined with lemon trees for some two hundred yards before the carpenter's house, and then a fifteen-acre field that almost reached the sea. It was a stunning location and no mistake, but during one of my visits to the workshop, I noticed that the lemon trees were looking a little sad and thirsting for water.

I asked the carpenter if there was a problem, whereupon he led me solemnly out to a spot amidst the lemon grove and showed me a well that he and his brother had dug. And then another. And another. The latest only just begun, fifteen feet or so deep, and all of them bone dry. Just thinking of all the work they had put into searching for water, the sheer cost in sweat and toil and now for the trees to be dying anyway, it made me feel sorry for the man, so I asked him what it would be worth to have enough water for all his needs.

He shook his head sadly and simply said that there was no water, that the land had dried up and that digging this last well was just one, final, desperate act before he gave in and grubbed up all the lemon trees.

"If it were possible though," I pressed him, "what would it be worth to have that water?"

The man thought for a moment before pointing over his land towards the sea

"A double building plot," he replied, "anywhere along the waterfront. Anywhere on any land that I own, I would gladly give it up for free." He eyed me suspiciously. "But how is this possible?"

Evidently, my reputation, such as it was at that time, had not preceded me. I explained in Turkish since the man spoke little English and would not understand what a dowser was, that I was a water Osman. This had the effect of making him stand back and observe me with even more bewilderment.

"What do you know about such things?" he snapped. Apparently, it was a skill usually only claimed by 'wise' old men and even then not in enlightened times such as ours. They were almost magicians, he said, and in this modern age who believes in magicians anymore other than children?

Well, I don't know if he realised that the things he said were offensive, but I let them wash over me calmly as is my nature. I did let him know, however, that I considered his words a challenge, by taking out a little crystal pendulum that I carried with me for just such a purpose and checking the final well. It was dry, as we both suspected, and I told him so. Go ahead and keep digging, I said, if you wish to sweat unnecessarily.

Then I did another little test, just for myself, to find out if there was actually any water going under his land. My senses told me that there was plenty, and at high pressure too, more than enough for any purpose to which the carpenter may wish to set it. Saying nothing, I allowed myself a little smile before pulling my face straight again in a deliberate theatrical manner, making sure that the man saw it before I turned and started to walk back towards the road.

"Well?" he called out after me. "Is there water on my land or not?"

"What would I know of it?" I replied with a smile, climbing into my car. "I'm not a water Osman, am I?" Then I started the engine and drove away, leaving the carpenter to stew in redress for his poorly chosen words.

A couple of days later, he came to my house unexpectedly on some pretext or other, and we chatted a while. I hoped that he had learnt a little courtesy and was happy to allow him the opportunity to demonstrate it, but alas he continued where he had left off, telling me that he didn't believe in such superstitions, and asking what made me think I could do as I claimed. He said that coming from England I should be thinking more technologically, not in terms of mumbo-jumbo which was for old heads who only knew old ways.

I kept a straight face and let the insults simply pour off me, one after the other, until he was done. Then as calm as you like, I told him that I was not insulted by being called a fool, which was what he had done, and that if coming all the way here to have his little rant had in some way eased his worry at not finding any water, that was fine by me. But if he did wish to approach the problem with a more open mind, he might do well to contact the two people whose details I wrote down for him on a piece of paper before showing him out.

The names I had given him were the owners of the first two wells dug following my dowsing exploits on the Island. Both now enjoyed lush gardens and more water than they knew what to do with. I suspected that I would be hearing from the carpenter again before too long. He did not disappoint. Within twenty-four hours, he was back at my door and the first words out of his mouth were gushing praise. Not for my skills, as one might expect, but rather for my generosity. Evidently, he had heard that I dowsed those first two wells not only perfectly, but also for free. What a kind person I was, he said, how good and generous and full-hearted.

Well, I can't deny that I was pretty pissed-off. One minute I'm some charlatan, perhaps attempting to perpetrate a confidence trick upon him, the next I'm the best thing since sliced bread. His doubts were gone, sure, but greed and duplicity had replaced them quick smart.

I kept my temper, however, remembering my manners as I had been taught and invited him in for coffee.

"Nescafé or Turkish?" I asked.

"Turkish medium," came the reply. I busied myself making it when after a moment my wife Barbara appeared at my side, shaking her head. Why couldn't I leave the poor man alone, she asked. Couldn't I see he was terribly desperate? She took over making the coffee and I walked out onto the balcony to ponder the situation. It was a beautiful day, and standing in the shade of the house, overlooking the sea with a nice breeze on my face, I felt that under such conditions most differences could be overcome, so I waved the carpenter out to join me.

"We're off back to the UK in two days," I said, "and we'll be back next year."

"But the trees will be dead by then," replied the man in an almost child-like voice.

"What did you say this was worth to you?" I asked, casually sipping my coffee.

"You want… payment?" he replied, with more than a hint of surprise and disappointment in his voice. "They said you were a kind man who would not take advantage of people. A real gentleman and a true water Osman of old who never failed to find water on land where people thought there was none."

Good grief, where was all this nonsense spilling from? A day or so earlier I doubt even the Spanish Inquisition could have wrenched such generous words from him, yet now it just kept on coming.

"A kind man?" I said, raising an eyebrow. "Who says I am? Besides, you have a talent. You are a very skilful carpenter and you charged me thousands of pounds for your work. You have land, lots of it. You are not poor. What, then, do you expect of me?"

I spoke quietly, calmly, yet the words clearly had a certain force the result of which could be seen in his expression, one of shame and discomfort. I made it clear in no uncertain terms that I was greatly offended by his attitude and questioned how I could work for such a person now, before returning to my coffee as I watched the water sparkling far below.

"Two of the finest plots," he replied, "anywhere you want, they're yours if you find me water to save my lemon grove."

Again with his precious lemon grove. I knew he wanted to develop his land with houses, all of which would need water and all of which would turn him a substantial profit. Lemons? Money more like was what he cared about and trying to take me for a lemon. Still, he was a pitiful sight and my natural inclination was to help him, so I told him that I would do so. Could he be trusted to fulfil his commitment, I asked, or did we need to have a contract drawn up? Not that I was really bothered about the financial benefit, as I was already fairly comfortable by then. Still, two sizable plots where I could have built a couple of houses a stone's throw from the beach, that was nothing to sniff at.

I was naïve, I admit it. I still believed up to that point that a man's word was his bond, it was the standard I lived by myself and expected others to do likewise. Unfortunately, such morals are not always reciprocated.

I found two aquifers under the carpenter's land, one twenty feet down and the second, more powerful, at thirty-six feet. The deeper of these lay upon black clay, a thick layer laid down millions of years ago and above which all water flows. That single well would supply the lemon grove ten times over, plus as many houses as the carpenter cared to build. It was a triumph by anybody's standards, and I looked forward to drawing up plans for my new beachfront properties.

Alas, that was not to be. When I returned a year later to check on the progress of the wells, I was greeted warmly for sure. The carpenter thanked me and his family fed me generously with many pats on the back for my good work. But no mention was made of the reward he had promised, then or at any time since, though there are quite a few expensive houses down there now with beautiful gardens.

Experience is the name everyone gives to their mistakes, or so a wise man once wrote. I ought to have learnt from this experience never to take a man at his word in matters of land or money. Life, fortunately, is a diligent teacher and has an obliging habit of testing a man on what he should have learnt. I was about to receive such an examination.

My gardener, a certain Mr Aslan (which means 'lion' in Turkish, like the famous children's stories), knew much of my work as a dowser. One year after the lemon grove fiasco, while we were out in Cyprus again enjoying a holiday, Mr Aslan came to me in desperation. It transpired that a good friend of his had spent thousands of pounds drilling and digging dry wells to try to revive his land and was in the process of digging another that did not look hopeful. Please, the gardener pleaded, could I help this acquaintance who was at his wits end?

As I say, dowsing was something I enjoyed doing anyway, and it only took a moment for me to agree to let him drive me over there. I didn't want or expect any payment for my assistance, so what could possibly go wrong? It still puzzles me today how things turned out the way they did.

Chas was a well-educated young Libyan man married to a nice Turkish woman by the name of Leila. They owned hundreds of acres of beautiful land rising from the main coastal road up a mountainside, high up where his house could just be seen. Mr Aslan drove me along a dirt road into a large walled area with majestic gardens, a beautiful house and a swimming pool to die for. Everything was built to the absolute highest standard, from polished marble to gleaming gold fittings, opulence the like of which I had rarely seen and truly breathtaking to behold.

When I met the owner of this incredible property, I couldn't help myself but ask how he had managed to accumulate such wealth. Chas explained that he rented the back end of leases on high street properties in London, Brighton, Manchester and other places, sometimes a month or two and sometimes a little longer, and packed these temporary shops full of cheap clothes, end of line stuff and rejects bought in bulk and sold for £5 or less. It's a strategy that was popular in the high streets of Britain, and back then it was making this man an absolute killing. With ten shops currently open and more on the way, Chas was absolutely awash with cash.

Having explained all this to me proudly, he then raised the issue of water. He wanted to enlarge his garden, he said, but was unable to do so at that time because all of his wells were dry and he was barely able to bring in enough water by lorry to keep what he had lush and green. He took me outside and showed me several of the wells, which were indeed dry, and one that was in the process of being dug. Standing over the top of the newest well was a very large man, dressed immaculately all in white and with skin to match which seemed impervious to the darkening effects of the hot Mediterranean sun. He was introduced to me as the most experienced well digger on the island, and the craftsmanship of the construction that his workers were currently toiling away at was certainly impressive. The problem was that they were eighty-eight feet down by now in this new well and yet to see a drop of water.

Chas whispered to me that this well digger was also a true water Osman, so I asked the man himself if that was so.

"That's what they call me," he replied with a smile and a shrug of his shoulders. His English was good, and he explained that he was never wrong about these things. So sure of his skills was he, in fact, that he had pledged to work for nothing unless water was found.

Well, that was a bold claim indeed. I considered myself a fairly accurate dowser, but nobody was one hundred percent accurate, certainly not to my knowledge. Another little concern that I had was that finding water halfway up a mountain has its problems so I asked him how he could be so sure, at which point he took out a little pendulum, just a stone tied to a length of string, and showed me roughly how he undertook his calculations. I asked him how deep he thought the water was, and he suggested that they were just off of finding it, any time now.

Something told me that all here was not as it seemed. I asked if he minded my checking his location, and upon receiving the go-ahead produced my own pendulum and did a little dowsing work myself. When I was sure of my findings, I looked at the man without a word. Our eyes met for what felt like an age but must only have been a few seconds, before he blinked and grimaced. I nodded a negative agreement, and he admitted to me with shame on his face that this one had him baffled. He'd never been wrong before (so he said, but I don't believe it), and not finding water here would leave him with a huge bill to pay his workers and suppliers.

I commiserated with the man and asked who it was had taught him his skills. Perhaps one of the old heads, about whom my carpenter friend had been so dismissive? But no, apparently a British army Colonel stationed in Cyprus during the sixties who had retired and bought a house in the eighties had hired him to help dig a well and shared with him some of the tricks of finding water. The Colonel hadn't taught him how to gauge things like depth and flow, however, I spent a little time explaining those things and sharing with the island's premier well digger a little knowledge he could work with that would no doubt be hugely valuable to him, but then wondered how that three minute lesson might help considering it has taken me over two decades to get right. Together, we dowsed down to the black clay far below, and both agreed that there was nothing but dryness where he was digging this well.

Not to be discouraged, I returned to the car and took out my dowsing rods made from six-millimetre bright steel in an 'L' shape, thirty-one inches long with handles around six inches. Holding them loosely in front of me, I lined up the first triangulation line. Directly behind where I was standing was a large tree, and looking directly ahead of me in line with the rods there was a wooden post sunk into the ground and barely visible above the scrub. The ideal spot must be somewhere along that line, I knew, so I walked around at an angle of about ninety degrees to the first line and found the rods pointing to a spot somewhere near the wooden post. After a little pinpointing, I explained that the best place to dig was in what seemed like an inaccessible area of rough scrub, a short way down a hill and with no obvious path for the necessary machinery and materials to reach it.

Chas took this news with surprising good cheer. Money was no object, he said, and he would make the necessary arrangements immediately. How much water though, he asked, was there?

Dowsing takes something out of you. I cannot explain why, or how it works, but take it from me that it drains your energy for sure, especially when you have to fight through dense brush in the hot sun. I was gasping for a cold drink, so we walked back to the house and sat by the pool with a Pepsi, under a huge umbrella-like structure built from brick and tile and sprouting phones and other gadgets.

They seemed like nice people, polite and well-educated, and their two children were a particular delight. The company was good and the conversation light-hearted, and at some point, I happened to mention that in my haste to leave with Mr Aslan that morning, I had forgotten to pick up my hat, and the sun was really punishing me for it. I'm not much of a fan of the sun as I darken virtually by the minute and always return home several shades darker than before, which in any event is a light brown.

Chas disappeared inside the house and returned a moment later with a huge sombrero, which he plonked on my head and asked me what I thought of it. Well, I think I could have shaded my entire family under there, and must have looked a comical sight standing up and walking back to the site, hat flopping either side of me, to work out the depth and flow measurements.

Underneath my new portable canopy, I did a little more dowsing to establish that the water was about one hundred and twenty-five feet down through clay-type rock, easily broken up with a compressor, and it flowed at a good pressure which would easily fill the well for some thirty feet from the bottom. I shared this information with Chas and warned him that the pressure was so great that far down that no man must be left to work past a hundred feet without another man present and a rope with knots fixed ready in case the water rushed in, which I believed it would.

I repeated this warning to both him and to his wife before I left, emphasising that the water would be very cold and any man left alone in it for too long could easily drown. I told them that I would return later in the year to check on the progress of the work and bid them farewell.

Come late October that year, Barbara and I were preparing to fly back to Cyprus for another short break, and I thought it worth just calling ahead to see how things were going. Leila answered the phone, and as soon as she realised it was me she blurted out, "Oh, you were right! The poor man nearly drowned!"

About two weeks earlier, apparently, the workmen had dug down to around a hundred and twenty-five feet down and were still breaking their way through muddy clay with the compressor, when the man at the top of the hole wandered off to fetch something, leaving the man down below on his own. That's when the floor of the well erupted and filled it to over thirty feet while the poor workman struggled to keep himself afloat by holding on to the rubber hose feeding the compressor breaker at the bottom of the well. He knew that if he pulled too hard, the whole thing would come tumbling down and almost certainly kill him, so he just steadied himself as best he could while the freezing water rose all around him.

By the time help arrived, the poor chap was so cold that even when a rope was thrown down to him, he could not make his hands hold fast to it no matter how hard he tried, and eventually, another man had to be lowered down to fetch him out. He was alright in the end, said Leila, but it was very close and all because they hadn't listened to the warnings I gave before I left.

A couple of days after arriving in Cyprus, I went to see the new well for myself. On arriving, Leila directed me towards a new roadway extending from the house down towards where I remembered dowsing months before. It was properly constructed for sure, some hundred and fifty yards long, coated with tarmac and easily wide enough for a large lorry. Alongside the road was a trench with galvanised 3" water pipe and alongside that an armoured electrical cable all in preparation to pump the water away. At the end of the road, I found a concreted wellhead with a square base a foot above the ground and a well some five feet in diameter which was another foot and a half higher. The whole thing was very professionally built, and I imagined that the great white water Osman I had previously met at the property had been given the job to help claw back some of his losses.

As I waited for Chas himself to join me, I thought that I would just check a few things out for my own satisfaction. I took out a ball of string and tied a little rock to act as a weight, lowering it into the well where I could see the water reflecting some way down, until the string slackened, at which point I tied a knot in it and lifted it carefully to the top of the water and tied another knot before fetching the whole lot back up again. This little exercise told me that the water was about thirty-five feet deep and fully one hundred and twenty-five feet down to the bottom of the well.

Just as I was rolling my string back up, along walks Chas who had just flown in that day from London. Feeling rather satisfied with my work, I asked him what he thought about his nice new well. To my utter amazement, he told me that he wasn't happy at all. I asked if he was joking, but he insisted that the well was dry, that he had wasted his money again and that he still had to have three lorry loads of water delivered every day.

Well, I couldn't believe what I was hearing and asked him to explain why, if the well was useless, there was thirty-five feet's worth of water at the bottom of it. He said that there had been a flash flood some days earlier that came down the mountain and filled the well. Now, I am not Sherlock Holmes, but there were absolutely no signs of what he described. I saw little twigs lying broken all around that would have been washed away in a flood, as well as many footprints in the dirt and all kinds of contrary indicators. I pointed these things out to him, as well as the fact that the water would need to have jumped up two feet and six inches to get into the well, but all Chas would say was that there had been a flash flood, and the well was no use.

I didn't have the heart to say that his wife must have told me a pack of lies on the phone just a few days earlier, which I am quite sure that she did not. I just couldn't understand the attitude of this man at all. I hadn't asked a thing of him, nor presented him with a bill for my services or anything of the sort. In fact, I had made it clear from the start that I was happy to help as a favour to Mr Aslan. I can only assume that it was in his nature somehow to not wish to be beholden to anybody. Still, a simple 'thank you' would have been nice.

I looked him straight in the eye, shrugged my shoulders and left without another word. Chalk it up to experience. That was lesson number two, but life wasn't done testing me just yet.

A year later again, whilst out in Cyprus, I received a call from a lawyer asking if I would search for water on his land. It's always nice to meet new people and add another dowsing project to my list, so I told him it would be my pleasure and off I went.

On my way to see this lawyer, I saw Chas's house far off in the distance and noticed a string of trees lining the road that had definitely not been there previously. Everything looked very lush and green up there and I couldn't help but marvel at what he had clearly managed to do with no water of his own. But that was all in the past now and I was happy to leave it there, except that the first thing the lawyer mentioned to me when we sat down for a drink was how he'd heard all about the work I did for Chas.

"Terrible, isn't it?" I replied, quick as a flash, "All that work for a dry well and now the poor man has to buy water by the lorry load. I let him down very badly." Then added, "Are you certain you wish to take that chance with me?"

Whether it was the words themselves or my overacted remorse I couldn't say, but the man stared at me for a moment before bursting into laughter.

"Who do you think recommended you?" he chuckled, "Chas's well is the best in the whole area and everyone knows it's thanks to you."

So that was how it was, eh? Not gracious enough to say thank you for a job well done but pleased enough to boast to his friends. The lawyer went on to say that he was happy to pay a fee for my services or just say thank you if that was all I wanted. The whole thing was starting to leave a bitter taste, as though I was having a Mexican hat plonked on my head all over again and ushered out to work for these arrogant rich men for free or else for some nominal tip.

I did the job anyway since I was already there, but it was the last time I dowsed for free. Sometime later I heard on the grapevine that Chas built a large holiday complex on his land and was short of water to service it. Word of mouth was that he wanted me to go and visit him again, to which I replied diplomatically that I would pop over if I had the time. Mind you, I don't think I will ever have the time where he is concerned.

For me, dowsing is a great challenge as it gives some insight into things that cannot be explained, though many have tried. Several controlled experiments over the last century or so have found that self-described dowsers are, under test conditions, statistically no more able to find water than anybody else. Experts have hypothesized that perhaps dowsing is an electromagnetic effect, and devised trials with buried wire and metal rods to try to prove this, again with little success. I consider myself a rational person, and surely any rational person would be forced to conclude that it is all nonsense based on all of the available evidence.

Except that I know something else. I know that it works. I know it from first-hand experience. How and why it works? I couldn't tell you. But it does.

It seems to me that mankind, in its slavish devotion to science, has built a brick wall between proof and possibility to the effect that unexplainable phenomena are too quickly dismissed as nonsense simply because we cannot fit them into our current understanding of the universe. A quick look back through history would suggest that this is a rather arrogant and misguided attitude, and I suspect that many great scientists who were mocked in their day for valuing imagination over conventional wisdom might agree. But that thought will have to wait just a moment, as I still have one final dowsing story to tell.

Many years ago, I attended a meeting of the British Society of Dowsers, at which one of the things demonstrated to us was 'map dowsing'. The premise of map dowsing is that one does not even need to be in the same location as the thing they are trying to find, but that a simple map of the area would be enough. Well, for a pragmatist like me who only reluctantly accepted dowsing in the first place because I found myself able to do it, I was very cynical about this idea.

I decided to test it out for myself, so when I got home I set about drawing up a plan of my bedroom and dressing room in as much detail as I could manage; bed, bedside cabinet, pillows, wash basin and taps, everything I could think of. Having completed the plan, I left the room and asked Barbara to place a miniature framed picture of my daughter somewhere in the room, and I would try to find it on the plan.

The first time, she placed the photograph on the left-hand corner of my pillow, right at the edge, before returning to me and watching as I attempted to dowse the position. When I was sure, I pointed to where I thought it was and made a mark on the plan. Barbara, not giving anything away, suggested I should go and look for myself to see how close I was. Well, I was spot on, absolutely perfect.

We did the same again, only this time she placed the picture in the middle of the wash basin's drain. Again I dowsed, and again I hit the mark exactly. The same thing happened a third time, but on the fourth things began to go wrong, until eventually, I was just getting it wrong every time.

I will never lie to myself as it is counter-productive and leads to all kinds of problems, but what I took away from this little learning process was that I am the bee's knees at dowsing. I can be super-accurate at finding something even using nothing more than a rough plan that I have drawn myself. I was sure that, contrary to the various studies on the subject, dowsing was possible.

On the other hand, the experience also showed me that the whole thing can go badly wrong just when you least expect it, and for no apparent reason. It was a puzzle alright.

Professional dowsers are very aware that dowsing relies on 'a need to know', something special inside you will consent to allow you to learn and show you how it works. But try to show off, or push your luck, and it shuts down. But then it's much more than that. For myself, I suspect that the ability to dowse relies to some extent on a psychological 'need' to find whatever it is we're looking for. Human beings are capable of superhuman strength in times of great stress. Variations on the story of the mother lifting a car off of her injured child have been witnessed since time immemorial and nobody can adequately explain how they are possible. Perhaps dowsing relies on a similar mechanic, only mental rather than physical.

At any rate, the defining moment in my dowsing career came a few years ago, again in Cyprus, when a local estate agent and acquaintance of mine, a man named Ian Smith, came to see me. He knew of my dowsing ability and wondered if I had ever used it to search for anything other than water. Specifically, missing people. Well, I didn't have to consider that one very hard, of course, I'd never before been asked to try such a thing.

Ian explained that a certain Brian McManus had gone missing earlier that year while walking his two puppies along a mountain road near to where he lived. Brian was recovering from a stroke and needed the exercise to help his damaged leg recover from the accompanying paralysis, so he went out for a walk every day, I was told, at twelve noon until two pm, since he was also insulin dependent and had to be back in plenty of time to get his injection. He was a true fighter, Ian said, who wouldn't let a silly thing like a stroke slow him down, so out he went every day at noon without fail.

One afternoon, however, Ian received a call from his wife, whilst he was still at his office, who had heard from Brian's wife that Brian hadn't returned from his walk, and now it was getting dark, and she was very worried. The three of them went out in the car, following Brian's usual route, to see if they could find any sign of him. When they came to a certain area they found the two puppies, lost and disoriented in the headlights of the car and reasoned that Brian might be close by. Forgetting the dogs for a moment, they searched the area fruitlessly before running to fetch the local police for help. Everyone searched as best they could until it became too dark and too late to continue.

The next morning the police alerted the local army base, who mustered some five hundred men to sweep the mountain at first light looking for Brian. They found nothing. Even the dogs were now missing.

I stopped Ian at this point and advised that he ought to be very careful not to give me any more information, since this can impair the dowsing process, and to ask if he could simply supply a plan of the mountain showing any roads that were there, along with some personal item belonging to Brian. He returned presently with an old map dating back from when the English ruled the place (I think I saw '1947' in the margin), and told me that it was mostly accurate except that some of the roads had now been widened and straightened to allow large lorries to pass. Then he gave me a jumper of Brian's, which I draped around my shoulders as a witness, and left me to my work.

I knew that they had seen the puppies that night, but I had no idea where, so I decided to try to find that spot first as a guide to whether or not the whole venture was going to be of any use. I thought about the dogs and where they might have been seen, moving my pendulum over the map as I triangulated, not knowing which road Brian had taken or even where he lived. To my surprise, it felt very easy. I marked my first cross with a pencil where I thought the puppies had been seen, and moved on to Brian himself. Almost as quickly, as I moved over the map, I made another cross not far from the first before sitting back in my chair and trying to understand where on earth all of this was coming from.

Early next morning, Ian returned to enquire how I was getting on. I told him that it had been very easy for me, but the proof was in the pudding and he would have to vouch for my accuracy himself. I pointed to the first cross and explained that this was where I thought the puppies had been spotted on the night of Brian's disappearance. Quite honestly, I expected to be told that I was way off, that it was a different road entirely and that the whole thing was indeed a waste of time.

"That's impossible," said Ian, looking hard at the first cross. "It's not even close."

"Sorry," I replied, my heart sinking, "I did my best."

"No," he said, "I mean it's not close. It's spot on. That's the place we call the parking area, where we saw the dogs that night. How did you know that?"

With a shake of my head, I motioned to the second cross and explained that I thought this was where Brian was.

"But that's the side of the road," muttered Ian, "how could that be?"

I understood his confusion. After all, if Brian was just at the side of the road as I suggested, they would have found him by now. They would have found him within twenty-four hours. Nevertheless, Ian said that a team would be sent up later that day to check the area again. I emphasised to him that I had never done this sort of dowsing before, and I could be completely wrong, though I was encouraged by the accuracy of the dogs' position and quietly confident that I was right about this too.

The next day Ian returned to break the news that nothing had been found, even though they checked very carefully for a quarter of a mile either side of the mark that I had made. He said they would go up again later that day, but he wasn't optimistic, and sure enough again there was no sign of Brian.

This was obviously discouraging, but I wasn't about to give up just yet. Armed with the map and my dowsing rods, I drove off up the mountain myself, applying a little dowsing as I went, until the rod told me to stop which I did next to a fairly large parking space at the side of the road. I walked to the edge and looked left and right, seeing nothing extraordinary but feeling very strongly that Brian was not far away.

As I pondered the situation, Ian pulled up next to me in his car and advised me that I was in the wrong spot and to come away from the edge as snakes liked to nest in the cracks down the side of the road. He went on to say they were especially plentiful that time of year. I felt silly at having missed my own mark, while simultaneously putting myself in danger out of ignorance of the local conditions, but I tried to shake it off as Ian drove me further up to the parking spot where the dogs had been seen, and then back down to where Brian should have been found according to my original finding.

Well, confusion was the name of the game at that point. I dowsed the area again just to be sure, and each time my rods pointed back to where I had first stopped by the side of the road. I scratched my head and resolved to return the next day, as it was now getting dark.

The map I was using was old and, as Ian had said, much of the road had been widened and straightened since it was drawn. Upon closer inspection, I decided that the difference in my and Ian's estimation of where exactly the second cross placed Brian was due to some inconsistency in the old map compared to the present reality of the road itself, and that the spot I had stopped in the previous day may well correspond with the mark I had placed on the map.

My suspicions were confirmed when that day's fresh dowsing led me back to exactly the same spot again. And the next day again, and again. By now I was convinced that Brian was under the road. So I spoke to Ian, who in turn contacted the police to voice my fears. The police eventually confirmed that the road had been widened at that point around the time Brian vanished, but they were also adamant that the works had been completed just before Brian had gone missing, so in their opinion, he couldn't possibly be under there. It didn't add up, and no amount of thinking could seem to fit the pieces together. The trail seemed to have gone cold.

That evening I arrived back at my house around five o'clock and assured Barbara that the dowsing was over and forgotten about, and we could get on with enjoying the rest of our holiday. There were two workmen there who had been laying tiles, and they would need a lift home which would have taken an hour or so, but Barbara saw how tired I looked and suggested that she took them home while I prepared the ground for the carpenters who were coming to fit our new kitchen a few days later.

I thanked her and then fetched out my plumbing gear to cap the hot and cold water and make safe the piping. I remember vividly being on my own in the house that evening, gently cleaning and fluxing the copper parts and soldering end feed fittings, and feeling so completely calm and free and peaceful as though the burdens of the last few days had lifted off of me. It was a moment in my life that I have returned to many times since, for reasons that I will explain shortly, but sufficed to say for now that it marked the end of my dowsing adventures for another year.

The story was not quite over yet, however. Just prior to arriving in Cyprus again the following year, Brian's wife and sister came to see me at my home in London. They told me a very strange story about how they had been to see a clairvoyant to ask about Brian's disappearance, and she had told them that he was at the side of the road, just as I had suggested.

Now, as I have said, I consider myself a practical man and I trust what I know. Dowsing works. But clairvoyance is a complete mystery to me and therefore not deserving of a place in the little box of tricks that I know I can rely on. Nevertheless, these women were convinced at what they had heard, and I simply repeated to them that I too believed Brian to be under the road and that I would go back again to have another look for whatever it was worth, though bearing in mind what the police had previously told me about the roadworks having been completed before Brian's disappearance.

Well, I tried approaching the problem from a different angle, but yet again my dowsing led me to the same spot near the edge of the road. Then as I stood there, looking down over the edge and wondering what on earth to make of the whole thing, I caught just for a fleeting moment a sickly-sweet smell in the air. Human decay has its odour that cannot be taken for anything else, and I was convinced that I had found what I was looking for, so I climbed carefully down the side of the road to sniff between the rocks. There was no smell, but as I wandered further down the embankment on to flat ground covered in dried long grass I came across a snake about a metre long, thick and grey with a large head.

The deaf adder is what they call this particular reptile. Deaf because apparently you can walk right up to one and it will not shoot off like others of its kind are wont to do. Most snakes will scarper from human beings, but if you surprise this one you're quite likely to suffer a bite and many had fallen victim to them around those parts. The deaf adder was very close, just half a pace in front of me, and it was well camouflaged in the dry grass. I was wearing shorts and boating shoes, an easy target for this one if he felt so inclined, but I stayed still and calm and surprisingly felt no fear, almost as though I were 'in tune' with this poisonous reptile.

"Come along, move on, little fellow," I said encouragingly, at which point he glanced in my direction before slowly slithering away.

I turned back towards the road, and was about to lift my foot onto the first rock to climb back up again when I spotted another snake, thin and tightly coiled, and almost certainly poisonous, right next to where I was about to step. He looked ready to strike to me, which was understandable given that I had been almost about to crush him, but again I simply stopped and said, "come on, I'm not going to harm you," and off he whipped even faster than the first. Two snakes within a few minutes of each other, and they were the first I'd seen all year. But more than that, they hadn't bothered me a bit, and normally I'm fearful of any snake. That was a bit strange. Even stranger was the fact that I had moments earlier pushed my face between the cracks in the side of the road to sniff for evidence, knowing full well that the snakes liked to nest in there. What was I thinking?

Well, I was sure that Brian was there but had no idea how to proceed. My best guess was that he might have tripped and fallen, and been somehow covered up by the great earth-moving machines that widened the road by breaking off great chunks of rock from one side and dumping it down the other. But several people had assured me that, although such work had been going on along that road, it had finished before Brian disappeared. I tried to gauge a depth reading the same way I did when locating water flows, and guessed that Brian was probably around a metre and a half down below the surface of the road.

I was still standing there on my own, feeling more than a little frustrated, when an athletic, well-tanned man wearing shorts and a t-shirt came running up the mountain. I stepped aside to let him past, but he stopped and asked me if I required any assistance. I told him that I didn't think anyone could help, to which he responded somewhat philosophically. I should stop dwelling on whatever the problem was, he suggested, and go back to my family who were probably missing me. Then he offered to accompany me back down the mountain.

He had a point. I had been dowsing again for some days on this lonely, little used mountain road and it was getting to the point where I really ought to get back to the holiday as it wasn't fair on Barbara.

I assured this friendly chap that I was not, in fact, suicidal, and pointed to the road to indicate what I was doing.

"There," I said glumly, "that's my problem."

"The road?" he replied.

"No, time. The time is all wrong," I said unhelpfully. And then, "Sorry, none of this is making any sense to you. Perhaps I should explain."

"I bet this will be good," he said with a quizzical look, folding his arms. "I can't wait to hear about why this little bit of road is so important to you."

I explained the situation in detail while he listened along patiently, and when I was finished he said something I was definitely not expecting. He said that he was about to help me.

"Help?" I asked, frowning. "How could you possibly help?"

"Just listen, brother," he replied, "I have information you might be interested in" before launching into a story about how he had been for several years a Sergeant in the Turkish army based at the bottom of the mountain. He told me that he ran up and down it most days to keep fit, that he knew the place from top to bottom, and that on the day the Army went looking for Brian, the men with the road-widening machines were still working flat-out as his soldiers past them on their way back to camp, having failed that day to find the missing man.

Well, this was a revelation. I asked him to describe the machines themselves, and he explained that one was a JCB-type digger that broke off chunks from the cliff edge on one side, and the other was a bulldozer which shoved the broken rock down the other side of the road in order to widen it.

Everything clicked into place. Brian must have fallen, perhaps lost his footing on the broken road, or else become distracted by the work itself. Maybe his bad leg just gave way. The workmen hadn't seen him, maybe because they had gone to lunch, or maybe their vision was impaired by their machines. Even if he was conscious and calling out for help, with all that racket going on they probably wouldn't have heard him anyway. And then, horror of horrors, they had scooped up another pile of broken rock and unknowingly dropped it on top of poor Brian, covering up any trace of him.

The sergeant seemed to read my thoughts as he looked down at the road beneath his feet.

"He was an English man," he said simply, "maybe it would be a kindness to say nothing." And with that, he turned and he was off.

When I saw Ian later that day, I told him what I had learnt. But when he contacted the police again, they simply reaffirmed to him that their information was correct. The digging work had definitely been completed before Brian's disappearance and the Sergeant must have been mistaken. Except that they couldn't trace any Sergeant from that base anyhow, so who I had spoken to that afternoon I have no idea.

I couldn't do anything else at that point but turn my back on the whole thing. I suppose we will never really know what happened to poor Brian, though I still believe very strongly that the version of events described above is probably accurate.

It is only human nature though to shrug our shoulders at a situation, no matter how extraordinary, and move on to the next order of business. So that is what we shall do. In any case, I haven't told you yet about the strangest thing to come of my involvement in the matter of Brian's disappearance.

Chapter Six
Doppelgänger Fetch
1971–2000

An idea, like a ghost, must be spoken to a little before it will explain itself.

~ Charles Dickens

If you thought dowsing was strange, this is going to knock your socks off...

How many times in your life have you had an experience that you thought was strange, unbelievable even, but which you accepted based on the assumption that there must be a logical explanation? I have long since lost track of the number of times this has happened to me. Caught up in the pressing business of earning a living, we drift through these moments with perhaps a brief surge of curiosity before relegating them to the secret cache of things we don't talk about with friends or associates for fear of being thought odd. This is not an irrational anxiety. We all have a need to be taken seriously, to be trusted, especially when there are people depending on us to get things right at home and at work. Still, the temptation to share can become overwhelming, and should you succumb to it, you may be surprised to find that you are not alone. You may also be surprised to discover that your own desire to find tolerance and understanding in others proves somewhat less than reciprocal.

This happened to me one evening, on a beautiful night in Cyprus, sitting outside around a large table after a rather nice meal, the wine had flowed and we were all well relaxed and enjoying the company of friends we know and trust. Such times are when we tend to open up and reveal, against our better judgment, those hidden things we normally keep to ourselves. I'm sure we have all been there at one time or another.

At any rate, I was relating to my friends the story of an encounter I had once had with a ghost not long after moving into our first house. I explained that it had all seemed very real, but covered myself at the same time by keeping the anecdote short and qualifying it by stating my belief that it was probably just a dream. For reasons you are presently to know, this was not entirely true, but I had no desire to make myself nor anyone else at the table feel uncomfortable or embarrassed, so I censored myself somewhat and the story went down rather well. So well, in fact, that our host then felt confident enough to share with us her own strange and troubling experience a few years back, when she claimed to have awoken in the middle of the night to find herself floating out of her bed, out of the window and up into the sky.

Well, okay, I thought. We've all had dreams like that. Then she tells us that she floated up into a spaceship, where aliens did all kinds of experiments on her (the finer details of which she declined to elaborate upon, except to say that she was unable to move the whole time), before returning her to her bed. The next morning she awoke naked, with no memory of her clothes being removed, and found her nightdress folded neatly and clenched underneath her hands. There was also a painful puncture mark, she claimed, in her navel, where the abductors had inserted a rather large needle during one of their many tests.

The poor woman almost broke down in tears while relating the story, as if it were a great burden that she had been carrying around for many years and was now so relieved to finally get off her chest. Unfortunately, her guests, including myself, were somewhat less sympathetic than we perhaps ought to have been. As a pragmatist, I judged her story on the basis of my own knowledge and experience, as no doubt, did the others, to be either a dream or a fantasy. A couple of the guests present evidently chose the less charitable of those two options, judging by what was said after the fact.

Nevertheless, the lady very clearly believed that something very real had happened to her, and she had as she saw it tangible proof of those events. If she had said, like I did, that she had seen a ghost, we would likely have been much more comfortable entertaining that notion. Some of us may even have believed her. But the story was so far-fetched and impossible to make sense of that our judgmental inclination kicked in and rather than us all empathising, one or two chose instead to question if she was becoming delusional. More fool them, perhaps, as there are thousands of people all around the world with a similar story to tell. Is there a truth hidden amongst them all that might shed some light on this particular matter? How many more people may have had similar experiences but decided to keep them private for fear of losing their jobs, their friends, or their place in society?

Ask yourself this: have you ever experienced something that you couldn't explain, something so strange that you feared to tell even your closest friends because you were so sure they wouldn't believe you?

Mankind has the ability to spin lies as truth and make truth of lies, to the point where it is one hell of a job to identify what is real and what is not. Even the teller of a story may not know how much of it is real. For many, the only way to stay sane in such an environment is to enforce a simple, empirical rule – do not believe in anything that is not proven. One might characterise such an attitude as diehard pragmatism, and for the longest time, I would put myself squarely in that category. But practicality means more than just taking things at face value, and today my scepticism is tempered with experience.

In a way, nothing has really changed in regards to my outlook on the world, except perhaps that I have become a little braver in saying out loud things that seem to me to indicate that the world is much more than simply what we see, far greater than just a means to an end.

I promised to tell you about the strangest thing to come out of our search for poor Brian on the side of that mountain in Cyprus, and I will. But we need to go a little further back first, in order to properly contextualise the event in question.

1971

Our next-door neighbours in London, a certain Mr Vine and his wife Elsie, were an old-fashioned pair. He was a draftsman, highly skilled in technical drawing and so employed by a large electrical firm to illustrate their machines, while Elsie was a traditional stay-at-home mother to their son Chris, who wasn't so many years my junior.

Barbara and I had started a family of our own, at a time when colour television was new and exciting, and I had just bought a whopping 26" behemoth which we all gathered around once a week to share an experience together. Afterwards, the four of us would usually sit around the table and play a few rounds of brag, enjoying each other's company and generally being satisfied with the world.

Well, brag must have gotten a little stale for Elsie after a while because one week (after an excellent programme about Henry VIII and his many wives, as I recall), she mischievously suggested that, since Chris and his girlfriend were there, we might try out an Ouija board instead. I remember dismissing the whole idea as nonsense, which must have upset Elsie, but she persevered until we all caved in and whipped up a homemade board. We laid it down on the table between us and placed a glass upon it face down, to which we each touched a fingertip.

Immediately, the glass began moving.

"You're all pushing it!" I complained, yet one-by-one they lifted their fingers off to leave only Elsie and me in contact with the glass. I was determined not to help move the thing, but move it did and began to deliver a message. The word 'pop' was spelt out, followed by the beginning of our address and the number of our house where pop used to live.

"It's Pop!" Elsie exclaimed excitedly, at which point I lifted my finger away and the glass came to a standstill. "But," she continued, frowning, "how can it be? Pop is alive and well, I saw him at the old people's home just two days ago, fit as a fiddle." She shook her head. "Not sure what that was all about."

Again, I dismissed the whole thing as nonsense, which earned me a telling-off later on from Barbara for upsetting Elsie, who was after all only trying to inject a little variety into our post-TV Brag sessions. I changed my mind, however, two nights later, when I awoke at about one-thirty in the morning to find an old man standing by the side of the bed watching us.

"Who the hell are you?" I mumbled. The figure didn't reply. I rubbed my eyes as my brain struggled to catch up with what was happening. "Come on! Who are you?"

Then I remembered that Elsie's Pop used to live in this house, and he being, I suppose, fresh in my mind from the other evening, concluded that this old man must be him. Pop had obviously run away from the old people's home, I decided in my half-awake state, and let himself in here, having nowhere else to go. I knew he hadn't wanted to be in the home in the first place, but the atrocious rain we had had a couple of years before had loosened the foundations of his house to the point where it wasn't safe for him to live there anymore.

"How the hell did you get in?" I demanded. "Come on, say something!" But Pop just stood there in his grey, three-piece suit, shirt and tie, impeccably smart with his thinning hair combed over, a slight curve in his back betraying his advanced years, a strikingly sharp nose bobbing up and down as he nodded his head in what seemed like silent acquiescence of who was now in his house. My mind was in overdrive by now, wondering how on earth the old man could have gotten in here since we had changed the locks since the time when this was his home. I blinked and squinted at the figure as though either expecting it to disappear or expecting myself to wake up, but neither happened, and the light streaming in from the hallway in one direction and the street lamp outside the window in the other left me in absolutely no doubt whatsoever as to what I was seeing. This was not a dream. I was sitting up in bed and now clearly awake.

I admit I became afraid, there was a ghost standing beside our bed just nodding. He was as solid as a real person which questioned my beliefs, ghosts are not real, yet here was one steadfastly holding his ground, intently looking at me as I questioned him. My mind was grappling with some form of reality. Yes, fear kicked in, along with my always inquisitive mind running at speed, wondering what next, but fortunately, I wasn't alone and I reached over gently to shake Barbara, who was still sound asleep. She had to see this. But the first shake didn't wake her, or at least she made no sound to indicate as much. My eyes were fixed on Pop so I couldn't be sure, so I shook again, and again, still no response.

"For goodness sake Barbara, wake up!" I said loudly, glancing down at her.

Finally, she rolled over and opened her eyes to see what I was so anxious about. But when I glanced around again to the place where our unexpected guest had been seconds before, he had vanished.

"Sorry," I said as Barbara began to sit up, groggily, "sorry. I had a dream about Pop being here, but it was just a dream. Go back to sleep."

As I say, I am and have always been very much a pragmatist, and as certain as I was in the moment about what I was seeing, still I put it down to dreaming and when I awoke the next morning I thought nothing more of it. Over the next few days, I managed to apologise to Elsie for my inconsiderate reaction to the Ouija board, which she graciously accepted and all returned to normal until about two weeks later when Elsie popped her head over the back wall. I say wall, but the top half of it was a kind of chain-link fence that you could look through, and up which climbers grew and tangled around from the other side. At any rate, Elsie looked very sad, and when she spoke it was to tell me that unfortunately, Pop had died. I said I was very sorry to hear that, and asked her when it had happened. A chill ran up my spine when Elsie explained that Pop had passed away the night of our Ouija board experiment, and while remembering the night of our unexpected guest I asked her if the following description was accurate; the smart, grey suit, slick, combed-over hair, sharp nose, curved posture, all-in-all the picture of a well-groomed gentleman of eighty-something years who had seen two world wars come and go.

"Yes, that's him!" Elsie said. "Have you found an old photograph of him in the house?"

With some misgivings, I began to explain to her what I had seen a couple of nights after we had messed with the Ouija board, and admitted that I had put the whole thing down to being a dream, but that hearing this news made me think that maybe I really had seen the ghost of Pop.

Well, Elsie looked a bit cross, told me I was talking nonsense and marched off back into the house. Funny how things turn about, isn't it? Just a couple of weeks earlier I'd been taking the mickey out of her and her Ouija board, and now it was she who thought I was the crazy one. Or perhaps she just thought that I was saying it as a joke, though I'm quite sure I've never had a form for cruelty such as that. Still, her confirmation of Pop's description, the description of a man I had never met until that night when he appeared in my bedroom, nodding silently as though approving of its new occupants, convinced me that there are aspects of this world which we still cannot begin to understand, but which are never the less real and tangible and important.

I was on the lookout over the next few weeks, but Pop did not reappear and so I supposed that at any rate that would be the end of the matter. I was wrong.

Some years and three children later, my eldest son, then ten years old and having his own bedroom, while the other two shared, came downstairs one night frightened. He wanted to know who the old man was who had been standing at the foot of his bed just moments ago, looking at him. We assured him that there was no old man, that he must have dreamt it, that sometimes dreams can feel very real just after you wake up and that it was nothing to worry about. Of course, in truth, my mind snapped back to my experience with Pop, and I thought it possible that the old man was back to keep a watch on us, but to what purpose I couldn't say.

He made another appearance not long afterwards when my daughter literally jumped out of bed and ran downstairs shivering with fright, swearing that she had seen a ghost and that it had vanished before her very eyes. She was about six or seven at the time, and there was no doubt in my mind based on her reaction that she believed she had seen something, but I didn't want the children to be afraid and so again I said that it was just a dream and there was nothing to worry about, which seemed to put her at ease.

Our youngest would similarly report sightings of Pop, and I would tell him the same thing I told the other two. The more I repeated that it was just a dream, the more it felt like I myself was in denial about the situation. Besides which, Barbara was completely immune to anything to do with Pop, and I suppose her calmness about the whole thing helped me to just shrug my shoulders and accept it, and move on. But ignoring a problem seldom makes it go away, and so it was with our persistent uninvited guest who would be seen from time to time, over a thirty-year period by all of us, except for Barbara who he seemed to keep away from.

Years later, when my kids had kids of their own and Barbara and I were spending a lot of time in our new house in Cyprus, my youngest son Lawrence and his wife Donna stayed in our London home with their two young children. One evening, as the story is relayed to me, Donna was at the kitchen sink preparing a salad to go with the barbecue that Lawrence was firing up outside. The two of them were having a loud conversation through the open doorway when Donna saw, out of the corner of her eye, a figure standing at her shoulder and lowered her voice, assuming quite naturally that it was her husband. She muttered on for quite a while apparently until she came to a question which Lawrence didn't answer, at which point she turned around to face him and jumped with fright at the sight of the old man standing there watching her. She had never seen him before in her life, and couldn't believe her eyes as he just stood there, nodding, and then faded away to nothing right in front of her.

Well, I'm told that Donna came flying out of that kitchen like a bat out of Hell. Lawrence called us later that night to remind me of all the times when they were children, and they would see this old man, and I would always tell them it was just a dream.

"You tell that to Donna," he said, solemnly. "She's just been face-to-face with him."

Lawrence and Donna continued to stay in the house while Barbara and I were gone and to take care of Tom and Suzy, our Jack Russells. But they weren't entirely comfortable there, and after returning from Cyprus one time they sat us down and flat out said that they thought the house must be haunted, big time. They hadn't actually seen anything on this occasion, apparently, but it was more of a general atmosphere that they could feel affecting them in unpleasant ways and they were surprised that we couldn't feel it ourselves.

The fact was that I could feel it, my acquiescence of this matter, over what must have been three decades of sightings and strange room feelings indicated that anyone could become used to a strange situation, till it becomes part of their life. I had not said anything because Barbara seemed immune to it all and it didn't seem like there was much to be gained from making a fuss. However, the fact was that my son and his family were not happy there and that wouldn't do.

I had seen a programme on the television about how to get rid of ghosts, and while thinking at the time that it was nonsense I had nevertheless remembered some of the techniques and decided it might be worth a shot applying them to ours. The programme suggested that ghosts are sometimes locked in a situation they can't get out of, being tied to one place for some reason or other and that simply talking to them might resolve the situation amicably. So I had a little think about what I might say to this trapped old man and prepared for a time when the room felt different, the uncomfortable atmosphere which Lawrence and Donna had mentioned.

That day came not long after. I walked into our bedroom and noticed immediately that it was not the light, airy room that I knew. It felt somehow claustrophobic and foreboding. Plus, it was the height of summer and roasting hot outside, yet the room was cool, almost chilly. I got the feeling that I wasn't alone, which you may scoff at but then I'm sure you've often sensed that there was somebody nearby, or somebody watching you without any rational way of knowing those things. These are well documented and yet unexplained phenomenon. Anyway, that was the feeling I had at that moment, so I stood still and calm and spoke just as if a real person had been standing there in the room with me. I remember it crossed my mind at the time that I hoped my wife didn't come in at that point and see what I was doing or she might finally decide I was ready for the funny farm.

"Pop, I'm glad you're here," I began, "I have some good news for you, but you must hear me out." I couldn't see him, but I took the continuing atmosphere as an indication that he was still there and listening and pressed on. "We've been very happy in your house, which you must be able to see is well looked after. But it's not your house any longer and you must let go. Your family, your brothers and sisters and loved ones have all been waiting for the time when you can join them. You must go into the light, the doorway, do you see it? Go there now. They're all waiting for you."

I know that all sounds rather corny, but it was almost word-for-word what the television programme suggested under such circumstances and who was I to argue?

For the sake of my own sanity, I convinced myself that it must have worked and that Pop was gone. I told no one what I had done, but some months later Lawrence reported to me that the house now felt completely different and no longer raised the hairs on the back of his neck when he came to open up for work in the mornings. Everything was nice and normal, he said and wondered if I had any idea what might have changed. So I told him that I believed Pop had left us for good, leaving out my own part in the matter as I didn't want him to think me bonkers. But it did at least appear to be true that the cold spots in the house had gone, and that our unexpected visitor had left us at long last. This pleasant atmosphere even had Barbara comment several times that the house was not drafty any longer and felt warm and different. Maybe she was not indifferent to our resident ghost after all.

Common sense cannot in any way explain the events I have just described, so I must attempt to judge for myself, impartially as is my nature, what the truth of the matter is likely to be. The facts to be pondered are that five different people claimed to have seen the old man Pop at some point during the time that we lived in that house. I suppose you could make a case that children tend towards fantasy with their overactive imaginations, but Lawrence and Donna had no reason to lie about it, and I've never had any reason to suspect that either of them were bonkers. Furthermore, I had seen these things with my own eyes. Did I believe in ghosts, after all, that had happened? I would have to say yes, I did. Did I understand them? Hardly at all. And anyway, as I was about to find out, there is a world of difference between seeing a ghost, and being a ghost.

The day we returned from Cyprus following my first search for poor Brian, I was met at my office by Lawrence, who was about twenty-seven years old by now. He briefed me on what I had missed while I was away, and then hesitated, looking at me in a strange sort of way as though he had been about to say something but checked himself at the last second.

"What's up, Lawrence?" I asked.

"I'll make you a cup of tea," he replied and disappeared off to the kitchen. That cup of tea was a long time coming, and when it finally arrived, it was accompanied by a strange story.

"Listen, Dad…" he began, the first of several false starts as the poor lad shifted uncomfortably in his seat, clearly bothered by something. "You're going to think I'm mad," he continued eventually, forcing himself to make eye contact, "but I must tell you what happened while you were gone. It was so strange, and honestly, it scared the hell out of me…"

Safe to say at this point that my attention was undivided. Lawrence went on to describe, by way of a preface to the event itself, how he would often have the office phone diverted to the flat next door, where he lived so that he could spend time with his wife and child when business was quiet. All he had to do was set the burglar alarm, then he could nip home and put his feet up for a while. Well, I had no problem with that, so I motioned for him to continue the story. He then told me that a couple of days previously, around three-thirty in the afternoon, he had popped home but forgotten to transfer the phone over first, so he had to go back in the office. He described opening the two Chubb locks on the two outer doors and then punching in the numbers to cut the burglar alarm. And then he fell silent, staring determinedly at a point on the ground somewhere behind me.

"You're not going to believe this," he said, wringing his hands, "it was just absolutely amazing…"

"Okay," I replied, reining in my impatience, "what happened?"

"Well," he pressed on, the words obviously costing him some considerable effort, "that chair that you're sitting in now… I saw you in it two days ago, while you were in Cyprus."

I looked at him, surprised, and nodded but didn't speak, as I felt that interrupting the flow of words now might cause them to dry up for good.

"I remember being surprised to see you back so soon," said Lawrence, "and asking you where Mum was, and how you managed to get in with the doors locked and the alarm set. You were looking straight at me, just smiling and nodding, and then you began to fade from being a completely solid figure to barely more than a wisp of smoke. And then you vanished."

Poor Lawrence had thought he was going out of his mind, he'd even called his sister Sarah right there and then and asked her to give us a ring and make sure everything was okay.

Well, three-thirty in London was five-thirty in Cyprus, and I remembered very clearly what I had been doing at the time. It was after I had finally returned home from dowsing for the missing Brian, while Barbara was out giving the workmen a lift home and I had fetched up my tools to do a little bit of plumbing, and a great wave of calm had washed over me as though the stresses of the past days were being purged away. It was at that moment, when I felt inexplicably at peace with the world, that my son had seen me, clear as day, some two thousand miles away.

I reassured Lawrence that I didn't believe he was out of his mind, though he himself still seemed unconvinced and obviously shaken by the encounter. Neither of us could explain what had happened, so we simply set it aside as I described earlier, and life went on as it always does. Until, that is, a little over a year later when more peculiar happenings brought Lawrence's story back to the forefront of my mind.

My auntie, my father's sister, rings Barbara every so often to see how we all are and exchange family news. On this particular occasion, she related with some concern a little turn that my father had experienced, which had frightened the life out of him.

I should explain that around four months previously, Dad had deliberately and, I felt, spitefully interfered in a little bit of business which cost me about £90,000. The whole affair had left me spitting nails and I'd made a point to avoid seeing the old man until such time as I had calmed down. Of course, blood is thicker than water, I always loved Dad and would later be able to behave as though nothing had happened. But at the time, he and I had not seen each other for a while and he knew very specifically why.

At any rate, auntie said that a couple of weeks earlier, again while I was out in Cyprus, Dad had been in the garden at his home at Shooters Hill reading his newspaper under the shade of some trees, when he noticed something moving out of the corner of his eye and upon looking up, saw me walking across the grass towards him. I had my arms out as though to hug him, and he likewise stretched out his arms to reciprocate.

"It's about time you came to your senses and came to see me," he'd said as we embraced each other. And then, yes, you guessed it… I vanished.

Dad's mind was always razor-sharp and the one thing he'd always been able to rely on, so to experience such a thing was unheard of for him, naturally, he was afraid that it might be the beginning of a mental disorder which would eventually cause him to lose control of his faculties. What he experienced scared him like nothing else he had ever encountered. He rushed to confide in his sister, who had no idea that Lawrence had experienced a similar thing not long ago since he and I had kept that to ourselves. So the two of them decided that it must have been a daydream and left it at that.

Perhaps the most difficult thing for my father was to admit to his son that he had a weakness, and so Dad would later deny these events when I asked him about them. As far as I am concerned, however, I now have two impeccable witnesses of an out-of-body experience when I apparently went walkies with little regard for the laws of physics. Not only that, but I myself had no idea at the time that people were actually seeing and interacting with me in a completely solid form, albeit without any words being spoken.

Obviously, I have no idea how this is possible, only that it seemed to happen at moments when I remember being particularly relaxed. It's a similar feeling to that which I experienced when faced by snakes on that mountainside in Cyprus. Normally, I am afraid of snakes, so why did I not pull back from them in fear? I only recall feeling like I was attuned to my surroundings, perhaps in some sort of altered state due to the mental and physical drain of extended dowsing sessions. Who knows?

People talk about the subconscious, and such things as a spirit and a soul. Was a part of me leaving my body while the rest of me was still wide awake and functioning normally? Bizarre as it sounds, there is plenty of precedence for this in the great gamut of recorded history.

A 'doppelgänger' or 'fetch' is what we commonly refer to as an out-of-body experience. My understanding is that a few notable adepts have been able to do this at will, but most cases have been seen to have occurred just as a person dies or is about to die. The great English poet John Donne is reported to have seen his wife carrying their stillborn child in her arms on the night of her miscarriage. She was hundreds of miles away at the time. Likewise Abraham Lincoln wrote about seeing a double of himself just after he received a telegram informing him that he was to be the next President of the United States. History is littered with honestly told sightings of 'ghosts' and other such apparitions, and yet even with the impressive array of scientific knowledge at our disposal today, we are no closer to explaining these kinds of events.

However, I believe that we may already be half-way towards an explanation if only we could put aside our stubborn perceptions of what is and is not possible. I believe that what we see is a glimmer of what is normally hidden beneath the flesh and blood that we carry around day-to-day, labouring under the mistaken and somewhat arrogant belief that we are all that there is. We are missing the true picture which would no doubt blow us away if we could only come to terms with what we truly are and more, what we truly might be capable of. If a part of you can travel in the blink of an eye to wherever it wants to be, then it stands to reason that our primitive bodies are barely scratching the surface of what it is to be human, a means to an end rather than the end itself. We see the façade rather than the person within, the spirit or soul or whatever you want to call it, capable in equal measure of supreme acts of kindness or the most desperate measure of evil. We are like Doctor Who's Tardis; walk around it in eight steps, but then open the door to find that what is inside is infinitely larger and more interesting.

We may not even have to find a name for it, as generations of human beings have already provided us with plenty to choose from. The Greeks called it pneuma, the Germans geist. In Sanskrit, it is known as akasha and in Hebrew, nephesh. To you and I, it is the spirit or soul.

No matter how clever we may think we are at this moment in time, we yet have absolutely no answers to so many of the questions that life throws up on a daily basis. Who are we, and why are we thus? Perhaps we will never know, but at least a measure of bold self-examination may help us on our way to a better understanding.

Chapter Seven
Bill's Bath Time
1965–1970

What soap is to the body, laughter is to the soul.

~ Hebrew proverb

Hall, Beddle and Co. were a good, old-fashioned plumbing and building firm not far from Blackfriars Bridge. They took me in and provided me with the security I was looking for at a time in my life when I had never worked for a company outside the family before, so it was all very much a new experience for me.

One of the first things I learnt was that there are plumbers, and there are plumbers. Hall, Beddle and Co. had a pecking order to be sure, and being the new boy I was very firmly last in line. To start with, I was given all the rubbish jobs nobody else wanted to do, while the big houses and cushier work was handed out to the brothers above me. There were five lots of plumbers, of which Bill was top of the tree as far as everyone was concerned, and it was a position he was rather protective of. I remember the second fellow in line casually took me aside one day and told me a story about how Bill had gotten upset with one plumber, the man I had replaced in fact, and punched him so hard that he was knocked out cold for eight hours and spent a whole week in the hospital. How Bill had gotten away with that I had no idea, but it was certainly a sobering thought.

I'm quite sure that he was telling me this for my own good, as people had noticed pretty much straight away that I was a bit of an odd fit and didn't seem to understand the usual standard they all worked by. Rube, the foreman, would try to give me little hints and tips when he saw me breaking the unwritten rules of the game, often saying with bemusement (or perhaps amusement) that he'd not seen anyone quite like me before.

The problem, apparently, was that I was used to working a certain way with Dad's company. When a job had to be completed, it had to be completed as soon as possible, so I would instinctively work quickly and my speed didn't seem at all odd to me or to the men I was used to working with. However, good old-fashioned plumbers do things their own way and at their own speed, and Bill and the other lads were becoming increasingly concerned that I was showing them up. They may have had a point.

One morning, I arrived at work a little late to be met with a message from Rube instructing me to take a toilet pan and other bits and pieces and get straight down to an Oxford Street shop to change a cracked one there. The note included a terse reminder that he knew I was late in that day. Well, off I went and did the job, and come ten o'clock that same morning Rube returned to the yard and found me enjoying a well-earned cuppa.

"Look here, mate," he began, wagging a finger, "you come in late and now you're sitting there sunning yourself? Get that pan and go and fit it immediately!" Then he turned to another plumber and asked, "Where's that pan?"

I must admit to enjoying the shocked expression on Rube's face when the man calmly informed him that I'd been and done the job already and arrived back in time for morning tea. I think he couldn't quite believe what he was hearing, and the shock of it rendered him speechless. If Rube was quietly impressed though, the other men were somewhat less so, tut-tutting and shaking their heads at me for not following the rules again.

That incident and others brought me to the attention of one of the senior surveyors and a partner in the firm, who soon had me ranking at least second in the pecking order. I was given houses of my own to sort out, as well as other big jobs like fitting bathrooms and the like to very expensive properties. Well, Bill didn't like that at all, and his irritation was only compounded by my acting like a bit of a big shot, showing off smoking fat President cigars around the place and driving my own car, which was a luxury on a plumber's wage.

Bill decided to teach this young usurper a lesson. I was doing a job at a very posh house near Harrods one day, installing a brand new bathroom when Bill showed up on the scene unannounced. What a lovely bathroom it was, he said, so much so that it inspired him to make use of the shiny new facilities. Stripping off all his clothes, Bill spun the bath taps and decided to kill the time while it filled up by strutting around the house, arrogantly flipping his didgeridoo up in the air like a rutting stag.

I didn't bat an eyelid, and nor did George, my plumber's mate. We just got on with our work and let it pass us by as though nothing out of the ordinary was happening at all. Even when Bill hopped into the bath and began scrubbing away the grime of a hard day's work with a block of soap he must have brought along himself. Well, if you're going to do something, you ought at least to do it properly. Maybe Bill and I weren't so different in our work ethics, after all, we just applied them in different ways. At any rate, I had just cleared away my tools and stepped into the hallway when the lady of the house returned unexpectedly. She was keen to see how her new, pink bathroom suite was shaping up, and headed straight off to look, only to find good old Bill thoroughly enjoying a nice soak.

"Pink will not do," she said in a perfectly dignified voice, breezing past me in the hallway again, "Change it to lilac. And do please ensure that I am the first user of my bath next time."

Oh dear, I thought, *we'll be in trouble for this*. But surprisingly enough when I went back to fit the new suite she came and joined me for a bit of a chat.

"So tell me," she began conversationally, "is it normal for plumbers to just jump into baths they do not own?"

Now, I had learnt a little diplomacy during my time at Hall, Beddle and Co., as well as in my dealings with Dad, and I summoned all of my willpower now to reply in an earnest voice and with a straight face.

"Madam, a plumber is not worth his salt if he does not test out what he puts in. How would it be if a bath did not work properly?"

"So you, er…" she said, a little flustered.

"Yes, madam, Bill is an excellent tester," I continued. "You were lucky he had time to come specially to test your new bath. He's a big lad as you saw, so he can really make sure that the fixtures won't budge at all even with a heavy cargo and all that water."

"And all that scrubbing he was doing," she said, suppressing a giggle, "that was part of your test procedure too?"

"Well, of course, madam," I replied.

"Then it could have been you scrubbing away in my bath," she said boldly, looking me straight in the eye.

"As I said, madam," I pressed on, not knowing where this was going but feeling like it was probably a good idea to see it through now, "Bill is just right for the job, he has experience and expertise and gets the job done properly. Me, I would probably just pop in and out and that wouldn't do at all, would it? No, it's experience that counts you see, so don't be concerned about Bill, you were lucky to have him."

She was shaking by now as she tried unsuccessfully to control her laughter, tears running down her cheeks. Between fits of giggles, she called for her husband to come and hear the story just as I had explained it.

"Tell him, tell him!" she gasped as the master of the house arrived, looking most bemused, and George shuffled into the corner of the bathroom wishing there was somewhere to hide.

"But, madam," I whispered conspiratorially, "these are the secrets of the plumbing trade. I would be in a lot of trouble if it were known that I had talked about what makes us at Hall, Beddle and Co. such extraordinarily good plumbers."

Well, that did it for her. I have never in all my years seen anyone laugh so much. What had begun as light-hearted banter and my feeble attempts to get Bill off the hook had turned into a proper good laugh that madam was certainly most appreciative of. So much so that after I had completed the work and was about to leave she handed me an envelope and a hand-written note expressing her appreciation for my good humour that had brightened her day. She suggested that I opened the envelope later when I was alone, as 'no one earns well working for another', and with that cryptic little message ringing in my ears, I took my leave. When I got home that evening I opened the envelope to find the sum of £50, which in those days was the equivalent of two-and-a-half-weeks' hard graft.

Madam had certainly given me plenty to think on. Yes, there were plumbers and there were plumbers, some of whom enjoyed the calm and security of working for a firm, carrying out jobs at their own leisurely pace whilst still picking up the same wage at the end of the week. That wasn't really my style at all though, and I wasn't convinced that I could settle into such a lifestyle. Plus of course, there were other important considerations.

I was engaged to my Barbara at the time, and her family came from a small town called Horley on the Brighton Road. Her father was a cable jointer working for the electricity board and making, by all accounts, less than a plumber, yet he had brought up two girls in a council house and from what I could see they were all very happy and content with their lot in life. The place was always spotless and very comfortable, with an overall air of peace and gentleness that reflected in the two girls Fred and Kit had brought up. They were a post-war family with strong financial ethics that were evident in everything they did, perhaps most strongly of all for me in Fred's devoted tending to the prize Chrysanthemums and vegetables in his garden, and the impeccably cut lawn. Barbara's family had built a grand life for themselves whilst living within their means and that was something they could be rightfully proud of.

Perhaps because of my somewhat unconventional family background, however, I looked at life more in the round. Would I be happy to keep working for bosses who reaped the rewards of my hard work and left me just enough to settle into a quiet life growing my own vegetables? I think only one of the many girlfriends I had during the sixties had a family who owned a car, and her father was a prosperous builder who answered only to himself and his clients. The evidence was mounting up. Fred had settled for a comfortable life that suited him and his family perfectly, and that was the right decision for him. I wanted more than that though, not just for myself but for my wife and my children when they came along.

I knew there was risk lying in the direction I was about to take, but I felt like it had to be done, so I left Hall, Beddle and Co. and started out on my own in a small way at first, picking up jobs where I could and employing the men I had used before. The first week we brought in £44 profit, then the second it was £99, then £102. Cash in hand for my workers was about £16 a week or so, give or take, so that wasn't a bad start at all.

More jobs meant more men, which didn't worry me at first, but I soon discovered that the number of problems you get is roughly proportional to the number of lads you have working for you. Sixteen men meant juggling about eight problems at once, which I could handle quite comfortably, but when we went up to twenty-four men it was like juggling twelve problems at once, and that's when you're likely to let one fall. It's that one dropped ball that then causes you a massive headache as you spend most of your time dealing with it, making it more difficult to juggle the rest and risking everything cascading out of control. Something needed to change before the situation drove me mad. I had managed all these men before without much trouble as they all worked for me on our properties. The situation was different, it was the several jobs and the clients, wanting to query this or that on site, now, that was the problem and delegation was not exactly part of my nature at that time.

An American walked into the office one day looking for a specialist plumbing service which by chance I had the expertise to be able to offer. Having carried out the work to his satisfaction, the man promised me a little tip, which naturally I assumed was going to be a little extra money.

"No, not money," he said, smiling, "better than that. I'm going to give you a little bit of advice instead."

I was intrigued. Someone had told me a long time ago that good advice can be worth more than a handful of gold, so I kept an open mind with respect to what this man was about to say.

"Specialising is where the money is," he said with a nod and a wink, and that was that.

I thought on this for a bit and came to the conclusion that the man made a lot of sense. Doing the general building work we were doing we had to compete with virtually every other building firm in London, as well as independent contractors and odd-job types, it was chaos and margins weren't great. But what to specialise in, if that was indeed the route to go down? Well, I knew plumbers by now, and I knew that they didn't like to get their hands dirty. Dealing with drains and other mucky business took a certain skill that most plumbers had never bothered to pick up, and the competition for those jobs was low. Most guys in the building industry would much rather build houses and walls and plumbers fit bathrooms, simple things like that.

I made the decision to switch. It was a gamble, but one that paid off handsomely as turnover doubled while the number of men I employed dropped to just seven, which was much easier to handle. A couple of years on, I did so well, my accountant at the time told me that he'd heard of a pig farmer who took the Inland Revenue to court to claim that his Rolls Royce ought to be allowed as a business expense. He won the case and was the first blue-collar worker in the country to be allowed such an expensive car on his books for tax purposes. I was the second.

The pig farmer's assertion, incidentally, was that he was every bit the equal of any rich industrialist or banker, such professionals who were in those days allowed to write off their expensive cars. The judges agreed with him. How times have changed.

Forty years on now every plumber seems to be a drain specialist, but at the time that American's advice had been spot on, and proved to be much more valuable than a little extra money would have been. People are worth listening to at times, the trouble is that most of us have heard bad advice at one time or another and so we block out all advice from then on, refusing to listen and learn and dismissing suggestions in a plainly arrogant way that may be to our advantage.

Going back a little, nine months after leaving Hall, Beddle and Co., my turnover had reached a fairly decent sum. There were still no loans going around as inflation was soaring, but thanks to our new specialisation in the market I was able to raise my fees from one pound, two shillings and sixpence per hour to a whopping £5 in a single stroke, no questions asked. Fortunately, I judged the situation well and had a little luck along the way, else that gamble could have cost me dearly.

I discovered that Dad's old offices had never been sold off, which was a surprise as he usually wouldn't have missed a trick like that, but so much the better for me, I took them over and set them up properly, paying the rates and bills and making sure everything was up to date. I needed someone in the office full-time though, to look after the phone mostly but also do other very necessary administrative tasks. Mum suggested that it might be a good job for Barbara, with whom she and Nan were very taken, and that she ought to come and move in with us as well in our four-bedroom house at Shooters Hill. Well, that seemed fine to me, and it didn't take Barbara long to settle in at all. She was and still is at the time of writing a huge credit to the firm with her untiring attention to detail and devotion to her work.

But more than that, Barbara always had a sharp mind that was very much on the same wavelength as my own. I was always talking about how I wanted to get back into the property game, but that I needed more than the little capital we'd been able to muster so far. Bills were creeping up and the profit margins shrivelled, especially after purchasing all sorts of equipment and vehicles for the firm that were necessary just to keep ourselves competitive.

Upon returning to the office one day after a job, I was asked by Barbara if I was interested in purchasing a gas water heater that had only been fitted a short while ago. I said no and dismissed the matter out of hand, but she was quite insistent.

"It's hanging on a wall in one of those houses," she said with a glint in her eye, "you know, the ones you said you'd like to get your hands on."

"Well, in that case," I replied, cottoning on, "do you have the details?"

There were three large empty houses on the main road in Lewisham that I'd had my eye on for a while now. They all had foundation problems and two would need their large bay fronts pulling down and rebuilding with deep piled foundations that could cost more than the houses themselves in their current state. This was a huge risk but that work having been done I was sure they would turn a tidy profit, especially with inflation taking off like a rocket. Fortunately, thanks to a little foresight and the timely advice from that American client, I had the money to take advantage of the situation.

I arranged to view the water heater in the first of those houses, all of which were vacant and two were condemned as dangerous by the local council. I was shown inside number 47 by Mr King, a middle-aged Jamaican gentleman who introduced me to a heater that turned out to be not nearly so new as I had been led to believe. I said I wasn't interested in buying it, but how would he like to sell me the house instead? I made him an offer on the spot of £750, which he accepted at once to my great surprise. Shortly afterwards, I received a letter from Lewisham Council demanding that any sale should go through them as they held the mortgage on the property. Fair enough, I replied, how would £750 do? Very nicely, as it turned out. One down, two to go.

I sent a letter to the owners of the second house, letting them know that I had bought next door for £750 and enquiring as to whether they might be interested in selling me their property for a similar amount. They replied that they were indeed interested, but wouldn't accept any less than £1,150. Done. Two down, one to go.

The owner of the final house which had a dangerous structure notice attached to it, wrote to me stating in no uncertain terms that he had no intention of selling, as he was considering putting it right and moving back. So I turned my attention to the best of the two, which I had bought, that did not have a dangerous structure notice attached to it, though the foundations did need attention, so following certain works I set about modernising it in order to please my darling wife, who was by this time expecting our first child and wanted a nice family home for us all to live in. Personally, I had no intention of moving in, my idea being to do up the properties, convert them into flats and sell them on, but in the meantime, we got on with the work.

I remember Barbara standing on a scaffold board in the front room, helping me to line the ten-foot-high ceiling with paper before it could be painted. Looking back now, I have no idea why I let her do that in her condition, but she was keen to help as the carpets would be arriving soon and so would the baby. That was on a Friday evening. Come two am Saturday morning I was rushing her to the hospital to deliver the little one, and the two of them stayed there for two weeks, which was typical in those days, being looked after while I kept working.

When Barbara and the baby came home, I showed no desire at all to move into the half-finished house, which was clean and smart but still had some way to go.

"It's best we stay here with Mum and Nan," I told her, "they can look after you when I'm not around."

But Barbara had her mind set, and she had accomplices I was powerless to resist. Coming back late one night after a hard day's work I put my key in the door to find that it wouldn't turn. After ringing the bell and knocking for what seemed like an age, the letterbox slowly opened up and I heard my mother's voice.

"Go home," she said. Then both she and nan started to laugh, though I couldn't see the funny side of the situation at all. "Go home to your wife and son," Mum went on, "There's nothing here for you today."

It's sometimes hard to think straight when you've had a long day, and standing there in the rain, hungry and dirty, all I could think about was having a bath and eating a meal for the first time in about twenty-four hours. It took a further jab through the letterbox before I finally got the message.

It turned out that while I was at work, Barbara had enlisted the help of a mutual friend, who owned a van, to move our meagre possessions; bed, table, sofa and chairs over to the 'new' house. When I arrived there she even had a meal ready and a hot bath drawn and waiting for me, doing everything she could to try to make our first night in our new home a special one.

I could resist no longer. We moved out of Mum's house and into our first proper home together with our newborn son Denis, and in no time at all, I put plans together to sort out the rest of the building work that needed doing, in particular, to deal with the foundations that were pretty shaky. It was clear that the work would take quite some time and even more money, but the business could cover it just fine so that wasn't a problem.

I contacted the owner of the third house to ask who his surveyor was, as I wished to carry out work to the adjoining party wall. This was a perfectly normal procedure, yet I was rebuffed by the fellow once again who said that they weren't ready to start the rebuilding work themselves. I had to remind him that the emergency wooden raking shores that were holding up his property were on my land and that since I would be pulling down the front of Mr King's old house next to his, I was concerned that his might come down on top of my men while they were working. I also pointed out that according to the Greater London Council rules in force at the time, a party wall notice could be served on them to ensure that they complied with a works notice to remedy the faults of a dangerous structure, i.e. their own house.

I knew that he had been quoted more than £5,000 to undertake the rebuilding work and that the house would only be worth around £4,250 when it was fixed up and in good order, so when they offered me the place for £1,250 I accepted without a fuss. It was a good deal for all parties. A small risk for me, sure, but one well worth taking. My risk was that it could cost me dearly yet inflation was rocketing, whilst there were no loans to be had people were starting to invest in property to protect their cash as I was about to see first-hand.

By the time I'd completed work on the two houses we weren't living in, transforming them into three self-contained flats a-piece and casually putting them on the market for £20,000 each, there was a line of potential purchasers at the door. Wow. I owned £40,000 worth of property, not including the very nice house we had taken as our home. Not bad for an outlay of £3,150 and a couple of years' hard work.

Still, inflation was up and down at the time and there was no real urgency to sell, so I decided to hold on to them for a while. Forty years on, I still own them. However, back then business was booming and Barbara and I were quite content to keep doing what we were doing, enjoying our new surroundings, settling into our first home, and making friends.

Chapter Eight
Learning to Fly
1961–1990

I fly because it releases my mind from the tyranny of petty things.

~Antoine de Saint-Exupery

I had a fear of flying ever since the age of seventeen when I was in a plane coming back from Ireland in the most atrocious storm and it was clear that the pilot was having difficulties. Not the least of which was that one of the two propellers kept stopping.

I remember that while others onboard the flight showed their nervousness quite plainly, I held my nerve, I'm quite sure nobody noticed at the time that I was just as terrified. But something about the event, the lack of control, the internal panic, the feeling of utter helplessness, it changed me.

As you might have gathered from the fact that I am able to tell this story to you now, we landed okay in the end and all was well. But that incident haunted me for a long time, to the point where I found myself in the position of being a successful businessman with a nice life and a notion to have some adventures abroad, hampered only by the fact that such adventures would involve the little matter of overcoming my fear of flying.

Not that anyone else knew about that, no, I kept it hidden even from myself as I was a bit embarrassed to tell you the truth for being afraid of such a silly thing. Well, finally, I decided to do something about it and confront my fear, so off I went one summer afternoon to Biggin Hill Aerodrome and just stood watching the little Cessna planes take off and land for a while. I was plucking up the courage to go into a flying school I had noticed nearby and ask them what would be involved in my learning to fly a plane for myself.

Eventually, I did go in, and a pleasant chap by the name of Peter Burn told me that the first step would be a thirty-minute flight to assess my aptitude and see how I coped with the conditions up there.

"Most people just love it," he assured me. "I've got half an hour right now. Shall we go?"

No. No, I wasn't ready, or so I convinced myself. Chickening out some might say. I went back to the car, parked it up at the public parking area and watched the planes some more. Even though I'd turned down the flight, I felt afraid as though I'd agreed to do it and was aware that I would be up there any minute now. Maybe because I knew this was something I had to do, and the inevitability of it was impossible to escape.

Sure enough, after what felt like ages there came a knock on the passenger side window and I saw Peter Burn smiling at me. I waved him in.

"Nice car," he said.

"Thanks," I replied.

"What do they cost?" he asked.

"Enough," I replied.

"You're not convinced, are you?" he asked.

"Did it show?" I replied, knowing full well that it must have if he was asking.

"Yep," said Peter, "but I can guarantee you that whatever you're afraid of now, as soon as you start flying you'll get hooked." He looked at me seriously. "But you need to do it." I didn't reply. "I'll take you slowly through it and you can stop any time you like. We're using runway two-one, which is long and I can land there safely in a hurry if you want to get down, but I know that won't be necessary anyway because you'll love it. I'll be back this way in fifteen minutes."

And with that, he got out of the car and walked away.

That conversation left me feeling very, very silly. There was me, a grown man, afraid of flying just because I'd had one bad experience when I was seventeen. What was I hiding from? It was ridiculous. Chastising myself for my cowardice, I drove around to the flying school and waited for Peter to return.

When he did, I thought it only fair to explain what had caused my little upset, and then with that out of the way we set about the trial flight. Peter showed me how to pre-flight an aeroplane before we got in and strapped up.

"You okay?" he asked.

"Yep, let's go," I replied.

"Biggin Tower," he said into the radio, "this is Golf, Alpha, Bravo Sierra, Charlie taxi for local."

"Sierra Charlie read you, strength five, QFE 998, QNH 1005 two-one right," came the reply. Having repeated this unfathomable string of information back to the tower, off we went. Peter went to a corner of the airfield and did a full engine run-up just to make sure everything was in full working order, then he taxied to the holding point and stopped before turning to me.

"You okay, John?" he asked.

"Yep," I replied.

"Biggin Tower," he said into the radio again, "Sierra Charlie at holding point, ready for line-up and takeoff."

"Sierra Charlie hold," came the answer. The delay was playing merry hell with my frayed nerves. Apparently, a business jet was coming in and we were asked to hold again for what felt like ages. It felt a bit like when you're strapped into one of those big rollercoasters after it's left the station but before it begins to climb.

The radio crackled into life suddenly.

"Sierra Charlie, are you ready for immediate takeoff?"

Peter looked at me.

"We can't stop now," he said.

"Go, Peter," I replied, feeling a bit sick.

"Sierra Charlie immediate takeoff," he barked into the radio, applying power to the throttle and turning the plane ninety degrees in a wide arc so that we found ourselves facing down this huge runway with the engine now at full power. In no time at all, we were up and away. It was amazing. I realised that I'd let this fear of flying fester inside of me for so long that it had become almost instinctive, just as many people fear snakes or spiders. Now I had conquered it in an instant. Peter was right, I loved it at once.

The minute we were back on the ground I made arrangements to take flying lessons of my own. Whilst it was not made obvious to others, I was unbelievably excited about this new freedom that had opened up for me out of the blue (so to speak.) Peter was an extraordinary teacher, young but wise and extremely talented. Just about knocked my socks off when this brilliant pilot confessed to me that he didn't have his full drivers' license yet. In the air, he was a pro. On the ground, he was still technically a learner. It's a strange world sometimes.

Anyway, after several hours of lessons, we got to the stage where Peter was to show me how to recover from a dropped wing in a stall, which in effect is the precursor to a spin.

"Are you ready for this?" he asked, the trace of a glint in his eye. I replied in the affirmative, even though I knew from our time together the past few weeks that Peter could be cruel when he wanted to be, and I sensed now that he was about to have a bit of fun with me.

I was right. Rather than gently easing into the manoeuvre with a dropped nose, then power on to recover a.s.a.p., Peter chose instead to yank the nose up high and apply full rudder, which caused us to then pitch down violently. As my stomach lurched, he applied opposite rudder to stop the turning and full power to build up speed and prevent us from falling again as we had been practically hanging in the air after he cut the spin short.

His skill was very impressive, but with my sense of balance thrown completely out of whack, I had no sense of what had happened or what he had done to recover.

"How was that?" asked Peter casually.

"Well, Peter," I replied in an equally measured tone, "I have no idea what you just did."

"Alright," he said, "well, we'll do the next one to the right, just follow me through."

I don't know what happened after that. I know we were upside down at one point, I think, or were we? And then there were huge G-forces, and then phew, we were back on the ground and the lesson was over.

I drove home that day in a daze. I remember lying on the sofa, having not touched my meal, my legs still frozen rigid as they had been while we were throwing the aircraft around the sky at three-thousand feet. There was no way I could do what Peter had done, no way at all, my senses had just abandoned me and left me completely helpless. It was not a fun feeling. I couldn't understand what had happened, or what Peter had done to recover the situation each time. If being a pilot meant I needed to be able to do this, then in my mind at least, this was my brick wall. Do I stop now and forget it, or what?

The very next day I decided to ditch work and go confront the problem.

"Now look, Peter," I said when I got to the flying school, "I haven't been able to stop thinking about what happened yesterday, but it is still a complete mystery to me. We have to go up and do it all again, and you explain to me how to recover, because last time you did my learning faculties were frozen and I didn't take any of it in."

After trying to explain everything to me again using a model aeroplane, what caused the situations and how one was supposed to go about recovering from them, Peter suddenly asked me if I had a problem with the two manoeuvres he'd performed the previous day.

"Well, yes," I replied, frustrated, "isn't that what I've been saying all along? I still have no idea what was happening to us or what I'm supposed to do about it. How can I learn if I don't understand?"

Overhearing the conversation, the chief flying instructor came over and asked a few questions, then he and Peter said something about the 'A to Z of Recovery', which meant so little to me that they may as well have been talking in code. Then the CFI shook his head at Peter, tut-tutting as if to admonish him. The gist of the conversation, or so I gathered, was that Peter ought to follow this 'A-Z' procedure, take me back up and show me the ropes properly. So off we went again.

Having taken off, we flew to a stretch of open land over Kent where Peter showed me clearly how to recover from a stall when the nose drops. Nose down, power on, recover. Easy. Blimey, it certainly didn't feel this easy yesterday. But then I supposed this was probably the 'A' of the 'A-Z' they had been talking about, and it would likely get more adventurous as we went along.

"It feels worse for a passenger," said Peter casually as we flew along, "because you'll lag behind your senses as you try to process something that's already happened. It can be very disorienting."

Well, that is interesting. He hadn't bothered to venture this little pearl of wisdom the previous day, had he? That was a bit sadistic. I gave him the benefit of the doubt though and assumed he couldn't possibly have known how thoroughly disoriented I had been. With hindsight, I'm sure he was just looking for a reaction from me and knew fine well that the manoeuvre he was executing was not for a novice as I was then.

The problem for Peter, for anyone dealing with me in fact, is that I can be disarmingly calm and collected, not reacting to situations as most people would. All hell could break loose and still, you wouldn't find me in a flap. That's just my nature. So when I showed no response to Peter's showing off with his skills, he probably assumed I was just taking it all in my stride and might enjoy being thrown in at the deep end with his rather roughneck teaching process, when in actual fact, it had been downright traumatic.

Still, today was much better, and by the end of our hour-long lesson I was able to recover not only from a stall but also a full-blown spin, as well as that nasty situation when the wing drops and you can sense a spin coming on, but you pick it up at the last moment. That one needs a bit of skill to be sure, but I pulled it off three times and it was absolutely cracking fun. As the hour came to a close, Peter told me I was his best pupil, and admitted that he might have been a bit cruel the day before.

"Okay," he said as the airfield hove into view, "you can land the plane yourself to end a perfect session."

Gulp. We were vectored to join runway two-nine, a fairly short one with a huge dip in the middle and a big bunch of tall trees on the approach. It wasn't a simple task, and I showed my inexperience by not judging the dip properly and allowing the crosswind to float us off to the right. Peter had to take control finally to bring us in safely.

"Oh well," he said, "eight out of ten anyway."

I'll take that, I thought.

It wasn't long after my first solo flight that Peter was called away to help fetch back a Dakota DC/3 aircraft situated at Entebbe airport, Uganda, where President Amin was in charge of a particularly bloody mess. Worse, just as Peter's plane was about to take off, the Israelis were beginning to storm the airport and retrieve a bunch of hostages being held there. That must have been a nerve-wracking experience.

Meanwhile, in Peter's absence, I was taken under the wing of the chief flying instructor, a certain Ron Brown. At first, I found Ron to be a perfectly nice, calm, polite gentleman. An old-fashioned flyer, no doubt, and a touch red in the face, he had a big bushy beard that reminded one forcefully of Santa. But this gentleman proved to be a little less than jolly.

"Okay, John," he said as we settled in for our first flight together, "let's go and do some circuits, and you can show me what you've learnt. Give me two perfect examples and I'll let you go off on your own to practice."

"Sounds good to me, Mr Brown," I replied, giving it full power to the engine and off we went.

Towards the end of my first successful circuit, having turned onto base leg and reduced my height in order to turn and make the final 500 ft descent straight down towards the runway in landing configuration, it began.

"Take your hands off the controls," said Ron. I did as I was told, and watched the nose of the aircraft drop a little. Then a little more. "Take control and trim the aircraft properly," he said. I did. We landed fine and Ron instructed me to take off again for another circuit.

"That wasn't good, was it?" he said as we rose into the air again. "Your trim was out. Let's get it right this time."

The same thing happened again, Ron instructed me to let go of the controls, I did, the nose dropped a little, I immediately trimmed back and recovered, and carried on with touch and go. I thought I was doing fine, but each time Ron found something different to be unhappy about. By our fourth circuit, he had begun to shout. I didn't react. By the fifth, he was all-out screaming and practically incandescent with rage. I took it all in my stride and calmly made my adjustments, bringing the plane down each time in a controlled and accurate manner. It became evident that not only was Ron Brown a perfectionist of the old school, he was a proper verbal bully as well.

By the time our seventh circuit came around, Ron was suggesting rather forcefully that I must be a very particular part of a lady's anatomy.

"What are you?" he barked at the side of my face. I didn't answer, just kept telling myself he was doing it for my own good, that it was just part of his teaching method, and that I really was learning a lot. Our eighth and final circuit came up, and I fully expected Ron to instruct me to apply power again and take off, whereupon he would find something new to be furious about even though I'd done everything virtually flawlessly. But that didn't happen. Instead, just as we should have been about to land, Ron gave a new instruction.

"I have control," he said.

"You have control," I replied, taking my hands off the control column. I was surprised, but I knew to defer to my instructor in this scenario and so I did so without question. I kept looking around though, ahead and to the side, left and right, up and down, checking that no other planes were heading our way.

"Look at me!" barked Ron suddenly as the wheels touched the ground. In an instant, I had a flashback to something Peter had told me before he left on his Ugandan mission. 'Never stop a good lookout when landing and taking off,' he'd said, 'especially with the CFI sitting next to you.'

It had all seemed really rather cryptic at the time. But now, with his hot spittle showering my cheek, I thought I understood what Peter had meant. I ignored the command and kept up my observation.

"F...g look at me, will you?" yelled Ron furiously.

For a split second, instinctively, I complied. But even as my head turned to look at Ron, I saw a fist hurtling towards me and managed to look away just in time to catch a painful knuckle sandwich right to the ear. As my head swam, Ron applied full power to the engine.

"You have control," he said, calm again.

"I have control," I replied. I had tears in my eyes now not from self-pity but from sheer pain. That had bloody hurt, but there was no time to dwell on it, as Ron had ordered me to take off for another circuit.

"Look out! Look out, you bloody fool!" yelled Ron, again trying to distract me. It wasn't like I didn't understand the point of the lesson; a young female passenger could be flashing her knickers at you, and in the time it took to sneak a peek, two aircraft could have drifted onto a fatal collision course. That didn't mean his methods were right.

"Look out, you bloody fool!"

I was being bullied, there was no other word for it. I didn't think that would ever happen to me again, and I briefly wondered how my younger self would have dealt with a bully like Ron Brown. Ultimately, that wasn't much help though. I mean, a fistfight at eight hundred feet wouldn't have been very good for either of us.

What I didn't know was that Ron had lost a former student who had just passed his test and was killed flying Ron's aircraft, with a passenger and he blamed himself for being too soft on him during his training. Well, he was making up for it now, more than making up for it. Ron wanted to make sure that everyone he passed in his capacity as an accredited civil aviation examiner was up to handling a plane under the most trying conditions. Evidently, the punch to the ear really was for my own good.

"You're beginning to learn," said Ron brusquely after we landed. Not sure I appreciated that sentiment.

I stayed away from the flight school for a week or so until Peter had returned safely from his trip to Africa. I went to Maderia with Barbara for our first holiday, and a rest bite from Ron. When I went back to book an hour's lesson with Peter, I thought I ought to mention that punch.

"You were right about Ron," I told him, "Bloody well punched me in the ear!"

"Sorry about that," replied Peter, "but he is prone to that sort of thing. I did try to warn you!"

Even so, against my advice, Peter went off to have a word with Ron, while I waited outside wishing I had not said anything. There was an almighty row in the clubhouse that I could sort of see and certainly hear, the upshot of which was that Peter walked out and suggested that I continue my lessons at the nearby Biggin Hill Flying Club which I was a member of anyway, "I won't be beaten, Peter," I said. "I'm staying on."

Truth is, I did think about leaving. It would certainly have been the easiest, most sensible and happiest solution for all concerned, but I felt strongly that I shouldn't let myself be bullied. I'd already been there, seen that and got the T-shirt a long time ago, and while Ron never punched me again after that, taking his verbal assaults became like a game to me. I don't think I could ever have walked away from a challenge like that. Besides, the man was clearly possessed with an almost religious zeal to teach safety in all aspects of flying, and that's certainly no bad thing.

I remember a lesson where I was to navigate through to Brighton and then overhead Brentwood then return to the aerodrome, a simple enough matter for a pilot of my experience by then. Ron, at first, sat all calm and quiet in the co-pilot's seat on the right of the aircraft with the simple request that I merely give him a 'good, safe flight' and all would be well with the world. Not bloody likely.

Along the way, we came upon a huge snow cloud that was precipitating right in our path. Now here was a test. If I deviated from my current course, Ron might yell at me. If I ploughed on through the snow, Ron would yell at me. I made a quick decision to dogleg the cloud and get back on course as soon as possible after it was passed, however that decision was too slow coming for Ron before I could begin the manoeuvre that thunderous voice erupted in my ear. I froze, today was not a good day for Ron to shout at me.

"What the f*****g hell do you think you're doing?" he screamed. "You're a c**t, aren't you? Well? Come on, what are you?"

I declined to answer the question but took a moment to reflect on my good fortune that most of my sessions with Ron seemed to fall on blustery days with rough conditions that gave him all manner of opportunities to bluster at me. Today was obviously going to be no exception, except that I was especially tired due to the relentless schedule at work. Maybe I let my guard down. Maybe I was about to show the emotion at last that Ron had been fishing for.

While I hesitated over my next action, snow began to smother the front of the plane and the leading edge of the wings.

"You have control," I said finally, lifting my hands off the control column. I'd had enough of Ron, let him fly us back and to hell with his nonsense. Ron folded his arms and said nothing. I did likewise. It was a standoff. After a few ridiculous moments, I decided that Ron obviously wasn't about to take control unless the aircraft was in real danger, and I couldn't let that happen.

"I have control," I said, taking the column back. "Sorry about that." And then, "Dog leg…" naming the village to the right of the cloud and steering us calmly out of it. Doing what I should have done much quicker in the first place.

After that, the flight was entirely uneventful, but I will always remember that day. Not for the shouting, or the weather, but because of the words Ron Brown spoke to me when we returned to the clubhouse for a coffee afterwards.

"I have broken you," he growled, in the manner of a sadistic old Sergeant Major, "and now you will learn."

At the time I just shrugged my shoulders and let it wash over me. I wanted my pilot's license and I wasn't going to let anything get in my way, least of all a bully like Ron Brown. Only now, looking back on it, I find myself amused by what happened that day.

A little while later, with my flying test rapidly approaching, I was booked to carry out some circuits of the airfield, which usually meant around eight complete circuits assuming nothing got in the way. By this time, Ron has condescended to allow me full range in solo flying, so his input into the session was simply to warn me that there was a front moving in quickly and to inquire whether I thought it was worth going up.

"If it becomes difficult, I'll stop," I replied simply.

"You're the pilot," said Ron. And off I went.

After the first circuit, the weather began to make an impact with blustery winds and rain like a giant wet broom sweeping through the countryside. I noticed all of the other aircraft in sight busily landing, and by the time I began my second circuit they were all down bar one or two latecomers. As circuit number three got underway, the control tower, realising I was a student, offered me a little advice.

"Sierra Charlie, suggest a full stop, there is a front passing through," came the crackling voice over the radio.

"Negative," I replied at once, "touch and go."

As I applied full power and rose up into the air again to begin my fourth circuit, the control tower had more to say.

"Sierra Charlie, suggest a full stop next pass. Full stop next pass."

It was clear they meant it, and to be fair they weren't wrong either. The weather was the worst I had ever encountered, but it wasn't so much worse than I'd dealt with before and I felt confident that I could safely handle it, which is the most important thing.

By now, the rain was thundering off the fuselage like machine gun bullets and the aircraft was being thrown up and down, side to side. It was difficult going, to say the least, but also incredibly fun. I was having a whale of a time, and feeling very much at home up there in that little aeroplane. As I prepared to touch down again I radioed my position to the control tower.

"Sierra Charlie, suggest a full stop or we will notify your club."

Well, that was new.

"Negative, touch and go," I replied defiantly, and off I went again. This went on until my eight circuits were complete, and as I came in to land for a final time I noticed that the front had cleared and that many of the little aircraft down below were queuing up to take off again. Oh well, that was no matter to me, I'd gotten my eight circuits in.

"Biggin Tower, this is Sierra Charlie final full stop," I said, and with that, I landed, taxied to park the aircraft where it belonged, and made my way back to the clubhouse. Ron Brown was making coffee as I pushed the door open, and he casually offered me one. This was new. I accepted his offer and signed out, making sure I was near the door before turning to Ron with a little trepidation.

"Mr Brown," I asked, "has the tower phoned you by any chance?"

"I told them to f**k off," replied Ron casually. "Will that be one lump or two?"

What I didn't know was that each of the clubs using the airfield at the time had been listening out on their radios, as had Ron in his office, and word quickly spread about the odd pilot refusing to land and forging on through such atrocious conditions. Apparently, people had even taken to placing bets on the outcome. Down on the ground, the weather was so bad that the clubhouses had closed their windows to prevent the rain from lashing in, yet up in the sky, this lone little plane was pottering about as if it were a calm summer's day.

Having finished my coffee, I popped over to the Biggin Hill Flying Club to meet a friend whom I had arranged to take back to London. They weren't ready to go just yet, so I went to the bar and ordered myself a cold Pepsi. As I was drinking it, I overheard some of the club members roundly criticising 'that bloody fool' who had refused to land. What was he trying to do, kill himself? People like that bring flying into disrepute! I could hardly believe my ears.

"What do you think, John?" asked a vague acquaintance of mine who was participating in the debate.

"Well, er… legally it was the pilot's call you know," I began. But I was saved from the rest of that awkward moment by the 6'4" club owner John, who draped his arm casually over my shoulder and proceeded to introduce me to the aghast group as 'that bloody fool', going on to say that if any of them could fly like the man standing next to him, he would be a happier man. Good grief. Two compliments in one day! It was almost too much to bear.

Some years later, after I had passed my flying test and my license was up for its annual renewal, I returned to Biggin Hill Flying Club, to meet the instructor who was to test me this time around. He was a lanky man, six foot maybe, maybe a little more, with an odd, unkempt little beard, tombstone teeth and an old tweed jacket. I'd never seen him at the club before and assumed that he must be fairly new. Anyway, off we went on what was for me by now a run-of-the-mill outing, conducting all the usual turns, climbs and recovery scenarios in a Grumman AA5B four-seater, which was a rather forgiving aircraft but still bigger, heavier and more powerful than the smaller and nimbler two-seater Cessna 152. You would never deliberately send the Grumman into a spin as they just do not like to recover, which is why it simply isn't allowed. Though the Biggles among us would argue that it can be done with some consistency.

So off we flew over the Kent fields and away from any trouble, and since I didn't know this chap at all I felt obliged, as I had several years' experience over him, to remind him of our situation with the ground being around 600 ft above sea level and the clouds 2,200 ft or so, giving us a maximum 1,600 ft to play with when planning manoeuvres. Which frankly isn't nearly enough to try anything risky, so I wasn't expecting to be recovering from any fast or dangerous manoeuvres as there simply wasn't enough room for it that day.

While I wondered what was to be on the agenda, however, the examiner made his move.

"I have control," he said.

"You have control," I replied, taking my hands off the column. Straight away he applied full power to the powerful engine and then, once we had built up enough speed for his liking, pointed the nose straight up vertically. All I could see were clouds rushing towards us, as I crossed my fingers that he wasn't about to do what I thought he was about to do. He was.

Without conducting HASELL checks for safety height above ground level, without checking the Airframe Flaps to make sure there were no loose bags that could fly up and hit one of us in the face, knocking us out, without conducting any kind of engine checks, location checks, or taking any kind of precautions whatsoever, my instructor dropped the right wing and pointed the nose straight at the ground with full power. The powerful engine dragged us down, fast.

Completely gob-smacked, I waited for the 'you have control' order so that I could try to save the situation. That was a mistake. The man was clearly a lunatic and the order wasn't coming. As all of this went through my mind, seconds passed, maybe three, maybe four, but that was all it took in such circumstances to cause certain disaster.

We were now in a fast, spiral dive towards the Earth and the conflict that had been taking place in my mind the past few moments as to whether or not to wrest control from this lunatic finally resolved itself, when he gave the order "you have control". There was no time to think, but the steps flashed through my mind in a split second; power off, level wings, pull back on the controls. I did all three at once.

Travelling at fully 150 knots now with a big white house directly in our path no more than a few hundred metres away, it was crystal clear to me that we weren't going to make it. As I yanked the controls back as hard as I could, veering away from the house, and felt the shuddering wings being forced back so hard that they felt like they might break, indicating that a high-speed stall was happening. Not that it mattered much with the solid ground only seconds away. I took one last look at my killer, who was just sitting there staring, his face frozen in a grimace that showed his large, plate-like teeth. He was gone. He was of no use now. Bugger it, pull back harder still and let the bloody wings come off if they're going to.

As the shuddering increased dramatically, everything seemed to go into slow motion. I ducked my head instinctively and silently said my goodbyes to the world, thinking in that instant what a waste it was to go like this. I had to have one last look at what I was leaving behind, so with a tremendous effort I forced one eye open and peeked out of the side window to my left. There was a flash of green, a tree, oh God, this was it. My eyes clenched shut again as I waited for the crash.

But it didn't come. Instead, I began to feel G-forces pushing hard against me. What the hell?

"Look out quick!" said a voice next to me. We were just above a high ridge and about to go into a loop, so I pushed down at the top of it and my guts and eyeballs changed direction suddenly as our trajectory began to level off. If I'd had lunch that day, it and I would surely have parted company.

I regained my composure, like a duffed-up drake smoothing its feathers, and calmly asked the flight examiner what was next. His eyes were wide and vacant.

"You okay?" I asked. No response. I did a few checks, ailerons, rudder, engine power all working fine so, I asked again. Still nothing.

"Back to Biggin," he muttered finally. We hadn't nearly completed all the tests we were supposed to do, but I wasn't about to argue with him. I'd had quite enough excitement for one day. I remember that flight back to the airfield well as, whatever I asked him, there was no reply, except for just one word that he muttered from time to time, which was "impossible" and that glazed look which I will always remember, It looked as if he hadn't returned to the real world and might have been playing over and over, in his mind what had just happened, who knows?.

I landed the plane safely, brought it to a stop and turned off the engine. As the instructor, my examiner for the day climbed out of the plane I realised he had soiled himself. No wonder he was so keen to get back down to the ground. As we walked back to the clubhouse, I stopped and pointed at him, and in the gravest voice, I could muster said, "Don't ever do that to a novice, as they won't save you. What you did was suicidal, and what's worse, you completely froze up there."

I do believe he thought he was about to be on the receiving end of a punch, but that was not the case. I did not even report him to the club in fact, as I was sure, the experience itself had been more than enough to teach him a lesson. Some months later I heard that that man had given up flying altogether.

What I still can't understand though is how on earth we survived. I mean, simple common sense and experience tell me that we didn't have enough height to start with, that's just a matter of mathematics. Plus, whatever room we did have was considerably lessened by my hesitation to take control away from the examiner straight away. Besides that, I saw a tree rocket past the window and yet we didn't hit anything. How is that possible? I was absolutely certain even in the first few seconds of that dive that we weren't going to make it. Any experienced pilot will tell you that you learn to have a sense of these things, and it is very rarely wrong. Plus, I've flown over that area several times since eventually locating the exact path I remember taking on that occasion and finding it lined with tall trees and a chalk cliff that we should have hit even if we'd missed all of those trees. I saw the white house that we were careering towards and replayed the whole incident in my mind, but I still cannot for the life of me fathom how we escaped with our lives. I remember vividly peeking out of the side window as I prepared for the end, and seeing the tops of those trees so close I could have reached out and touched them.

Common sense would suggest that I must have had enough space to recover the aircraft because I did just that. The pragmatist in me can come to no other conclusion. However, common sense and pragmatism cannot answer the questions that still nag away at me to this day. How did we manage to miss all of those trees when we must have been almost at ground level and with the nose still pointing mostly down, as I distinctly remember still struggling to wrestle it back up at that point. What did my instructor see that turned him to stone and seemingly prevented him from trying or helping to recover the situation? He had his eyes open the whole time, and whatever it was he saw was enough to make him soil himself. I doubt that would have happened if he believed we were going to make it.

Now, I'm not going to suggest that a huge hand came down and lifted us clear of the ground at the last second, causing those massive G-forces I felt and leaving me free to complete the escape. Though I may as well say that since it makes as much sense as any other explanation. In all my years of flying, I have never seen or experienced anything that might explain to me how we managed to survive that day. Not one single, solitary thing. Maybe there is a logical explanation, but if there is, I am not aware of it.

Throughout the whole event, all I could think about was my family, and the instructor's family, the people we would be leaving behind and for what? Such a waste. Other than that it was a strangely calm and peaceful affair. Well, up until we reached the top of the loop when I pushed down, flicked the aircraft level and applied full power because that kind of forces can make you physically sick.

Facing my own mortality, I found that I wasn't afraid to die so much as I was sad for the people left behind who would be affected by it. I didn't panic, scream, cry or soil myself, but worked to retrieve the situation even though I was beyond convinced that it was hopeless. I kept battling even after I'd said my goodbyes. That tells me something useful about who I am, I think.

Peter Burn once said to me that good pilots are too busy to worry about a crash, as they're constantly flying the aeroplane and the second they stop doing that, all is lost.

As for the instructor, well, a good wash and a change of trousers later and I'm sure he was fine. Still alive, after all, which is better than the alternative.

I think the thing I love most about flying is how the realities of our everyday lives pale into insignificance when viewed from way up high in the air. We are mere specs on the face of the planet, our choices and actions utterly insignificant in the great scale of things, though we try our best to convince ourselves otherwise. For me, coming to terms with the idea that none of the things we worry so much about on a daily basis really matter, has been incredibly liberating. Flying never fails to remind me that all life is simply a matter of perspective.

It reminds me of a story I heard many years ago about a Dutchman who was said to be one of the richest men in all of Holland. He wore an old (but superbly tailored) tweed jacket, smart old trousers and an antique waistcoat, and carried a silver pocket watch. People would ask the man why he didn't just buy expensive new clothes, a gold watch to replace his old silver one and a nice big Rolls Royce rather than the battered old Land Rover he drove around. The man's simple reply was that his vehicle got him where he needed to go, his clothes were warm and adequate and his watch still kept perfect time. Why should he want to change them? For me, that is a truly special character, and I believe that understanding that kind of mindset is one of the keys to finding peace and happiness in the world, and understanding better what man is and what we're all about.

For all that we think about who we are, we take ourselves and our trivial day-to-day dramas far too seriously. Ironically, it may be this unwitting overestimation of our own importance that prevents us from seeing the big picture and realising how special we could be.

Perhaps if everybody learnt to fly, we would get there sooner.

Chapter Nine
Rocky's Little Problem
1976

Throw moderation to the winds, and the greatest pleasures bring the greatest pains.
~ Democritus, Greek philosopher, 460-370 BC

We can all be naïve in our own different ways. One of mankind's particular traits is a willingness to settle into routines and comforting, familiar ways of thinking, without ever stopping to check whether we have the right end of the stick. Every society has its taboos, on top of which people tend to add their own personal issues which pride forbids them to discuss, all of which can lead to otherwise completely normal, happy, healthy people getting things that the rest of us take for granted spectacularly wrong. In such instances, the smallest revelation can move mountains and change a person's life dramatically, as happened to a plumber of my acquaintance, who went by the name of Rocky.

As a plumber running a brisk business, dealing with local authorities and suchlike, I have over the years had occasion to hire a number of plumbers looking for work. Usually, I would speak to the local labour exchange, who would notify suitable candidates and send them around. In those days (the early seventies), jobs could be hard to come by and there were plenty of good men after each one, so it was common for them to present themselves in a formal and professional manner, stating their credentials and explaining why they were a first-class prospect for that particular job. Rocky did exactly this, and as I took his labour exchange card and glanced up at his face, I recognised him immediately.

You see, in addition to being a professional plumber, Rocky was also a wrestler on Saturday afternoon television. On the small screen, where I had seen him several times grunting and groaning and throwing other men all over the place, he was large, and fierce, and aggressive. In person, he was disorientingly slight and charming.

"I'm Rocky Hargrove," he said, offering his hand for me to shake.

"Yes, I know," I replied, "I'm just wondering what on earth a television star wants with a twenty-pound-a-week plumbing job."

Rocky explained that he had hurt his back and that his doctor had ordered him to take it easy else he might damage himself beyond repair. *That would explain it*, I thought. At any rate, he said all the right things, and after a successful interview, I offered him the position.

But then there was something else that troubled me. Rocky said that he had a wife and four children in Kent, some thirty miles from our office. That was a long way to commute in those days, and I enquired as to why he couldn't find work a little closer to home. He replied that mine was the first offer to come along in over a month. I knew times were a little tight, but that sounded a bit odd to me for a trained plumber.

Well, there was a reason for that, as it turned out. Sensing that I had his number and wasn't going to stop asking questions until I figured out what was troubling me, Rocky came clean and admitted that he hadn't exactly completed his apprenticeship, and was therefore really more like 'half a plumber', and did I mind? The answer was yes, I did. But on the other hand, I did like his tenacity in going after the job, so I agreed to a trial period to see how he got on. The answer was pretty well. By today's standards, he was quite an accomplished plumber and managed most tasks just fine, even with me watching over his shoulder like a hawk to make sure he didn't screw anything up. The things in which he had little or no training, such as lead burning, I taught him myself over time, and as the months went by Rocky became a complete plumber and a valuable member of my team.

The only issue really was his temper. Rocky could be aggressive at times and became stressed easily, especially when you were trying to teach him something difficult. He had a lot of pride, more than a lot of men I would say, on top of which I suspect his small stature contributed to the problem as he tried to overcompensate for it in other ways. I remember more than one occasion when he glared at me like a wound-up bull after I'd tried to correct a mistake that he'd made or offered some well-meaning advice, and sometimes I think I was a hair's breadth away from Rocky offering me a knuckle sandwich for my trouble.

I was to learn to be 'respectful', that was his word. He wanted everyone to respect him or else risk ending up eyeball to eyeball, even if that meant Rocky standing on a chair. He was very athletic and would literally jump onto a table to make his point, gesticulating flamboyantly just as he used to do in the ring. At times, it created a difficult working environment but it certainly was interesting. He was 'good value', you might say, and to be honest, he was usually a happy sort of guy and good to have around. It was only when the smile went away that you knew he was about to blow up, and the phrase "now what, Rocky?" would be heard in wearied trepidation. Sometimes after he'd blow up he would storm out, returning either within the hour or at the latest next morning with a profuse apology, saying that his anger had gotten the better of him and promising that it wouldn't happen again. I knew it was all bravado, Rocky never actually hurt or attempted to hurt anybody, and I was sure he never would, so I always forgave him.

I had the policy to keep a certain distance between myself and my employees, for business reasons. It's hard to be the boss and be everybody's friend at the same time. But Rocky was an emotional chap and we were always quite close, to the point where even though he was some fifteen years my senior, Rocky would come and seek my advice on certain matters from time to time, and I was always happy to help if I could.

So it came about that one morning in July 1976, at the ungodly hour of six-thirty am, my doorbell rang. Scrambling bleary-eyed to answer it, I found Rocky standing on the step with a look of abject misery on his face.

"Sorry," he said, taking in my just-out-of-bed appearance, "I'll come back later."

"Come on," I replied, grabbing his shoulder as he turned to leave, "come in and tell me what's up."

I lead him through to the kitchen and put the kettle on while Rocky sat slumped in a chair, looking as though he had the weight of the world on his shoulders. A few minutes passed and the kettle boiled, but Rocky hadn't said a word, so I made us both a cup of tea and sat down opposite, waiting patiently for him to start. Well, we went through the process of sipping the too hot tea, past the phase where it was cool enough to drink in a pleasant manner, to the point where we had both drunk more than half a cup, yet Rocky still didn't speak. I thought I saw tears welling in his eyes, so I averted my gaze in the hope that he wouldn't feel like I thought him a weak person.

"You've been a good friend, John," he began finally after a few false starts, "and a good boss, and you've helped me out from time to time. But I'm not sure what you can do about this one."

I was rather worried by this point and said so, suggesting various things that might have caused poor Rocky such consternation. But he assured me that his family were all fine and that he didn't have any money problems, so I was at a loss to imagine what it might be.

"Okay, Rocky," I said at last, "so what's the real problem?"

Speaking very slowly and looking determinedly at the floor, Rocky began to explain that after work the previous night he had returned home, as usual, parked the van around the back of the house and made his way through to the kitchen where his wife, June, was entertaining a few friends from where she worked. They were trying to persuade her to come for a girls' night out, as he understood, but she hadn't really been up for it. At any rate, they were having a good old natter and he thought he'd best leave them to it, so he made himself a coffee and was on his way upstairs to take a well-deserved soak in the bath when he caught a snippet of the conversation from the kitchen that made him stop dead in his tracks.

Apparently, one of the women had said that her husband called her his Colt 45 because he could trigger her off six times, every time. The girls all giggled, then another said sadly that she was lucky to have an orgasm once a week as her husband was totally selfish and only cared about himself. The laughter died down for a moment before exploding again as she went on to say that at least the new bloke at work made up for it. Well, Rocky knew he shouldn't be eavesdropping, but he couldn't help it, and he stood perfectly still on the stairs as the girls turned their attention to June. Surely, they supposed, an athlete like Rocky must be able to go a few rounds with her, and could he last all night, and how many times did she orgasm?

There was a pregnant pause before June admitted, in a quiet, sad sort of voice, that her husband only lasted a couple of minutes if she was lucky, and that he'd never given her an orgasm at all, not once. Now there was more silence before one of the women asked crudely whether Rocky might be… short in any other areas.

"Oh no!" replied June aghast. "He's all man in that department. He just can't satisfy me. Never has."

Shocked by what he had just heard, Rocky quietly let himself out of the house, got back in his van and drove around the streets aimlessly before finally pulling into a lay-by to get a few hours' kip. At around six-fifteen, he was awoken by a concerned policeman, and now here he was in my kitchen looking for an answer to the big question. What could he possibly do to satisfy his lady?

I hated to see Rocky like this; the dynamic, muscular hero of the small screen who roared and prowled and heaved up men only to hurl them down again in the ring, banging his chest in triumph, now reduced to a sad little heap whose whole world had come crashing down around him. Oh well. A little knowledge, as I said, can shed a whole new light on things. Rocky was about to find that out.

"I've tried," he said miserably, "but damn it she's just so beautiful I can't help myself."

I suggested he might try looking away or thinking about something else to take his mind off of the act in progress, train himself to last longer. But he said he'd already tried that and it didn't work. *Hmm*, I thought. Well, there is one other thing that might work.

Before I explain, for health and safety reasons please don't try this at home. Back in the seventies, we were all a lot more casual with our bodies and besides, we didn't know any better. Things are different now, especially legally speaking, and I have no desire to be sued by would-be Casanovas who get it wrong.

Okay, so I must admit that I had gone through a similar experience to Rocky's as a young man, when luckily for me one charitable girl took me aside and explained that a leg-over takes more than a couple of minutes, and that contrary to popular belief (by boys of a certain age), girls tend not to be simply grateful for the service. It's a bit of a slap in the face to hear that you're pretty much useless in the bedroom department, but I suspect most of us have been there, done that, and have the t-shirt sitting in a drawer somewhere. Anyway, this girl didn't give me instructions exactly, but being the creative sort I had a think and changed my ways, and luckily it worked. But now what to do about poor Rocky's particular situation? I had an idea.

"Well, Rocky," I said carefully, "I might actually be able to help you, but you must take extreme care."

I went on to explain about a certain kind of cream, used to treat wasp stings, which contained an anaesthetic that would render the affected area numb. Perhaps Rocky could make 'creative' use of such an ointment to help him with his oversensitivity.

"But be careful," I warned, "it may take a few tries to get used to it."

Looking a little bit more cheerful, Rocky thanked me for the help before going home for a good sleep.

For the next three weeks straight, Rocky showed up for work in a better mood than any of us had seen him in for some time. When I enquired about his little problem, he merely gave me a wink and a smile as if to say that everything was just fine now, before carrying on about his work, whistling away and looking for all the world like a cockerel in full command of his hens.

Then, unexpectedly, a few weeks later, my doorbell rang again at the crack of dawn, and there Rocky was just as before, tears streaming down his face, stuttering something about having properly mucked his life up this time. I wondered with some apprehension what on earth could have gone wrong now. Had he done as we'd discussed last time, I asked. Yes, he had. Apparently, the first time it didn't work very well, but after that things picked up and now he could last as long as he liked.

"So then what's the problem?" I asked.

"You told me to be careful," he replied, "but you didn't explain what you meant."

"Just that you shouldn't over-do it, that's all," I replied, bemused.

As it turned out, Rocky had jumped in a little too enthusiastically, perhaps in an attempt to overcompensate for his previous poor performances. It was the honeymoon of honeymoons for lucky June and she was loving it at first, walking around with a new spring in her step and a certain radiance she hadn't had before. They were at it constantly from the moment Rocky woke up in the morning, then again when he got home from work, another session later in the evening and double-time at weekends. Eventually, it got to the point where the poor girl couldn't cope with him anymore and needed a rest. One morning after a particularly long marathon session, Rocky made his move bright and early at five am, whereupon he was gently pushed away with a 'woah, boy!' and an enquiry as to what could have brought this new-found enthusiasm on after all these years and four kids together. Poor June was getting banged up as though sex was going to be outlawed next week, and while she wasn't exactly complaining, she was certainly curious.

Rocky admitted that he had inadvertently overheard what the girls had been discussing that awful night, and how ashamed he was by what June had told them.

"Oh, honey," said June, "well, don't be ashamed anymore. I've confided in a close friend that you've turned into the most amazing lover, so no doubt half of Kent knows by now."

She went on to say, her friend couldn't understand what might have happened to effect such a dramatic change, and neither could June herself. She was delighted about it, no doubt, but now she wanted to know what Rocky had done to turn him into such a Superman.

Rocky hesitated and then out came the wasp sting cream and he explained it all. That was not a good move.

"You dirty little bugger!" yelled June, sitting up suddenly in bed and pointing towards the door. "Go away and leave me alone!"

Poor Rocky scrambled to throw his clothes on and left the house in a hurry, and now here he was again in my kitchen. Poor Rocky. We had another cup of tea and I sympathised with him, and then at eight am on the dot that morning I received a phone call from June. She thanked me for helping Rocky with his little problem, as the change had done wonders for their marriage, but would I kindly advise her husband that a little restraint was necessary. Well, I think that went without saying at that point.

Within a month, Rocky had left the firm to find a job somewhat closer to home. I gave him an excellent reference, so he had no problems at all on that front and hopefully, now none on the other. He was a good guy and a good worker, so it was a bit of a shame to see him go, but at least we all learnt a few good lessons during his tenure.

The whole situation reminded me of wise words I heard as a young lad, from a certain Christos, who suggested that I should always listen to other people's advice, as it always has the potential to lead to better things.

I wonder what value June would put on what Rocky learnt.

Chapter Ten
Good People and Bad People
1981–2010

With or without religion you'd have good people doing good things and evil people doing bad things. But for good people to do bad things, it takes religion.
~ Steven Weinberg

While Rocky and his wife were busy having their religious experience in the bedroom, I was having my own, of a very different kind, in my village in Sussex.

I should reiterate, just for the record, that I am not a religious person in the strictest sense nor an atheist, though I have no issue with it per se and in fact, I think religion has a lot to offer mankind. No doubt the Ten Commandments are good, common-sense rules of thumb to live one's life by, things like the Christian parables are well worth learning for the wisdom they contain and the Koran is full of all manner of good advice. However, I had it drummed into me as a schoolboy that being good was its own reward and that being bad usually ended in punishment (in those days a couple of thwacks on the hand with a stiff cane.) So I believe that it is not religion itself, but rather what a person makes of their religious beliefs that mark them out as good or bad. In short; actions speak louder than words.

If Christianity, for example, were really all about the teachings of Jesus Christ, I should have expected that visiting the church in my village would bring me into contact with plenty of good, honest, fair-minded people. In reality, I had cause to suspect that many of them went to church for the wrong reasons, mindful of appearances rather than actual morality, so I wasn't exactly keen to pander to this sanctimonious pretence and play my part in the superficial 'good neighbour' routine.

I knew some of them of course, and I like to think that I was always kind to them. Do unto others as you would have done unto you is another good example of common-sense maxims to live by, and I hoped that my local acquaintances would reciprocate whenever possible. Unfortunately, this wasn't to be the case.

The situation at hand was that I wanted to carry out some building work in the area. Anyone who has attempted to get planning permission for a new development out in the beautiful English countryside probably knows how much of a fuss the locals tend to kick up, even when the building work is of a high standard and certainly no detriment to the surrounding area.

In this particular case, the law stipulated that there were permitted development rights that I could count on, mind you there are conditions attached, which I must abide by. So if my plans were by the book, I didn't actually need planning permission to proceed, but I wanted everything to go forward in an amicable manner and so I petitioned the local council for confirmation that all conditions were met and that I could move ahead with the plans. The planning department was happy enough with that assessment and recommended an approval, but when it came down to the planning committee they disagreed and insisted that I needed planning permission, and furthermore that they would not grant it.

I knew that the law was on my side, but I also knew that there would be strong opposition to my plans. So although I could have pressed my legal advantage right away, I went and spoke to the local clergyman first to see if he might be able to facilitate a peaceful solution. I showed him proof beyond doubt that I would win any legal action and gave him the telephone number of the local planning officer he could speak to if he had any doubts about my truthfulness.

My reasoning was that if he could be convinced that the actions of the council were wrong, he may be able to induce some degree of shame in his allegedly God-fearing congregation and get them to back down. Were they good Christians or not, I asked. The answer seemed to be that this clergyman, at any rate, was less a creature of morals and more one of convenience. His congregation were up in arms about my plans and he was going to tell them what they wanted to hear for fear of losing his job. His last-ditch effort was to appeal for me to come along to church on Sunday and show that I was prepared to act more like them. Respectfully, I declined. I told him that I was always happy to hold out an olive branch to anyone with whom I have a disagreement, but that it would be morally wrong of me to pretend to be something I wasn't in order to appease these people, who had proven that their application of Christian teachings was somewhat less than consistent.

Well, this is where things all became very strange. I asked to meet with one of the district councillors, who also happened to be a magistrate and the chairman of the parish council in the village, she was known to be a very powerful influence in the area. She must have been well aware of the legal merits of the case, and I implored her to step in and end this whole saga, which seemed to be nothing but a gross waste of taxpayer's money. But rather than settling things there and then, the lady referred me to someone she was well acquainted with, the local MP, who was also a cabinet minister, who in turn suggested that I ought to simply file an appeal against the decision. Which I duly did. Besides, she said, she was entitled to her view. And what's more, she was acting on behalf of those she was representing, adding sarcastically that I hadn't voted for her anyway.

The appeal was heard and rejected by no less than the Secretary of State himself, and my plans to build seemed in tatters. The locals were overjoyed and let me know in no uncertain terms that I had been put in my place and ought to learn that nobody takes on "this" local council and wins.

Stop there for a moment and read that line again, because it is, for me, pretty astonishing. The law of the land, in this case, seemed crystal clear, and the Secretary of State had apparently gone completely against it. Now I could be wrong but he seemed to act at the request of his friend in government and by extension, the busybodies in the local council. From what was said at the time by the locals it was a matter of not what you know, but more about who you know.

I suppose you could say that they were simply exercising their democratic right to make that decision, knowing that my only recourse would be to the courts and that would be an expensive and time-consuming process which they clearly judged I wouldn't have the appetite for. So I imagine they were quite surprised when the case of Emin v Secretary of State and Mid Sussex District Council was scheduled to be decided at the High Court in London. I went right ahead and sued the lot of them.

Outside the imposing front doors of the court, the Secretary of State finally caved in and apologised to both myself and the judge, Sir Graham Eyre QC, stating that a mistake had been made and that he would take steps to rectify it immediately. To which the Judge remarked that he was pleased to hear it, and how refreshing it was to hear a Secretary of State admit to a mistake as that didn't happen very often.

The council's barrister, however, a short, tenacious man with a neatly trimmed beard, wasn't giving up so easily. He rambled on for some hours in front of an amused Sir Graham Eyre, trying to persuade him that the council's case had merit and that the Secretary of State had been wrong to change his mind in this instance because he had been right to say no in the first place. It was an impossible sell. I won the case hands down and set a precedent in case law that opened the floodgates for other developers to carry out similar building work unfettered by spiteful not-in-my-back-yard types. Until that point, councils had been abusing their position for years, handing out planning judgements based on their personal wishes rather than the law of the land. No longer would that be allowed to continue.

Of course, had my local council been flexible to negotiate with me, to begin with, no doubt we could have reached an amicable arrangement that suited all parties. But no, they were stubborn and petty and they paid the price for forgetting what their Bibles taught them once upon a time, that being a good person brings rewards while being a bad one attracts punishment. Their punishment was that I was given the go-ahead not only to construct the original building but also the second one as well and they could do nothing about it.

At that point, one might think, they should have learnt their lesson and we could all move on with our lives. But unfortunately for everyone concerned, spitefulness still lingered in the Sussex air.

The weekend after the court case, I popped along to the newsagent in the village, whereupon a discussion erupted about my building plans that soon drew a crowd of some fifteen or so people and spilt out onto the pavement. People were asking me why I was so intent on spoiling their beautiful countryside, some even went so far as to call me a vandal and suggest that I might like to bugger off back to London and leave them alone as it was costing the town a small fortune to deal with me. Wow. Well, those were clearly the opinions of people who had been spun a decidedly coloured picture, both by the council and the local paper that was reporting the case blow by blow.

There were so many people voicing their opinions outside the shop now that it was becoming difficult for me to make myself heard.

"Ladies and gentlemen!" I called out loudly. To my surprise, they all stopped and stared. Sensing that the shocked silence would not last long, I pressed on without missing a beat. "I am not sure what you have heard about my proposals," I said, "but I would like to assure you that everything is legal and above board. Should the courts deem otherwise, I will gladly purchase a half-page advertisement in the Mid-Sussex Times, apologising to each and every person who has fought so vociferously against me."

"Not only that," I continued, "but I will also donate to the local Boy Scouts the sum of £5,000, to do with as they see fit. And if someone would care to bring me a top hat, I will eat that as well. The law of the land is very clear, and it is there to protect all of us equally. But look at what we have here now. A lynch mob, no less. Just look at yourselves. This is never the best way to settle a dispute."

"Finally," I concluded, as there were calls again for me to pack up my bags and bugger off back to London, "I have always said that if anyone has an issue with me or my plans, they can come and talk to me with an open mind and I'm sure we can come to some equitable compromise. But none of you did that. Indeed, the parish council," I pointed to one of the councillors who was present, and indeed doing much of the shouting, "insisted on having things all their own way. They weren't interested in compromise." My feelings were I was being bullied by people that ought to have known better.

I admit I was having a little fun. I already knew the result of the court decision and these people didn't at that time, so I was making promises I knew I would never have to keep. But the looks on some of their faces were priceless.

The saga wasn't quite over yet though. It turned out, upon further examination of the plans, that I actually did need planning permission for a small part of the work. The council granted it, knowing that they were legally obligated to do so, but put as many petty limitations on the order as they possibly could, effectively making it impossible for me to proceed. If they couldn't stop me with fair terms, they would use every technicality on the book to clip my heels every step of the way.

I suppose I should have been upset by all of this stonewalling and prevarication, it still took several years to get right, but I just found it more amusing than anything else that these people who prided themselves on being good Christians were behaving in such an unnecessarily nasty manner. Periodically over the following months, I would receive a letter from the planning department threatening to put a stop to or limit my development, but each time I would go away, study the law, confirm that it was in my favour and hand back their red herring with a smile. In the end, it took almost five years to get planning approval that I could actually work with.

My patience didn't quite stretch that far, however. Two years into these shenanigans I had lorry loads of bricks and other materials all sitting around waiting for me to be given the go-ahead. But I was itching to pass the time, and Sir Graham Eyre had clarified the situation nicely already, so I altered the plans a little and set about building a bungalow-type ancillary structure behind the ten-foot-high walls within an acre walled garden.

There was a huge pine tree on the land that had a broken limb and needed to be trimmed, so I called in a tree surgeon by the name of John, who I then found out was also a member of the parish council. As John walked into the walled garden and caught sight of me digging the footings with a JCB, his jaw dropped.

"What are you doing?" he gasped.

"Building a bungalow," I replied simply.

"You can't do that!" spluttered John in disbelief.

I begged to differ.

There was plenty of chatter in the village after that, and as I understand it they all came to an agreement not to act immediately, but to teach me a lesson by waiting until I was finished and then making me tear down the whole lot. Well, finish it I did, a splendid property in the end at a cost of some £50,000 in 1990, with those generous walled gardens, grape houses and more, in a part of England that was soon after designated by law an area of outstanding natural beauty. Then even before the paint was dry, the District Council, following a complaint from the Parish Council, fell upon the planning officers and demanded that I be forced to demolish it. How on earth did I have the right to just go ahead and build a whopping great bungalow in the back garden without their express permission?

I received a curt letter requesting that I be present on site at an appointed time, when the Chief Planning Officer, his deputy and the council's enforcement officer, as well as a member of the council's legal team, would all be present to inspect the construction.

No doubt the chief protagonist in this affair knew all too well the legal situation, having no doubt spoken to the chief planner who had been given delegated powers to decide such requests. When the time of the inspection came around I had all my documents laid out on a table in the bungalow waiting for them. The planning officer didn't cast his eye over the papers, but simply waved his hand around at the building work and muttered a "yes, yes, Mr Emin, all by the book, by the book."

"Well, then," I said, "what on earth are we all doing here? What does an hour of your time cost the taxpayers?" I asked, pointing to the Chief Planning Officer. "A £100? And maybe eighty-five more for your deputy? Forty-five for the enforcement officer?" I gestured to each man in turn, "And let's say £80 an hour for your legal man over there."

"My lost earnings from standing here talking to you are in the order of £200 an hour. This is what we're all losing, what we've been losing for years carrying on with this ridiculous, fruitless fight. You knew before you came out here today that you weren't going to get me to pull this all down." I reminded him that not only was he the head of planning but also of the building inspectorate, in which case he must know virtually everything there is to know about this building, as no doubt his inspectors must have reported back to him on this particularly sensitive issue. He pursed his lips and scrunched his face, then with a deep breath, tried to look me in the eye, yet for me, his eyes said it all. This was a good man pressured by politics to do as he was told, this had been clear to me for years. "So," I said, "I think serious questions need to be asked of the main instigator of all of this nonsense. I pleaded with the local district councillor who seems to have enormous power over the planning committee and seemingly far beyond, who is also a magistrate and should have known the legal position better than anyone, and importantly used balanced judgment, to advise both the parish and take heed of the professional advice of the planning department. Instead, she has chosen, in my view, to behave vindictively, abusing her power and status and wasting not only my money but that of the taxpayers as well. Now," I caught the eye of the Chief Planning Officer and pointed at him earnestly, "why did we not have this meeting when the footings were put down? Why wait until the building was completed? You answer me that question and you will see where the real shame falls. Since she has now failed to have the building work undone," I said finally, "she ought to resign forthwith."

Predictably, the whole village got wind of this demand, and for whatever reason, she did resign about six weeks later, having been a councillor for over twenty years.

Now, as I said I am not a religious person, but I have a great deal of respect for those who are, and who follow the teachings of their chosen faith in a manner that helps them to be good people. I believe in something greater that comes from within us all, an echo which hints that we are more than what we see, call it a spirit or a soul, conscience, or whatever you like, that gives us a sense of good and bad and allows us to measure our own actions in those terms. If religion helps to guide us towards the good, then I am all for it.

What I cannot abide is people who pay lip service to their chosen religion, believing that simply the act of going to church, or mosque, for example, grants them some kind of innate goodness while their behaviour suggests anything but. The teachings of Christianity, of Islam, Judaism, indeed any of the major religions with which I am familiar, applied and followed in an honest way, will no doubt lead to people behaving kindly and charitably towards one another. The point of my story here about the parish council and the apparent long arm of influence they had is simply by way of demonstrating the hypocrisy, even on a relatively trivial level, of a large number of people calling themselves good Christians. My situation was certainly not unique. This kind of treatment by so-called good people is dished out daily all over the world.

The problem, as I see it, comes when we start relying on external factors like churches and scriptures, rather than paying attention to our innate sense of right and wrong. People use religion as a crutch or excuse rather than a guide, and such people almost always get found out in the end, as happened with the unfortunate councillor who chose to take me on. And also with a gentleman of my acquaintance by the name of Tim.

I came across Tim at a time shortly before the computer revolution began, when people actually had to type letters and invoices on typewriters and take shorthand. My trusted secretary Mandy had the ability to run my busy office, but she had just got married and would shortly be moving away, leaving me in a bit of a pickle.

The plan was to advertise for another girl immediately, whom Mandy could train up before she left us. I interviewed two candidates who turned out to have poor typing skills and no shorthand whatsoever, and I was beginning to fear that the search would be a painful one when Tim arrived in my office. He was a mousy little man in a grey suit, an old tie and threadbare cardigan, and he claimed to be an experienced secretary with excellent typing skills. He was a strange one to be sure, and I was understandably sceptical.

"Test me," said Tim, simply.

I picked up a full sheet of words and read it out to him at a brisk pace, easily over a hundred words a minute, and to my surprise, Tim jotted it all down in shorthand without batting an eyelid. Then when I finished speaking he took a clean sheet of paper from the drawer, placed it in the typewriter and began rattling the thing like a machine gun. The sound of it was so impressive that it made Mandy stop what she was doing and come and see what was going on. She gave me a nod of surprised approval, and then moments later Tim whisked the sheet from the typewriter and offered it to me. It was as complete and accurate as anyone could have wished for.

Well, I was convinced as far as Tim's typing skills were concerned, but now something else was bothering me. Back in those days, secretarial work was almost exclusively done by girls and women, and the pay was less than what a grown man could expect to earn in virtually any profession. I let Tim know that the wages I was offering were on a par with a regular office girl, to which he replied that he expected as much and it was no problem. But that only deepened my suspicions that all here was not quite as it seemed, so I carefully asked a few questions about Tim's personal life. If he had a wife, for example, and children, and a mortgage to pay, there was no way he could have afforded to do those kinds of things on the money I was offering.

Tim was single, he told me, and living in the house his parents had left him. So no real expenses there to take care of other than food, drink and utilities.

"Okay, Tim," I said, "you seem too good to be true. If I give you this job and find out later on that there's something you aren't telling me, I won't hesitate to terminate your employment on the spot. Do you understand?"

Tim opened his mouth hesitantly to speak, and for a fleeting moment I thought he might be about to tell me that he had just been released from prison. As a matter of fact, that would at least explain where he had learnt to type so proficiently.

"There's only one thing," began Tim, "and as you have asked for full disclosure, I will tell you. I am a Jehovah's Witness." We looked at each other. "Is that going to be a problem for you?" he asked.

So not a killer or a burglar fresh out of prison then, just a Jehovah's Witness. Now it makes sense.

"Well, Tim," I replied, "I would never discriminate based on a person's religion, but I'm offering you this job on a trial period to see how you get on, and on the strict condition that you must not bring your religion into the office. Do you promise?"

He agreed, and I took him on there and then. Tim was an excellent secretary and Mandy soon had him caught up on the workings of the office. After a while, there came hints that things were not going so well.

The main office was upstairs, and Mandy and Barbara would come down to see me from time to time and complain about little things Tim had done. They seemed pretty agitated, even going so far as to say that I would have to get rid of him. I didn't particularly want to do that, as Tim, as I say, was a skilled worker and seemed like a good person, so instead, I would go and have a quiet word with him about the things the girls had mentioned. Tim always thanked me for pointing out the problem and stated that he would do better in the future, and for a while, I was reassured.

Then one day about a week before Mandy was due to leave us for good, she came storming downstairs in a rage.

"I've been banging my head against the wall with Tim all morning!" she seethed, "But I can't do it anymore. It's those job tickets again. You'll have to deal with him yourself. If you want my advice you'll sack him now before it gets out of control."

A moment later she was followed by Barbara, who looked equally agitated and said almost exactly the same thing again. I was quite surprised, as Tim had seemed alright to me, but I couldn't ignore how obviously wound-up the girls were. Something was clearly badly wrong. At the same time though it was a very busy period and I didn't really have the opportunity to conduct another search. It seemed that Tim would get one last chance to prove he could make things work.

A few days later, after Mandy had left us for good and Tim was alone in the office but for a junior girl who helped out, he came downstairs to ask me a question. There was a job ticket in his hand for one of the jobs that we had ongoing at the time, and I could see that it had three men's names on it. Tim wanted to know which of them had actually done the work, but I couldn't tell him so I suggested he used the last name on the sheet. It was a touch pedantic perhaps, but in all fairness, Tim did have a point. I had a word with the men and found out who had actually done the job, which took me a day or so, then went back to Tim and told him that it was Harry. I also told him that if it happened again, for the sake of expedience, he could just put down the last name as I had suggested earlier, furthermore I said it wasn't really important enough to make a fuss and hold up more important work.

"I can't do that," said Tim, "I have to write down the name of the person who actually did the job, or I would be lying."

Funny, I distinctly remember telling him not to bring this kind of thing into my office. But I wasn't inclined to make a big deal out of it, so I said that I would have a word with the men and instruct them to sign out properly for each job so that it wouldn't happen again. Tim seemed happy enough with that, and I assumed it would be the end of the matter.

The problem was, however, that much of the work we were doing was for local authority housing, and my men would quite often find that they were unable to gain entry to a site for some reason or other, in which case the ticket for that job would be left overnight for whoever happened to be going in that direction the next day. The system had worked very well till Tim made an issue of it. I wasn't about to change the way we have functioned simply to indulge Tim's ethics.

Worse still, he had begun taking it upon himself to solve the problem that didn't need solving, by going down to the yard himself and giving all my workers the third degree trying to find out which one of them had done a particular job. Eventually, they just started owning up to work they hadn't done in order to get Tim to go away. It was becoming a joke.

At any rate, things came to a head a short while later, while I was in full flow dictating a letter to my 'friend' the Chief Planning Officer of Mid-Sussex District Council, who were being particularly troublesome regarding a planning application I had filed and I was taking them to task regarding the planning law that they apparently hadn't read.

"...he was wrong in what he was suggesting," I dictated as Tim scribbled away in shorthand, "as I'm sure you know yourself, sir, is complete and utter bullshit..."

No sooner had I said those words than Tim stood up, put down the pad and refused to continue.

"Sit down, Tim," I said, "and tell me what the problem is."

"I can't use that word," replied Tim, "it's not right."

I tried to explain the situation to him, that the Chief Planning Officer was deliberately wasting my time as far as I could see, and that the word I had used most succinctly described his reasoning for denying my original request.

"Why don't you just say 'rubbish'?" asked Tim.

"Look, Tim," I replied, frustrated now, "what did I say to you when I first took you on? You promised me that you wouldn't bring your religion to work. Your ethics are your concern. My concern is running my business the best I can, and if I need to say bullshit then I'm going to say bullshit."

I looked at Tim. He was still standing up, his pad left defiantly on the desk, and we both knew he was a whisker away from losing his job.

"Alright," I said wearily, "how about this. You type up to that word and then call me in and I will type it in for you."

Tim shook his head and insisted point blank that he couldn't be at all associated with such a letter. This must have been what Mandy meant when she told me to fire him before things got out of hand. Well, now this nonsense really had gone far enough.

"I know a way we can work this out," I said finally. "But first, answer me a couple of questions, would you?"

Tim nodded hesitantly.

"Do you think of yourself as honest?" I asked.

"Yes," replied Tim.

"I see. And have you ever stolen anything in your life?" I asked.

"Never," replied Tim.

"Alright, Tim, I didn't want to do this but you've forced me into it, and please believe me when I tell you it's for your own good. I am going to prove to you that life isn't as black and white as you think it is because even by your own standards you are a thief and a liar."

Tim stared at me, aghast.

"If I can prove to you that you are a thief," I went on, "will you agree to compromise on your strict interpretation of the Bible in future?"

"I am not a liar," insisted Tim, "and I have never stolen a thing in my life."

"Okay, Tim," I replied wearily, "are you sure you want me to do this? I'm going to drag you into the real world so fast your head will spin."

A smirk of confidence spread across Tim's face, the smile of the righteous who are so arrogantly sure of themselves and the fact that God is on their side no matter what. It was a smile that very clearly said, 'bring it on.'

"Right," I said. "Count one. You have lied to me when you told me that you've never stolen anything in your life."

"That's not a lie," replied Tim.

"Really?" I said. "So tell me please what are your working hours?"

"Nine am until five pm," stammered Tim. "Why?"

"What time did you leave work yesterday afternoon?" I asked.

"Err... three-thirty," he replied.

"And what time did you arrive this morning?"

"Nine-thirty," replied Tim.

"So you stole half an hour's pay from me this morning, and an hour and a half's worth of pay yesterday. That's not even taking into account all the other times that you've come in late or left early. You stole from me, Tim. You are a thief and a liar."

The poor man may as well have been struck by a bolt of lightning. Obviously stunned and without another word, he turned, walked past me out of the room, went upstairs to fetch his overcoat, and left.

I felt a little guilty. Even now I think that must be one of the most unkind things I have ever done to another human being. Obviously, I thought that would be the last we were likely to see our Tim, but no, nine am sharp the next morning he was in the office and removing his coat. He came down to see me straight away with an apology and a promise that if I calculated all of the time he had 'stolen' from me that he would pay it all back from his savings immediately, and that it wouldn't happen again. He told me that he'd been to seek advice from the elders at his church and that they'd told him he had indeed stolen and should make amends straight away. Perhaps they had also suggested to him that if he were to correct his mistake in an expedient manner, the whole incident could be swept neatly under the carpet and all would be forgotten.

That's what people tend to do in my experience, pretend to adhere to a particular belief system but then bend the rules and bend the truth to suit themselves and their particular situation, convenience over morals every time. Well, not this time I'm afraid.

"Tim," I began sadly, shaking my head, "this isn't about the money. In fact, your offering to pay it back after consulting your church elders sums up the real problem all too well. You just don't know how to use your brain properly, that's the problem. No doubt you are a good man and I have overlooked your little problems so far, but you follow this religious dogma almost blindly and without applying any common sense whatsoever, and it makes running a business practically impossible. Don't you understand that?"

I don't think he did, to be honest. I told him that, reluctantly his trial period had come to an end and that I was going to have to let him go, but that I would send him on his way with two weeks' worth of pay to help him while he looked for another job that might suit him better. Finally, I left him with a reminder, again for his own good, that he had broken his promise to me not to bring his religion into the office. I hoped that he might go away and think about that for a while, and perhaps realise that he would have to adapt his behaviour if he wanted to get along in the real world. Then he went back upstairs, picked up his coat, and left.

I thought that was that, but seconds later there came a crashing sound, and then another. Tim was kicking out squares of glass from the front door. I couldn't believe what I was seeing. I ran outside to try to stop him, taking him forcefully by the arm as he continued to aim kicks at the panes of glass and escorting him back into the office where I sat him down in my chair.

"What the hell do you think you're doing, Tim?" I asked, perplexed. He didn't answer. "Alright," I went on, "well, you can just sit there while I call the police." Still nothing. "See, not only have you lied to me and stolen from me, now you've deliberately damaged my property. That's criminal damage, Tim. What have you become? Fingerprints, mug shot, criminal record. You're far worse than I ever expected. There's no excuse for that."

Tim sat silently squirming in the chair, his eyes darting left to right as though considering making a break for it. I told him he could leave if he wanted, but that I would send the police after him if he did, the choice was entirely his. Then I went to make him a cup of sweet tea, which I knew he liked and added a little extra milk so that he could drink it more quickly. This seemed to help him relax a little, but still, he said nothing, just sat there hunched in his overcoat with his little bible clutched in his hand and the bag he always brought his sandwiches in sitting sadly by his feet.

The police arrived finally, a male and female officer together, and took in the damaged front door.

"Do you know who did this, sir?" they asked.

"Well, yes," I replied, "he's sitting in my office."

They asked me if I had any idea why he had done it, to which I replied that I wasn't entirely sure, before adding that I was surprised since he was a Jehovah's Witness and that he was inside having a cup of tea to calm down. The police officers looked at each other and then burst out laughing. I couldn't see the funny side at first, but then it dawned on me that they'd imagined me slamming the door on some particularly persistent Jehovah's Witnesses, who had then taken it upon themselves to kick the glass in. On the one hand, it was a comical notion. On the other, it was a comical notion largely because you wouldn't expect that kind of behaviour from that group of people, nevertheless here was one in my office who had done just that. The police officers dried their eyes before going in to see Tim, but they were still giggling when they entered the office. It was a bit unprofessional really, and I'm quite sure poor Tim had no idea what was going on, but you can't hold it against them really. We're all only human after all, and doing a tough job like police work, no doubt a situation like this can tickle a person more than usual.

They had a quick word with Tim, then came back out and advised me not to press charges. The experience would be enough to make sure he didn't do it again, they said. They asked how I knew him, and when I told them he was an ex-employee they both cracked up again, the girl with tears streaming down her cheeks and the man leaning over his car howling with laughter. Passers-by were looking on puzzled about what must be so funny.

I can't help but smile now when I remember the incident, and I'm sure those police officers went back to the station that morning with a great story to tell. I didn't want to cause Tim any real trouble, only to shock him into realising that common sense is an important part of life and that he wasn't living in the real world. You might look at a man like that and say he's harmless, but he was definitely hurting himself and making the lives of the people around him much more difficult by adopting such an inflexible manner.

For me, religion is a positive thing so long as it is taught in a way that allows people to also think for themselves. We have a collective mind that is expanding at such a rapid pace, making possible things like brain surgery and space travel, all manner of things our ancestors could never have imagined when most holy books were written. Yet, some people still insist on living by written words that have little or no relevance to the way we live our lives today. Every word in the Bible is sacred, they say, we cannot pick and choose. Yet pick and choose is exactly what they themselves do with the teachings in those ancient books.

If there is a God, and we will all meet him at some point when our skin and bone existence comes to an end, no doubt he will ask us what we have done with ourselves to warrant his approval. What will we say? How about those who buried their humanity, their instinct, the very thing that makes us who we are in order to live a strictly policed life based on what they perceive as unbreakable rules? Will they claim following the rules as virtue enough? And others who explain that they lived their lives to the full regardless of rules, loved every day, treated others as they would wish to be treated themselves, made work for others and helped them feed themselves and their families? If you were their creator, what would you think?

My own view is that he would want us to be creative and use the abilities we were born with to their fullest. Be good to each other, learn to communicate and take life's challenges in our stride. If there is another plane of existence to ascend to, and we are required to prove ourselves in order to get there, I cannot help but think that proving we appreciate and know how to use our minds and skills is far preferable to blindly following orders and burying our humanity under a rock.

Religion itself is not a badge of good, not one of evil. The most religious person in the world could be a devil and the least religious an angel. In fact, in some ways, the concealment of bad people within religious institutions only makes them more dangerous, as many people will find it more difficult to see them for what they really are.

The bitterness and spitefulness exhibited by the members of my local council does not seem to me to be something that would impress a higher being. Nor does the brainwashed life of Tim, who lived in his mind so meticulously by the book that it made his life and the lives of those around him miserable. Is that what the Almighty would want? Sometimes it seems like the most vocally devout are the most wicked, or at least the most hypocritical. Surely these people have moments of clarity when they realise how ridiculous they are being.

Evil comes from the most unexpected places, and often from those who profess to be working for the benefit of mankind. Tim's church would probably see me and my family as wicked people who need to be taught the error of their ways, yet what they did to him in terms of filling his mind with nonsense that only served to make his life more miserable was far worse than a few curse words or a little white lie on a job slip. I was the one who tried to help Tim and teach him a few truths that would have made his life much happier. His church may have meant well for all I know, but their actions were not.

Not that the church always means well, of course. What they used to do to those poor girls in Ireland not so long ago who had the misfortune to bear a child out of wedlock was disgraceful, it was a workhouse run by a veritable Gestapo of nuns who believed that they could do no wrong because God was on their side. But the punishments they meted out didn't come from the pages of the Bible, and even if it had surely their inbuilt humanity, their conscience should have told them that it was wrong. We all have an innate sense of right and wrong as I have said before that is nothing to do with religion.

To use a more contemporary example, Tony Blair is only one of the latest in a long line of men who have waged war in the name of right. Blair didn't outright say that he was doing God's work, but it was pretty thoroughly implied in his words and deeds, and whilst he still disagrees that he did wrong, many of us still feel that he lied to us regarding the reasons for going to war. As a result, he shows no shame for the hundreds of thousands of men, women and children that are now dead because of him. It amazes me that a person who undoubtedly believes in a Christian God can do such a thing and still believe that his God would look kindly upon him. You can almost imagine Satan disguised, whispering in his ear, promising him praise and glory for carrying out this work in the name of the Lord.

Ah now, though, evil, true evil is something else. It's hard to describe, but we know it when we sense it, as in the case of another secretary of mine. She was a nice girl, with a few A-levels to her name and she could type well, in fact, her CV suggested that she would be able to run my office just fine. The only thing, she said, was that she occasionally suffered from grand mal fits or epileptic seizures. I didn't know anything about the condition, but this girl explained that she kept it under control with tablets at any rate and that it was nothing to worry about. *Fair enough*, I thought and hired her.

Everything seemed fine until one day when she came into my office to take down some shorthand notes. She was sitting in the large, high-backed leather armchair next to my desk and looking a little miserable if truth be told, so I cracked a joke to try to cheer her up and we both laughed as I turned briefly away to retrieve some papers. I then heard as if in slow motion her laugh run down like a record player, her feminine laugh becoming deeper and deeper before grinding to a halt, and on turning back saw her body slip off the smooth leather chair onto the floor as if suddenly she had no bones to keep her upright. I called Barbara in to help and together we pulled the girl's legs out from under her and straightened them out before I noticed that her skirt had ridden up, and moved to brush it down. But before I could do so, her own hand reached down and she did it herself, even though she still seemed in the throes of this seizure. So she must have been aware to some extent what was going on.

At any rate, the moment passed and she seemed fine afterwards, and I found nothing else in what had happened to trouble me at all. That was Friday afternoon, and when work finished that day Barbara and I left London for our house in Sussex as normal. What happened later that night, I cannot explain.

I went to bed as usual, but that night I had the most vivid dream in which two grotesque, terrifying figures were hunched over me, trying to pull me out of my bed, I actually felt myself being pulled and saw what was pulling me. I frantically broke free and sat up. I had never before in my life had a nightmare, but I was having one now because I have never before or since been so thoroughly frightened.

Now, you could put it down to a coincidence of course, or an overactive imagination, or any one of the other excuses we use when we cannot rationally explain what is happening to us, though I am now fully aware that this kind of experience happens to many people and has a rational explanation. But I believe my experience that night may represent another possible piece of the puzzle in our quest to find out what man really is.

What if there was something about that girl, my secretary, that rendered her unable to control for a few seconds the evil that lurks in and around all of us, and that touching her during her seizure had caused the release of something inside myself that I had been adequately suppressing up to that point. I cannot shake the feeling that my dream, which was so real and frightening, was caused by something that happened in the seconds after that girl's face fell and she slid to the ground. I could feel the presence of evil, there is simply no other way to explain it.

I remember sitting up in bed and having to wait several minutes before I could contemplate going back to sleep. That simply isn't like me at all. When I saw pop the ghost I barely even stirred, just accepted it as something normal that was happening and nothing to be alarmed about. This time I was most certainly alarmed and then some.

Is there evil in all of us? Something lurking within, ready to spring forth in those moments when our usual checks and balances are tampered with? Maybe it is the same force that constantly struggles with our souls, allowing people to do varying degrees of bad deeds. Perhaps this evil is why the parish councillors could not recognise their hypocrisy, or why Tim didn't understand that his efforts to lead a good life were fatally flawed. Maybe he was battling evil the whole time, and his strict adherence to 'the rules' was the only thing that helped him keep it at bay.

Perhaps, in the end, the difference between good people and bad people is simply how effective they are at dealing with the unseen, intangible evil that threatens all of us, all the time. God help us if tampering with our DNA unleashes that in its purest form.

In the meantime we are left to deal with good people and bad people on a day-to-day basis, perhaps sometimes wondering where we ourselves fit on that sliding scale. No doubt most of us would consider ourselves to be good people, perhaps eighty or ninety out of a hundred if you wanted to put a weighting on it. That's bias for you, but we all do it, labouring under the delusion that other people will not apply the same unreasonably critical eye to us as we do to them. We decide we don't particularly like this person or that person because they're too loud, or too arrogant, foolish, irritating, pick your quality. Even physical attractiveness (or lack of), though many of us would never admit it, is used to justify why we don't spend time with people.

When you're a child, you tend to make friends easily and keep many of them around you. But as we get older we whittle down our list of acquaintances to few and fewer, leading to perhaps the biggest single cause of meanness of spirit in the world; loneliness.

Tim was a lonely man, you could tell. Probably didn't have many friends outside of the church that used his loneliness to exert power over him. I suspect, if the matter were further examined, this would be the main reason why he was so unhappy, and why he, in turn, spread unhappiness to those around him.

Likewise the busybodies on the local council. Had they all been preoccupied enjoying time with friends and loved ones, would any of them really have cared what kind of house a stranger built on his own land? I doubt it somehow. Loneliness and nastiness seem in my experience to be intertwined in a kind of vicious circle. Ah, but how does it start? And how to break it? Perhaps if we can figure out the answers to those questions we can stop being a society that becomes more and more miserable with each passing year. Because despite the dramatic increase in our comfort levels, education, sources of entertainment, and all the wonders of the modern world, statistics show that human beings are sadder than ever we were, and it isn't getting any better.

Are you lonely? You probably don't think so. Denial is the classic human emotion. We may be popular and have lots of friends, always around people, the life and soul of the party. But that doesn't mean we can't also be lonely. We convince ourselves that circumstances are our own choice, as though having control of them somehow makes life more bearable. I prefer my solitude, we say to ourselves, it gives me time to think. A little peace and quiet. Just what the doctor ordered.

We lie loudest when we lie to ourselves, is what a writer once wrote. If that's true, then the world must be a veritable cacophony of fibbing.

I loved my father, blood being thicker than water as they say, and would always forgive him his behaviour. He was one of the most difficult and selfish, but at the same time charming and likeable men you could ever hope to meet. He loved women and they loved him, and he unashamedly fathered a great many children in circumstances that were often less than honest or fair to those others involved.

One of these children became a world-renowned modern artist, of whom I am very proud. She and her twin brother were forged from the flaming embers of a relationship that saw them walking the streets like urchins at times after dear old Dad skipped out on their mother, leaving her virtually homeless and destitute.

Yet, he never stopped loving my mother, who stood by him through thick and thin.

My maternal sister, on the other hand, hated Dad. I mean she really hated him. Not only did he mess her about with money in the same way he did to virtually everyone else he ever met, but she could never forgive him for the way he treated Mum. She held some hard, uncompromising views, and she wasn't afraid to express them, even to the point where you'll come away from a conversation with her feeling scratched and abused. Particularly, if the conversation was about Dad.

"You f*****g mention him one more time and I will never speak to you again!" would be the scream, and down went the phone. At my end.

Now I loved my sister and would have done anything for her, but she didn't half make it difficult sometimes. Part of it is understandable of course, having been hurt in the past and suffered miserable experiences which were entirely of Dad's making.

"He's such a bastard!" she would spit, with venom in her voice.

"Well, he had a proper mother and father actually," I would reply coolly, "just as you have. So that's not exactly true."

"You know what I mean," comes the retort. "He f**ks up everyone he comes into contact with. Either takes their money or shags them. That's our Dad. Are you proud of him?"

All true, to be fair, but then he was what he was and no doubt will have to answer for it at some point if he hasn't already. Our place is not to judge, but to try to understand the actions of others and learn from them, so strengthening ourselves and hopefully making us better, more thoughtful, more considerate human beings.

Kindness is something we always ought to give. It doesn't cost us anything, in fact usually it makes us feel better afterwards even if at the time it might feel like a struggle to put our negative thoughts aside and do something for somebody else. But we don't seem to appreciate that we are all of us interlinked through the many tiny interactions we have with others every day and that our demeanour, our attitude, the way we treat others has a knock-on effect. Just like when a small part of a vast and complicated machine breaks down, the whole thing suffers. Mankind suffers collectively when we each as individuals cannot bring ourselves to be kind rather than cold.

And then there are times when otherwise good people can be reduced to meanness when certain buttons are pushed. My eight-year-old granddaughter is very bright, bubbly and popular, but not long ago she began to turn into a quiet, introverted thing and got us all worried. Was she suffering some illness? What could have happened to change this little girl's personality so dramatically and in such a short space of time?

It turned out that she was being bullied at school by a girl some two years her senior. The bully, whom I will call Tanya was a big girl, plump and arrogant, knocked my granddaughter over in the playground, fell on her like a ton of bricks, stabbed her with a sharp pencil which left a nasty puncture wound and threatened to kill her if she ever trespassed onto Tanya's territory again. Yes, kill her. Where does a ten-year-old girl get that kind of hatred from? Oh, but that is not really the point of the story. What was more disappointing than the bullying, which can be taken care of, was the reaction of Tanya's parents when confronted with the problem in a calm and reasonable fashion.

"My Tanya wouldn't do that," snapped her mother. And then having questioned her little girl about the matter had the audacity to suggest that the story was in reverse and that it was Tanya who had been bullied and knocked about. Well, if you saw the two girls you might even have laughed at the notion if it weren't so serious.

"Complain to the school then, if you dare," said Tanya's father. If you dare? Where did that come from? These were previously nice and friendly people. Well, a complaint was made as requested, and the headmistress called Tanya's parents in to explain in no uncertain terms that the incident with the pencil had been witnessed by several children and that if their precious darling had used a bit more force they might right now be talking about a murder as the wound had been made right over my granddaughter's heart. I believe social services were called in and counselling arranged, which no doubt forced everyone involved to examine the matter with clear and calm heads. But that incident was a classic example of how good can become bad at the flick of a switch.

Fortunately, the opposite may also be true. With a little more introspection, we can all learn to recognise our own flaws and traits that might rub others up the wrong way, and in doing so hopefully become more pleasant to be around and happier in ourselves. Wanting to be in the company of others is a natural and healthy instinct and one we should all embrace, but the flip side of that is taking a good long look at ourselves to make sure we are also the kind of person that others want to be around. Loneliness is both inflicted and self-inflicted, and we can do something about each of those.

On the other hand, maybe you prefer to be reclusive, inflexible and uncompromising. Maybe you believe life is all about getting what you want and letting everyone else worry about themselves. Maybe you think the world is against you and there's nothing you can do to change that. Or perhaps you don't think about such things at all, but just cruise through life from one moment to the next without worrying what tomorrow may bring or what anybody else thinks of you. That's their problem, not yours.

That's all well and good until you find yourself aged forty-nine, home alone, and sad, and hopeless. Another little piece of the great human machine broken. And the whole world is a worse place for it.

But then it's never too late to change.

Chapter Eleven
Mick and the Kuwait Oil Fires
1990–1992

Pride is a vice, which pride itself inclines every man to find in others, and to overlook in himself.

~ Samuel Johnson

Mick was a powerful-looking man with a portly frame, barrel chest and big, bristling ginger whiskers. After losing his mother at an early age, Mick's father struggled to bring him up alone, and as a young boy, he took it upon himself to cook and clean and help around the house. All of which, on top of his home studies, meant that Mick didn't seem to have much of a childhood, with no brothers and sisters, and no close friend to confide in. He had to grow up very quickly, in which respect I suppose he was a lot like me.

Perhaps it was this experience that shaped Mick into the die-hard pragmatist that I knew. He certainly had a way about him which left you in no doubt that he knew who he was and what he wanted. A supreme confidence in his own judgment that was, to be fair, not altogether misplaced, as Mick was also one of the smartest people I've ever known. Though his fingernails, always chewed to the quick, hinted at another side to his character. Nevertheless, I always felt that his unwillingness to open his mind to the possibilities beyond a limited world where two plus two equals four led to Mick chugging through life well below his potential.

Mick is married to Ann, a college lecturer, and they had two young boys at the time of these events, in addition to a mortgage and a modest income stream that saw them living month to month as most people do. Myself, I've never had a mortgage or had to live month to month, so I can't say I know exactly what it feels like, but I think I can imagine close enough. I don't mention that by way of bragging, incidentally, but just in case it helps people to get a handle on my perceptions and attitudes as a man who's never particularly had any financial worries.

Anyway, Mick was an expert in planning law, an area in which I was taking an increasing interest as my local authority started throwing up more and more roadblocks in the way of my building plans, and that's how we got to know each other. He was a good teacher and I a keen student, and once I got caught up a bit in my reading we would sit up together into the early hours of the morning arguing the finer points of planning law when his family would come to visit at our country home. Without Mick's help, I would never have had the knowledge, nor the appetite, for that epic struggle with the council, which saw me wind up in court with the Secretary of State. And for Mick's part, he said he found me to be a character that fascinated him and was interested to know what made me tick.

One thing about Mick though, being a pragmatist with a thorough logical approach to all things, he does not like to lose an argument. Mick was always right in his mind, which started to become a problem as my knowledge of planning law grew and I was able to make my case with a degree of authority. I remember the first occasion that this came to a head, when we'd been debating a particular point of planning law and come to a classic impasse with me telling Mick that he was flat-out wrong, and him refusing point-blank to accept it. Feeling confident, I bet him ten pence that I was right, to which Mick immediately responded with a characteristic flourish, "ten to one!" and slapped a pound coin down on the table next to mine. Well, I went and found the relevant line in the appropriate book, which I then handed to Mick, who went very quiet for a moment before flicking the money towards me.

"It's yours," he said flatly.

I had won the bet, but my relationship with Mick had been damaged. Here was a man with an almost photographic memory and a mind as sharp as a razor, and I was encroaching on two of his specialist subjects no less; planning law, and being right. He clearly wasn't happy with me, and I made a note to myself to be careful how I behaved around him in the future.

Several years went by, and I came to think of myself as being as close to Mick as any brother. His heart was as big as his brain to be sure, and he was always completely unselfish when it came to considering the needs of others, whether it was his own family or me with my ridiculous planning problems. I suggested to him many times that he ought to go into business for himself as he obviously had the brains and the savvy for it and would no doubt be successful. I would even have been perfectly happy to lend him the funds to get up and running until he found his feet, but Mick wouldn't borrow, he was an old-fashioned man with old-fashioned rules about money and conduct. If he couldn't afford something, he went without.

Nevertheless, there came a time when Mick came into a decent chunk of change, which he proceeded to sit on for a while before finally seeking my advice as to what he ought to do with it. He had the notion of buying into a small building firm that he worked for from time to time doing technical drawing and form-filling, and other strategic jobs while the builders did the dirty work. He could juggle that, he said, with his council job and see how it went for a while. *Well, that would be a start*, I thought, and Mick had clearly done his homework on the project, so I told him to go for it.

Things started off a little slowly and profits were thin on the ground, so I suggested they might consider branching out into house building.

"Just go out and find houses with nice big gardens in town," I said, "pay the owner for the land and start building."

After a fair amount of arm-twisting, Mick finally agreed that the firm would need to borrow in order to take this next step, which was against all his principles but there really didn't seem to be much choice in the matter. With a fresh injection of capital, the project was ready to go. First, they bought three nice plots, built, and sold, and then Mick found a bargain at auction; a large industrial building with foundation problems that he knew were a pretty straightforward fix. The company made a quarter of a million in less than three months. Around half a million in today's money.

But Mick wasn't done yet. He went out and bought what seemed to be a useless old quarry for around £30,000, which was a big risk at the time, but then Mick knew something nobody else at that auction did. The local authority was about to run out of space to dump the town's rubbish—a purpose for which his newly acquired piece of land was ideally suited. A quick meeting with the council made him millions virtually overnight.

Tenacity and the willingness to take a risk, that's what Mick learnt from me. The old Mick would never have taken such bold gambles, but they were paying off now and then some. I thought perhaps the success would mellow his inflexible attitude to life, but if anything the new Mick, whilst outwardly brash and easy-going, had less confidence than ever. He often told me that he didn't trust anyone, and I didn't even have to ask if 'anyone' included me because I was so used to arguing with Mick over the meaning of just one sentence, or even one specific word, that I knew he meant exactly what he said. Anyone meant anyone. Despite this, I trusted him implicitly and never questioned the walls he'd build up around himself to keep the world out. They were Mick's business. All I could do was be honest with him always, and never pander or just tell him what he wanted to hear. That was my way of trying to prove to Mick that he could trust me.

Unfortunately, it didn't quite work out that way.

It all started when there was an almighty fire on a North Sea oil platform, a blaze so fierce that they just couldn't put it out and eventually the platform simply melted and disappeared under the waves. Well, I was following the story on the news as it developed, and found myself thinking about the production line [usually called the string] coming up from the seabed, and how they could have saved the platform if only there had been a way to hot-tap it in an emergency. I pondered this problem for a week or so, night and day, coming at it from one angle until I hit a brick wall and then backing up, reassessing things and trying another way. I didn't say a word to anyone about it, it was just a private mental exercise and who knew if anything would come of it. Besides, with the countless billions of dollars floating around in the oil industry, surely if there was a solution to be found somebody would have done it by now rather than leave it to a London man who'd never even seen an oil well in his life.

Anyway, Barbara, Mick, Ann and myself were sitting around the table at Mick's house one evening that week after a splendid dinner, when it was noted that I seemed a touch subdued, and they all wondered aloud what could be the matter.

"Nothing really," I replied, "just a little problem on my mind."

They poked and prodded a little, but I refused to be drawn and presently the conversation moved along until, towards the back end of the evening, Mick asked if I would share the last of a fine bottle of whisky with him. This particular bottle had been a fortunate discovery when sensing something unusual about an old house he had bought, Mick knocked down one of the walls to reveal a hidden larder down in the cellar containing various valuables. We guessed that someone hid them away for safekeeping while they went off to fight the Germans during World War Two, but never could be sure. Either way, whoever it was, never came back to claim what they had left.

Barbara gave her approval and said that she would drive home, so Mick and I settled in. He had two large leather sofas facing each other, with a huge wooden coffee table in between. It was so big he had to walk around it to hand me my glass and show me the bottle. It looked about half full by my reckoning, with an aged label that read Morgan, or McMartin, or something like that. I've never been very good with names. It also bore the words '20 years old', and then underneath that, a date, hand-written on the label, faded but clear enough to read '1939'.

Mick poured out two neat measures into cut-glass tumblers that made the rich, caramel-coloured liquid sparkle like in a television advert, then true to form he raised his glass and gulped down most of it in one go while I nosed my own drink curiously. Neither of us was an expert in whisky, but we were experts in analysing a problem and the conversation turned to the question of whether whisky ages any further once it's in the bottle. We knew that it would be aged those first twenty years in an oak barrel or some such, with a burnt interior that gave the drink its unique colour and flavour. But surely some seventy years sitting around would give a stronger, darker whisky? Was the darkness commensurate with age? We weren't sure, but the topic was full enough of possibilities that we became engrossed in it, imagining the whole sordid saga of the rare old whisky that was vanishing now, little by little, down our throats.

I remember feeling thoroughly relaxed, sitting back with half a glass in my hand and thanking both Mick and Ann for having us around, it had been a great evening and the whisky was a real treat. But then almost as soon as I had finished speaking, something happened. I was in the process of lifting the glass to my lips for another sip when something stopped me. My eyes were wide open and it felt like everything slowed down for one long moment, the noise of everything and everyone else around me completely obliterated by an invisible veil that seemed to descend. And at that moment, no more than three or four seconds in real time, the problem of how to hot-tap an oil line through all the casings solved itself in my mind. I could see the design of a valve as though it were right in front of my eyes. It was extremely complicated, but also simple in a way since it seemed clear as crystal to me, and I knew instinctively how it worked.

"Mick! Mick!" I called out as the veil lifted. "I need a pad and pencil, quickly!"

There was an unwrapped parcel in the corner, and a somewhat puzzled-looking Mick handed me the loose wrapping paper and a pencil. It took three, maybe four minutes to sketch out the design, working quickly for fear that the knowledge would vanish again as swiftly as it had arrived, and when I was done I quietly folded it up and tucked it away in my pocket without a word of explanation. Then I finished what was left of my drink, thanked Mick and Ann again for their kind hospitality, and off home we went.

I considered the drawing for a couple of days, taking it out and examining it at length before putting it away again until soon enough I found myself back at Mick's place on an errand to pick up something or other. I took the drawing out of my pocket, showed it to him, and asked for his verdict. Mick stared at the crumpled piece of paper for some time as I tried to explain the workings of the valve, before finally handing it back to me with a curt, "Nope, it won't work."

"But it's easy, Mick!" I replied excitedly, "Can't you see the flows and pressure reductions and how it all comes together?"

"Can't work," he repeated simply.

"Alright," I sighed, a little exasperated, "well, can you draw this out for me anyway please so that I can apply for a patent?"

I could have done the work myself, but Mick was on his drawing board practically all day, every day, and he would be able to do the work much faster.

"I will," he said, "as a favour to a friend. But you should think about it some more because this is never going to work."

He then went on to elaborate in some detail as to why my new invention was complete junk, and I left his house that day feeling that Mick was probably right. He was much cleverer than me and, outside of our pedantic late night sparring, he was hardly ever wrong about anything. But something kept nagging away at the back of my mind, telling me that I should have a little more faith in myself and in what had happened in those few mysterious seconds that night at Mick and Ann's.

A few more days went by before I was summoned back to Mick's house again. He had completed his drawings of my hastily scribbled design, a creation I had labelled the 'Josher Control Valve', and I must say they were every bit up to his usual fine standard. Mick said nothing as my eyes roved over the pictures and I became more and more excited.

"Can't you see how it works, Mick?" I said, "It's so simple really, so obvious."

Mick turned to look at me, and then in a very low whisper he replied, "It will work."

"Sorry, what was that?" I asked, half-shocked and half-triumphant.

"I said it will work," replied Mick, looking away and sounding for all the world as though he was delivering the worst news anybody had ever heard.

"You mean," I said, playing along, laying my hand upon his shoulder and adopting the solemn, concerned tone of someone commiserating with a friend who's just found out they have terminal cancer. "You mean, you were wrong?"

I shook my head slowly and then let it fall in reverence. Okay, maybe I was overdoing it a little now, but Mick's attitude was so amusing to me that I just couldn't help myself. He must realise that it's not the worst thing in the world to be wrong.

Mick's reaction had convinced me of something else, however. I respected him hugely for his knowledge and intellect, and if anything were to come of this design I wanted to share it with him. He had done these beautiful drawings for me after all, and it was his whisky I'd been drinking that night when the epiphany came to me, who knows, maybe that had something to do with it as well. But I knew I couldn't go into business with Mick. The late-night discussions we had were all fun and games, but I couldn't do that day in, day out when there was potentially a lot of money on the line and I knew Mick would never defer to my judgment if he had reservations about something. We'd end up arguing endlessly about what to do with the valve, and I couldn't live like that.

"Here," I said, resolved, offering Mick the patent application I'd brought with me. "We'll go fifty-fifty, on the condition that we sell it outright for a lump sum and not enter into any form of business that might ruin our friendship. Is it a deal?"

It was. Mick signed the paper and we set about looking for a buyer for the new Josher Control Valve.

Around about that time, the Americans and the British were preparing to go into Kuwait and shift Saddam Hussein, who had invaded the country on some spurious pretext in 1991. Sanctions had already been imposed of course, but Saddam was a bad boy and he wouldn't be told. Something obviously had to be done.

I remember seeing Yasser Arafat on the news, seemingly speaking on behalf of the regime in Iraq and warning the West that should they try to take Kuwait away from Saddam he would blow up all 1100 odd oil wells and cause a global disaster that we might never recover from. Most people's immediate reaction to this statement was horror, or revulsion, or something similar. My first reaction was to get together the plans and documentation for the Josher Control Valve and mail them off quick smart to the then Minister of Defense, a certain Mr Tom King. I enclosed a note, in addition, suggesting that he might pass along the enclosed information to the Department of Energy as well, who may be better able to evaluate the possibilities of the device in a hurry since it seemed like it might be needed sooner rather than later.

I received a short note back soon afterwards advising me that they were reviewing my proposal and I should sit tight and wait for their decision. But as time went by and the war began, I started to suspect that my letter had been slipped in a drawer and forgotten about. We kept up with the conflict on the news, watching television footage, then one morning there were graphic images on the television of burning oil wells and thick, black plumes of smoke, and being told that the majority of the wells had been blown up by Saddam. Now I became increasingly frustrated. Kuwait looked like it was becoming Hell on Earth, and the seeds of possibly the worst environmental disaster the world had ever seen, were sown. I couldn't sit back and do nothing, so I wrote a short, curt letter to 10 Downing Street, which read something like this:

Dear Prime Minister,

You may not be aware, but I have sent to Mr Tom King, [Minister of Defense], details of the Josher Control Valve. Following the threat of Yasser Arafat some weeks ago that Kuwait's oil wells might be blown up, Mr King assured me that both his department and the Department of Energy, would look into the usefulness of this valve in dealing with that disaster, should it happen, as a matter of urgency.

What the hell are they playing at? Perhaps they have not properly appreciated the urgency of this situation? I write to you now in the hope that this will be speedily re-evaluated.

Yours Sincerely,

John Emin

I faxed that letter to Downing Street, and within two hours my office received a phone call from a woman stating that 10 Downing Street would like a word. My secretary handed me the receiver and I took it, expecting to hear a female voice on the other end of the line as she had just said, so I was a little taken aback when a man asked, "Is that Mr Emin?"

"It is," I replied, "who's that?"

"John Major," said the man.

"Who?" I asked again, confused. There was an awkward silence at the other end and I realised with a small start that I wasn't dreaming. The Prime Minister really was on the phone for me. "Okay," I said after a moment, "sorry, Mr Prime Minister, it's been a long morning, that's all."

"I see," replied Mr Major. "Are all you inventors like this?"

Well, we had a little chuckle about that, and then he asked if I could attend a meeting that he would set up urgently at the Department of Energy at Victoria in two days' time. Naturally, I replied in the affirmative.

On the morning of the scheduled meeting, however, a terrorist attack at Victoria Station caused the meeting to be shifted back a day. This wasn't my fault of course, and there would now be a delay. Unfortunately, the various experts and engineers who had been flown in especially for this meeting didn't quite seem to see it that way as it must have altered their planned schedules. I was shown in through one office, then another, then an outer office by a secretary before finally arriving in a boardroom with a large oval table. There were some fifteen, maybe twenty people sat around it with space for me two seats away from the Chairman, an engineer who had come down from Scotland in order to meet me.

"Mr Smith, your group are waiting for you in conference room five," said a woman who seemed to have appeared behind me in the doorway to one of the men across the table.

"Give them tea and biscuits and make sure they're comfortable," replied Mr Smith, "and I'll be with them in thirty minutes."

Then another girl appeared and said almost exactly the same thing to another of the men, to be given exactly the same instruction. 'Give them tea and biscuits,

I'll be with them in half an hour.' To my mind, this was clearly a less-than-subtle way of telling me I had thirty minutes tops to say what I had to say before I was thrown out. The looks on the men's faces left me in no doubt that they had all seen the plans for the Josher Control Valve and, like Mick, concluded that it couldn't possibly work. This whole thing was clearly, in their opinion, a colossal waste of time and energy and they were just going through the motions to appease the Prime Minister before they could get back to some real work.

I was a bit irritated by these silly intimidation tactics, to be honest, so when the chairman asked me to explain to the room how my invention worked, I first looked my watch, and then back at him, and said simply, "Mr Chairman, it seems that some of the men here are very busy and I wouldn't wish to hamper their work, so I can tell you all about how the valve works in thirty seconds. Now, if you would all like to look at the plans before us—"

"One moment, Mr Emin," interrupted the Chairman. "Of course we would be pleased if you could explain to us how the valve works, but it is very important that we understand every aspect of this device, its potential, how to fit it etc."

"Hmm," I replied, looking at my watch again. "I think I can do it in twenty-five minutes or so if I leave out a few things. We can always return to them later should you deem it appropriate."

The Chairman nodded his approval, and off we went. All of the men in the room had been introduced to me, but names are my Achilles heel and, although everyone was wearing a name badge, they were far too small to read across a huge table that we sat around. So I simply defaulted to the tried and tested method of not bothering but just trying my best not to call anyone 'mate' or 'oy you, what's your name?'. There was a stenographer there writing everything down, and you can be sure she wouldn't have heard me name a single one of them. I just got on with my unwritten presentation, which was pretty straightforward. To my mind, anyway.

The man to my immediate right, a scientist of some description, kept tapping his teeth with his yellow pencil while the one to my left was tapping the table with his. They were obviously very clever people and they didn't look at all impressed with what they were hearing. Almost twenty minutes in, in fact, everyone in the room who wasn't me seemed to be really rather bored. I wasn't put off. Now having described the process of dealing with the several casings around the production string, how we gained access safely with an inferno raging around the well, and showing how the valve is attached, now came the most important piece of information as far as these men were concerned.

"So now, gentlemen," I said finally, "if we look at the plans, I will show you how the valve actually works."

I talked them through how we could now hot tap the live flow then divert that flow of the oil and control a smooth shutdown, even produce oil continually and also a way to kill the well if needed at the touch of the valve's controls.

Using his pencil, the Chairman followed the different flows of oil that the valve offered, before exchanging a look of amazement with his deputy. They both nodded as though silently agreeing that it could work, and then looked towards the scientist to my right, who also nodded, as did the one to my left. Looking suddenly alert and excited, the Chairmen requested that everyone in the room make themselves available a while longer, before leaving the room to make some arrangement or other and presumably check in with number ten. While he was gone, I took the opportunity to ask the scientist to my right what he thought of my invention.

"I think you have something there," he replied, nodding sagely.

The Chairman returned presently, having instructed his assistant to cancel his appointments for the rest of the day, deal with the fallout as best she could and not allow us to be disturbed for the foreseeable future. It was obvious now that the place was being locked down with a flurry of activity as people stepped in and out, cancelling appointments and trying to soothe anxious staff on the other end of phones. I wonder how many people were turned away from meetings that day.

At any rate, the door was finally closed and the room went quiet. The Chairman asked me what I needed from the government in order to make the Josher Control Valve a reality. I told him that I would have to think carefully about that, and asked if I could drop him a fax next morning. By eight am please, he replied. He would be in his office by seven, and he needed an opportunity to look over my proposals and make his own recommendations before they could be passed up to the Prime Minister.

That being settled, it seemed that I would be required to go over the finer details of the system at least one more time, not least because many of the men in the room simply hadn't been paying the slightest bit of attention the first time around. I kept my composure and talked them through it all again patiently until one by one I saw their eyes open and stare as the penny dropped and they realised with amazement what they had missed the first couple of times. I had a feeling I knew why it was taking these doubtless highly intelligent individuals so long to cotton on. They were so set in their perceptions of what was and wasn't possible that they simply couldn't see what was literally right in front of their faces. Experts are much the same the world over, arrogant and closed-minded, unable to see the bigger picture or the new idea. I sensed when I walked into that room that they'd been looking down their noses at me, some crackpot inventor with a silly drawing. Well, now we were settling in to make a day of it, and they were all looking at me in quite a different light.

As the meeting progressed, various people digressed into subjects I knew little or nothing about; metallurgy, scientific principles and aspects of engineering practice that simply should have been beyond me. I think they probably assumed that my expertise was limited, and fired a lot of questions my way that they didn't think I would have any answers to. But strangely, I found that I was able to satisfy their enquiries every time.

At a certain point, when I insisted that the device would need a chevron seal rather than a more modern, synthetic 'O' ring, the Chairman and one of the scientists took me to task. In fact, it became almost what you might call an argument. The 'O' ring would be safer, they said, and capable of withstanding far greater pressure under the circumstances in which we would be deploying it. By all accounts, I should have deferred to their expertise, which was clearly greater than my own, but for some reason, I stood my ground and explained how it was important that the seal be directional, and gave my reasons. The Chairman looked to the scientist, which began a ripple as people up and down the table exchanged questioning glances before one man said finally, "He's right you know. Solid in one direction and a little give in the opposite. Perfect." They all nodded in agreement.

Those few minutes were possibly the hardest of the whole experience for me. I had no idea why I was pushing so hard on this particular point, especially when most of the men in the room knew much more about engineering than I did. I'm not particularly wise or clever, and yet I knew instinctively that I was right about this, and as I stood firm the greater minds gradually all came around to my way of thinking.

We worked through lunch, with tea and sandwiches and it must have been at least three and a half hours afterwards we came to a halt, and then as the meeting finally broke refreshments were brought in for those who didn't have to rush off immediately. I helped myself to a cheese sandwich and a cup of coffee, as I was exhausted by that point and it would be a while yet before I could get home. As I ate and drank, I got talking to the scientist to my left; a tall, thin, boffin-type man in a smart suit. He said he thought that there were forty-seven problems with my idea that had to be dealt with and that I had demolished each and every one to his satisfaction. Then he explained that he was one of the people who set exam questions for the higher engineering degrees at Oxford University, and asked me which university I had attended.

"I don't have an engineering degree," I replied.

"No, that's impossible," he said, shaking his head from side to side. "I bowled several tricky questions at you today and you answered them all without hesitation. Even one that would have tripped up many experts. I thought I caught you out with the chevron seal, but yet again you proved to be right. Come on, there's no way you haven't been through higher learning."

He raised his eyebrows as he waited for an answer, but I simply shook my head in the negative.

"Either you've been to university," he went on, "or you're … well…" but he never completed the thought. Instead, he asked me what else I might have in mind to invent, to which I replied that I was still chasing the elusive goal of cheap, everlasting energy.

"How far have you got?" he asked with genuine curiosity.

"It's difficult to say," I said.

"Cold fusion!" he quipped.

"Not exactly," I said, "but I'm sure the solution will be completely different to the way we're envisioning it at the moment. I think the trick is low energy in and high energy out, not the way we do it today with a whole power plant churning out plasma that's too hot to handle without huge physical and energy considerations." I think he liked what I had to say, and gave me his card with a private phone number to call if I ever needed any help. Predictably I mislaid the card and forgot his name before I'd even left the room.

So the British Government seemed interested enough in the Josher Control Valve. The Prime Minister stood outside 10 Downing Street the next day and talked about the British firm that was working on a way to help deal with oil fires. We had doors opening up for us, in essence, I required a specialists firm able to produce the valve in an emergency and importantly fit it on site. So it came to be that Chubb Fire International was introduced to us and even a promise of work from the Kuwaiti oil Company based here in London. But hearing about the Josher Control Valve, Red Adair who was in charge of putting out the fire's, rang me on two occasions to say angrily it would not work. I heard his view was, that I was a London spiv that hadn't been near an oil well, so what would I know. It was clear the people on the ground in Kuwait didn't want us there, and gradually the interest in our valve began to cool. Still, I wasn't about to sit around and wait, one way or the other, not when there were other oil barons and rich Arabs we could be selling to. If only we could find a way to reach them.

In our village, there was an ex-banker who had recently returned from Hong Kong. Apparently, as it turned out, he'd had to leave in a bit of a hurry due to some naughty business on his part and people in the know did warn me about him (though I never did find out exactly what it was he'd done.) For me though, as a pragmatist, I recognised him as a man who knew people. Rich people. Important people. The kind of people who might be interested in what we had to sell.

Chris was his name. He was a tall, Richard Burton look-a-like with a posh English accent and always impeccably turned out in the smartest suits. I thought he was the epitome of a rich banker. Not that I couldn't scrub up pretty well myself when the occasion called for it. I remember often being dressed in expensive business suits and plain black leather shoes with metal heels that clicked authoritatively when I walked down an uncarpeted hall or across an office. They were an integral part of the toolkit, portraying an image of power and confidence, and heads turned at the purposeful click-step of a man who clearly knew what he wanted and where he was going.

Chris came on board and played his part well, arranging high-powered meetings for us with potential buyers. The problem was that Mick would turn up in an open-neck shirt, jeans and sandals, giving a distinct impression that he just couldn't care less. One Arab businessman we were negotiating with took me aside after a meeting to tell me that while he understood Mick was my friend, he didn't feel that he was showing sufficient respect for the deal and that perhaps I would do better to leave him behind next time when there would be even more important people involved. Also, he wasn't wild about Chris, who seemed to have a wider reputation than I'd realised for having disgraced himself in the banking industry.

In retrospect, I think maybe if I'd listened to that man we would have had ourselves a sale, but instead, I sided with Mick and suggested to Chris that we look for another client. The Arab called back twice, the second time agreeing that Chris and Mick could be brought back into the negotiations so long as they stayed in the background and Mick at least wore proper shoes and a tie. But I'd already made my decision and we were moving on.

As the process of trying to secure a buyer progressed, Mick's behaviour seemed to become increasingly erratic and I started to worry about him. On one occasion, riding back from a meeting with the Chubb engineers, he was almost like a field mouse sat in the back of my car. In retrospect, perhaps he felt that Chris riding in the front with me and talking over some notes about the meeting had somehow relegated him to third place, a background character. As far as I was concerned, Mick and I were the bosses and Chris was just a junior partner with a 10% stake in the outcome. But I'm not sure now whether Mick quite saw things the same way. We talked less and less, and sometimes Mick would just completely go missing and we'd have to wait for him to turn up again. On more than one occasion, I would ask him to come with me to some meeting or other, to which he would reply that he was busy, and then say something like, "trust me" in a knowing way. Probably he thought the people we were dealing with were risky, though he never said that outright and his behaviour was becoming more and more of a problem as we started to lose control of our aims.

Once, just before an important, technical meeting with a chief design engineer at Chubb, Mick and I were at my house having a discussion about the design of the valve. He had come up with an idea that he believed would make it work even better. Naturally, I was all ears. Mick drew some freehand sketches of his proposed changes, which I looked over carefully before concluding that the changes would not work and explaining precisely why. If we did as Mick suggested, I said, the valve would close but not be able to open again, rendering it useless. Mick was adamant though that he was right and I was wrong, and we went round in circles for quite a while, me trying my best to remain polite while he became more and more angry with each passing minute. It came to a point where Mick flat-out accused me of being stubborn, banging his fists on my desk so hard that everything jumped a few millimetres into the air with each thump.

Well, the next day we went along to that meeting, and in the middle of it, hoping to either build some bridges with Mick or at least put an end to our current quarrel, I ventured the idea that he'd put to me in my office the previous day. No sooner had I finished speaking than the chief engineer let out a surprised laugh.

"But then it'll jam and lock tight," he said, "and you won't be able to shift it."

"Okay," I said quickly, "just a thought," and on we moved.

When we broke for lunch, I went to the men's room and found myself washing my hands next to Mike, the chief engineer.

"Where did that come from?" he asked, grinning. "The three guys from our design department couldn't believe you said that. It was so out of context with everything else you've been talking about that we've got a bet on that it wasn't your idea at all. So come on, what's the story?"

"Well," I answered hesitantly, "it's just that Mick was rather keen on that idea, so I thought I'd venture it for him."

I left it at that, and as far as I know, none of them said another word about it to Mick or anybody else, but the blunt rejection of his big idea had wounded him badly. The one-time mountain of a man with the intellect and know-how of a top lawyer, the man who was clearly head and shoulders above most of the people I've ever worked with in my life, intellectually speaking, diminished noticeably in size and stature. It was heartbreaking to see. I think maybe he'd always thought of me as the lucky businessman who thrived on risk and was always a cat's breath from bankruptcy. The realisation that I actually knew what I was doing and could hold my own on his turf was a shock to him.

At any rate, I needed to make a limited company so I had a chat with Mick and explained to him that I would rather keep him as my friend rather than an enemy to fight with in the boardroom. I suggested that maybe he trusted me enough to sign over his 50% of the patent application, and I would make an agreement to pay him half of any profits we made. Also that when any deal was to be finalised, Mick would be brought in by my side to advise on it. He agreed straight away, chiding me for even thinking that we would need a contract between us to keep our respective ends of the deal, and that was that.

The reason for the limited company was that our agent out there in Kuwait informed us that Red Adair was being overruled by the King himself because he had advised it would still take over a year to complete the work and that we were about to receive an invitation to go to Kuwait to sign a contract.

Well. unfortunately for us, it was discovered that soaking the ground around the 600 or so oil wells that were burning, combined with high-pressure water spraying in a particular way, was enough to effectively snuff out the oil fires. Virtually overnight, any interest in the Josher Control Valve dried up and we could all go back to doing whatever it was we did before. Except that Mick and I couldn't seem to just go back to our friendship the way it had been before.

I would happily have done so. I didn't hold any ill feeling or whatnot about our failure to make a deal for the patent. It was an exciting ride at least and we came pretty close, but in the end, it didn't work out. That's life. We move on.

Mick chose to move on though by relocating hundreds of miles away. He's been more than successful since, and we've had several long telephone conversations, but it's clear to me that the trust which was a long time coming in our friendship is no longer present.

I can't pinpoint why it happened. Maybe he didn't like that I brought Chris in on our previously two-way arrangement. Maybe he preferred to think of me as the chancer who got lucky rather than being genuinely smart. I know for sure he was gutted by the engineers' making fun of his design proposal at that meeting. Whatever it was, Mick lost a good friend and all because of his own damn stubbornness.

I'll never understand rigid people like that. Being flexible, learning to communicate and compromise and deal with changing situations without burning down the house is a mark of maturity, but it seems maturity doesn't automatically come hand in hand with knowledge or wisdom and vice versa. Mick was a bright guy and a good person, but he could never find it within himself to open up, empathise and trust other people. If you can't do those things, you're always going to find trouble waiting for you up ahead.

For me, Mick's attitude is typical of many so-called experts, or the clever people, as I usually call them and actually, in a way, of the majority of people on the face of this planet. We seem to cling to the knowledge we acquire and treasure it, guarding it jealously and never missing an opportunity to show it off. It comes to define us, and maybe we feel lost or worthless without it. But it is a form of arrogance to rely so blindly on what we think we know, to the exclusion of new concepts and ideas.

Human beings, as a rule, seem to have a strong desire to believe in a higher being of some description, hence the prevalence of religion throughout all the ages of man. Whether this need is impressed upon us early in life or grows with us as we age, or for that matter is always present in our DNA to be accessed at will, nobody really knows. The pragmatists of today, the experts, the so-called clever people, most of them would say that it doesn't matter. The notion of a higher being makes no sense to them, logically. Why should they trouble themselves with something that sits outside their strict definition of truth?

Well, the truth is, it does matter. Because it is a part of who we are, and how can we hope to solve the big problems of the universe if we can't even figure out and accept who we are and what our true purpose is?

When I look at the modern Christian and Muslim faiths, I see a whole mess of complicated nonsense and wickedness. Nevertheless, even as a pragmatist myself, I am on the side of the believers, as they have at least opened their minds to possibilities beyond our current level of scientific knowledge.

Besides, science can't explain how I was able to invent the Josher Control Valve during the course of no more than three or four hazy seconds at Mick's house. Nor how I defended the design in the face of some dozen or so experts, all of whom were much more knowledgeable than I in the field of engineering. Logically, I shouldn't have been able to do that. Nevertheless, it all happened just as I have described here.

Chapter Twelve
The Car Accident
2005–2009

He who suffers much, will know much.

~ Greek proverb

An insomniac I am not. My whole life I have been able to nod off to sleep almost at the drop of a hat, but unfortunately that all changed one fateful August day when a car travelling at tremendous speed collided with another pulling out of the junction I was about to turn into. The speeding vehicle lifted clear off the ground and soared sideways as if in slow motion towards me. I remember opening my mouth to say something. It might have been 's**t'. Whether the word ever actually left my lips I'll never know.

I am a pilot. I've had close calls before, some of them bloody close, but none that felt quite like this. This was it. This was how I was going to die.

All hell let loose, and everything in the vehicle I was driving that wasn't nailed down became airborne. I remember catching sight of Barbara and our dog, who had been sitting between us, as they hovered eerily for a split second before we all slammed to the left and then to the right. It didn't feel like the seat belts helped at all, not like you expect they will anyway when you imagine that sort of thing happening, but they must have done their job to some extent because none of us went through the windscreen.

When it was all over, the upshot was that the love of my life had suffered a mild case of whiplash but was basically, thankfully, okay. The dog was also fine. Nobody had any broken bones and there didn't seem to be any blood. It seemed like we'd had a miraculous escape, though I hurt all over and had a headache, dry mouth and vague sick feeling from banging my head hard against the door pillar. Still, common sense told me I'd probably be okay, so I went to check on everybody else.

My vehicle had been pushed almost clear into the next lane, but lucky no one had been following close behind at the time. The speeding vehicle, a medium-sized Vauxhall or some such, difficult to tell now, was so badly mangled that the wheels and suspension had been ripped clean off. I prepared myself for the worst, only to then see the driver's side door nearby as it had been also ripped off and a lady in an immaculate business suit emerge from the car virtually unscathed. She had a long gash down her right trouser leg but no blood that I could see, and her right sleeve was cut where I suppose sharp shards of metal or glass had whizzed past her. The woman smoothed her hair and suit and began talking in such a casual voice to her emerging, and also unharmed, male partner, and they both conversed as if buying groceries. Funny how shock affects some people.

The third driver, an old man in his eighties, had completed his turn out of the junction and tottered off, seemingly oblivious to the chaos he had caused by coming out of the junction without looking properly. He drove on for some hundred metres or so before his wife must have said, she thought they might have been in an accident, and maybe they should go back and check. Had she not said anything, I could well imagine him having gotten home only to find one side of his car caved in and wondering what on earth could have happened.

We all need a little understanding sometimes, and I don't bear any ill will to those others involved, even though their different sorts of recklessness led to the situation I now find myself in. Because it turned out that I hadn't had quite such a lucky escape as I'd thought after all. You see, when I banged my head, my body had bent up to such an extent that it burst the disc between the sixth and seventh vertebrae in my neck. And now there was a nerve trapped there. And it hurt like hell.

I went to see my doctor, a caring and pragmatic man in his forties whom I call Doctor Wiggles. I like Doctor Wiggles, his observations are always straight to the chin and he's the kind of person you can tell has your genuine best interest at heart. Mind you, if you were dying and had a month to live I could well imagine it being a case of, "the tests say you're a goner, you've got about a month, best put your affairs in order before you go. Have a nice day." But he's always been good to me and I trust his judgement. Doctor Wiggles gave me some painkillers, sent me for an x-ray and suggested we ought to see how it went. Surgery would be a big risk, he said. Might not even help at all. Best see if it calms down on its own first.

Well, at first, the painkillers and sleeping pills that he prescribed seemed to work pretty well, though there were still plenty of nights when I just couldn't nod off at all. So I'd get up and try to find something to occupy myself and take my mind off the pain and the pins and needles in my left hand. First I'd try making a cup of tea, then I might get on the internet and waste an hour or two just pottering about. But then you reach the point where you can't sit in a chair any longer because your arm hangs down and that hurts more with each passing minute. So then I might go and just pace up and down the living room carpet, wishing that I could just go to a private hospital, write them a cheque and have the nerve decompressed there and then.

"What about an operation?" I would ask when I went to see Doctor Wiggles. "I can't carry on living like this."

"There is a risk," he said gravely, letting his arms fall down by his side theatrically and his head tilts to one side to imitate someone on a ventilator. It was a point well made in his usual blunt fashion. "Now," he went on, "stick out your left arm and open and close your hand in a fist." I did as I was told. "See?" he said, "It works. Now if there comes a time when you can't do that anymore, I would consider an operation. But for now, we ought to wait and see. The neck is a tricky place to mess around with. The risk is just too great."

Doctor Wiggles must have been able to tell from my face that he wasn't winning me over, so he thought for a moment and then dragged his chair close as though about to reveal a great secret. He told me that once upon a time he worked at Stoke Mandeville, one of the best NHS hospitals going, where they specialised in spinal operations for those, such as myself, who were in dire need. Often people who had been let down by the private sector surgeons, he said, who commanded the power of life and death like gods and would frequently treat the whole process with a contempt bordering on the criminal, nipping into operating rooms while their car engines were still running and popping in a few sutures after their junior staff had done all the real work. Half the time, they didn't even bother to scrub up properly. Now, said Doctor Wiggles, it would be crazy for me to give up the full life I was still able to live today in the hopes of a possible cure, more likely a nasty infection and complications, or at the worst a careless slip of the knife that could finish me off for good just because some jackass doctor had a golf course to get to.

I wondered what on earth could have yanked his chain to provoke such a reaction. Professional jealousy maybe? Maybe not. But Doctor Wiggles wasn't done yet. He went on and on about the hospitals where paraplegic patients were farmed out to when their operations went wrong, where simple infections could prove disastrous and by the way, there was a much higher chance of contracting an infection in a British hospital than elsewhere at that time. I would be better off having it done in India or Serbia, where these new antibiotic-resistant superbugs hadn't had a chance to take hold yet. I wondered briefly at the management culture of a national health service that could pay ever-increasing numbers of managers hundreds of thousands of pounds a year, but couldn't afford to get the wards cleaned properly.

"But if the situation is as dire as you're describing," I said, "how come everyone doesn't know about it? Why is there no uproar?"

Covered up, he replied. Successful operations had a big deal made of them while the failures were quietly filed away, out of sight, out of mind. I wasn't sure whether to believe what I was hearing, but the man's manner and tone of voice made it quite plain that he had indeed seen some horror stories of neglect and poor treatment and didn't want me to end up the same way.

I sat and stared at him for what seemed like ages while my mind raced. I thought of the master of my lodge, a chunky six-foot-tall police inspector from the Flying Squad whom you wouldn't have wanted to argue with down a dark alley. He had had an operation to put right a cartilage problem in his knee suffered while playing rugby. He never woke up from it.

I remembered the most recent occasion I had been in the hospital myself, for a simple hernia operation. The anaesthetist, a pleasant German woman, interviewed me some hours beforehand to find out about my medical history and what kind of precautions she might have to take. But then my operation was pushed back three hours or so and she couldn't be there, so the responsibility for keeping me unconscious was handed over to a large Nigerian gentleman who presumably knew nothing about me at all and just guessed what would be okay and what wouldn't. It took me fully two hours to come round afterwards, and when I did the surgeon was standing over me in his street clothes, a scarf and heavy raincoat. Odd attire for a man who was supposed to be checking to see if my brain was still working properly.

I had been under the knife longer than expected, due to him finding not one but three hernias and deciding to fix them all in one fell swoop. That's the magic of the NHS right there, you can bet your bottom dollar that had that been a private procedure, they would have closed me up after the first one and scheduled two more at full price. Anyway, the surgeon asked me what my name was and if I knew the time.

"John Emin," I replied, "and I went in at two, and they said it should take about an hour, so it must be about three o'clock I should think."

It was five past six. Un-phased, the surgeon told me that he'd booked me into ward twenty-four for two to three more days, to allow me to recover from the extended procedure. I suppose that was what he was meant to do, by the book and all. But then after he'd said goodbye and made to leave, no more than three or four steps passed before he turned right around and came back.

"Mr Emin," he said quietly, "do you think you would be more comfortable back at home?"

The look in his eyes said it all. You'll be safer at home than in this bug-ridden hospital. He had to book me in for a few days by the book, but if I wanted to leave there was nothing they could do about it. Barbara was there to pick me up by nine, and she followed as the nurse pushed me to the lift in my wheelchair as carefully as she could, with me staying as still as possible because every movement hurt despite the hefty dose of painkillers I was on. By the time we got to the car, there was a saucer-sized escape of fresh blood staining my clean white shirt. Something clearly wasn't right. My three wounds were all left undressed, and while two incisions were sealed and glued together (without sutures), one was bleeding freely. I held it together with my fingers and showed the nurse who had come down with us, presumably to take the wheelchair back upstairs. She took me to a little room and applied some kind of sticky device, and that seemed to do the trick. Off home, I went. It hadn't been the most comforting experience of my life, and now my doctor was telling me that I could be in for even worse if I couldn't put up with the pain in my neck for a bit longer.

"It's up to you," said Doctor Wiggles as I turned to leave finally, "but you have my advice. Oh and by the way," he went on, "I'm stopping your sleeping tablets, so you should start to cut down to half a tablet a day for a week or so and then you won't be getting any more."

"But I came to get a new prescription today," I protested, now standing in the doorway to his office, "I've only got one left."

"There you have it then," he answered with a smile, "two nights on half a tablet. Have a good day, Mr Emin."

Despite what felt initially a bit like unexpected cruelty, I appreciated what Doctor Wiggles had said, and moreover that he obviously cared about what was best for me rather than just what I wanted to hear. That kind of person, be it a doctor, friend or otherwise are priceless. But then more weeks of sleepless nights passed and the pain didn't seem to be easing. I considered flying to America, to a hospital in Boston that apparently had an excellent record with this sort of thing and where hopefully some careless playboy surgeon would not leave me in a wheelchair for the rest of my life. Money was no object, the pain was.

Eventually, I cracked and went for a private consultation at Brighton Hospital. They did an MRI scan, and then the surgeon came and had a chat with me, and explained that the nerve needed to be decompressed. It sounded like a simple enough procedure; cut a chunk of bone from my hip, then slice through the side of my throat to get to the damaged joint, remove the prolapsed disc and replace it with a ring like a large polo mint with my chunk of hipbone in the middle. Apparently, that would then fuse together over time and become like permanent connective tissue. The surgeon said that in the weeks following the operation, I would hear cracks and grating sounds in my neck as the fragile new bone bonds broke over and over, but eventually after six months or so they would fuse tight.

Well, if it needs to be done, I said, let's get me booked in right away. No, no, said the surgeon, I should probably wait to see if it settles down. That was what Doctor Wiggles had said! I should have known he would be right all along. I suppose the National Health Service being free does not jump to every marginal request to fix people up with expensive operations as would most private hospitals where cash is being paid. I knew very well if the situation became worse the NHS would carry out whatever was necessary and for free. So chastened a little for wasting the surgeons time left to do as he suggested.

But still I had not learnt my lesson, it seemed because a year later I booked another private appointment, this time with a retired surgeon who claimed to be an expert in neck problems. He rented a room on Harley Street to see patients, which ought to have been my first warning bell as that's where most of the quacks that get exposed seem to base themselves. But I was desperate and in pain and wanted a specialist's opinion.

I sat down across the desk and offered him a copy of my MRI scan on disk.

"I've already got a copy," he sighed, flicking it away contemptuously with a finger. "Patients shouldn't be allowed to see those," he went on, "it only causes problems."

Well, here was a dismissive attitude. Never mind. There was only one question I wanted answers right now, and that was whether or not my condition would get better, or should I now seriously consider going under the knife possibly in that Boston hospital I had learnt of.

"You don't need an operation," he said, sounding bored.

Wow, what a relief! And he didn't even need to examine me! This man must be really good. Hey ho, at least I didn't need the operation, no risk of paraplegia. But then this retired surgeon went on to say that he couldn't see how I could have sustained such an injury in the crash, seeming to imply that it was either already there or didn't exist at all. I asked if he had read my medical reports from two years previously. He said he hadn't. I felt like I was really getting my money's worth here. I tried to explain about the accident and what had actually happened with my body being forced upwards and bending my neck so.

I got the distinct impression that he had some kind of problem with me, which was very strange because I never usually think in terms of prejudice or what not, it's just never a factor. But now hearing this man's South African pronunciation popping in my ears I felt uncomfortably like a black man caught on a white bus or something. There was a wall being built up between us with each passing word, yet we were both smiling and pretending that nothing was happening. Very strange.

At any rate, the man simply told me not to worry about it and sent me on my way, now feeling very much like a second-class citizen with my tail between my legs. The whole experience was like something out of a Victorian novel, with the arrogant doctor putting the poor, stupid commoner in his place. No wonder he was smiling the whole time, I'd just paid him £1,000 for the pleasure of insulting my intelligence. I found myself longing for the honest, plain-speaking and completely free counsel of Doctor Wiggles. I suppose there are experts and there are experts.

In spite of the discomfort and the pain, the silver lining to all of this is that I have been given the luxury of time that few people ever really have until perhaps it's too late. Time to ponder the more unusual events of my life which are all in their own way wonderful experiences that have taught me a great deal. If it hadn't been for that car accident, it's likely that those eureka moments, and all the times when I saw pop, and the strangeness of dowsing, would all just be added to that long collective list of things we don't talk about for fear of appearing strange. I have begun to tug at the threads of mystery wound tightly in my mind that, who knows, may someday lead to an explanation for it all that will blow our minds. Life is certainly a puzzle that needs solving, fit the pieces together and see what appears. But I feel as though I can see the shape already, not clear or defined yet but definitely there and waiting to be discovered.

The best way I can think to describe it is like finding a huge ocean liner carrying a thousand people suddenly appear in the middle of London. The people all peer over the sides wondering what the hell is going on, but the fact is it is there and there's no getting around that. The first question that those people will naturally ask is, "where are we?" But that's the easiest question to answer. Of course, they're in London England. That much is obvious. But how and why are they there, those are the difficult questions, the ones I can't quite answer yet. Metaphorically the liner represents all of the strange things that I have experienced throughout my life. I know they exist, that's the easy part. Explaining them is where the problem lies.

As a pragmatist, I've always held that black is black and white is white, accepting grey areas reluctantly, a necessity in order to get through a life in which compromise and expediency is often the best way to get where you're going. But on a scientific level, proof is the name of the game. We shouldn't be dissuaded from searching for that proof just because things make no sense to us now, or because certain possibilities are unlike anything we have known before. It was ever thus in the field of discovery throughout human beings' time on this planet.

Lo and behold, after almost four years now the discomfort is much less than it was, and the sleepless nights fewer and farther between. And when the pain is finally gone, at least I will be left with the journey that my mind has been able to take these long months, and the promise that someday it may end. Perhaps in a place where no one has ever been before.

Funny how things work out sometimes. Almost as though they were meant to happen for a reason.

Chapter Thirteen
Beginner's Luck
1977

A person does not seek luck. Luck seeks the person.

~ Turkish proverb

Sometimes we let the most amazing occurrences slip past us quite deliberately. So long as we can put a name to something inexplicable, like 'déjà vu' or 'intuition', we're surprisingly content to just accept it, however incredible, and move on to the next order of business.

Beginner's luck at the roulette table is something that we recognise as 'just one of those things' that seems to happen to people. So when it comes to being our turn to experience it, we'll probably just shrug our shoulders, say something like, "well how about that," and then either keep rolling the dice (and inevitably lose it all) or collect our winnings and be thankful for our fleeting good fortune.

Back in the seventies, I had such an incident myself. At the time, as most people do, I simply chalked it down to experience and didn't think much more on the subject. But as the years have passed the memory has once again risen in my thoughts to be considered as one little piece of the puzzle that we are, a hint perhaps of something special that lurks within us but rarely makes itself known.

Of course, I hope that each of you will draw your own conclusions about what this phenomenon may or may not be. My wife Barbara, being far more sensible and grounded than I, maintains that what I experienced as 'beginner's luck' was, in fact, a perfectly normal series of events. Perhaps she's right. I have her to thank for keeping me on the straight and narrow all these years after all. Yet I still consider myself something of a hardened pragmatist and not prone to flights of groundless fantasy. Having applied reason to the facts of this matter, and been unable to conjure an explanation in keeping with conventional wisdom, I am forced to conclude that something very unusual happened to me that day.

Judge for yourselves.

We went to Madeira in order to stay in Funchal for a few days.

The view flying into Funchal bay is quite breathtaking, with majestic, curved slopes covered in trees rising up from the sea all around. Though the sense of awe was somewhat tempered with anxiety as we closed in on the single landing strip carved from the mountainside and noted with raised eyebrow a crashed plane protruding from the waves below. I hoped our pilot wasn't one of those who enjoy a drink or two before setting off, and thankfully that did not seem to be the case as we landed safely and were able to get on with the business of enjoying our holiday.

We rented a little Austin Mini and toured the island, taking in sights like the world's second highest vertical cliff (so they claimed), some one-thousand, nine-hundred feet straight down. There was plenty to see and explore during the day, but the nightlife was somewhat lacking in variety. There are some cracking restaurants in Madeira to be sure, and if you like fish you really ought to stop by sometime and try the Espada, a local speciality that's a bit like fresh cod but maybe better in my opinion. Though if you're of a squeamish disposition you might want to avoid getting a good look at the creature before it's been cleaned and cooked. Madeira pops up out of the crystal clear Atlantic water like a huge mountain, which means that the sea there gets very deep very fast. In most places, one step in and you're up to your knees, another and you're waist-deep, and by the third step, the water's above your head. The little fishing boats have an easy time of it, floating out a short way offshore and putting their lines down to the seabed far below where the Espada swim. Any fish from that depth is likely to look a little odd. The Espada are no different; maybe four feet long and covered with thick slime and shaped like a conger eel, but different, with great long jaws full of spiky teeth and big, bulging eyes. Enough to put you off fish for life maybe, but damn me if they aren't delicious.

Anyway, we'd just enjoyed some of this lovely seafood at the hotel, when another couple there, a gentleman by the name of Simon and his wife Sally, suggested that we might like to go along with them to the gambling halls down the road. Well, there wasn't much else to do and our choices seemed to be to either accept the invitation or spend the evening, instead, in one of the town's rather tedious bars. So off we went to the casino.

Simon changed up around a hundred pounds into Escudo chips and we went for a wander around the tables, just watching people at first. There were maybe a hundred people there spread across various tables that offered a variety of different games, mostly dice and cards. I should confess at this point that gambling was a nonsense to me, a complete waste of time. But then, that was why we were there after all because there wasn't anything else to do. When in Rome, as they say.

Okay, I thought, *time to try and learn a little something*. Maybe some insight into human nature could be gleaned by observing the people around these tables. The evening needn't be a complete write-off. I picked a table that seemed to have attracted the most serious gamblers, the ones who were fingering bigger and more expensive chips than the giggling holidaymakers dotted around the place. The players at this table wore sombre expressions, their brows furrowed in thought as they tried to decide where next to place their bets.

The first hour or so, all I did was watch these people play. Their game was roulette, and as the little white ball clicked and clacked around the wheel my attention was caught by two people in particular whom I would see playing this same table three nights in a row. The first, a local Portuguese lady, in her sixties by my reckoning, was dressed all in lacy black and must have had a few quid judging by the way she was feeding that table with chips. She was there alone and never spoke a word to anyone as far as I saw. I thought she seemed a little sad, probably lonely if she did have family presumably they didn't live nearby or didn't visit very often. She didn't seem to be doing very well in terms of the game, but neither did she seem to care at all.

The second character was another local, a gentleman, maybe fifty years of age. I supposed he must be a professional of some sort judging by his dress and the enthusiasm with which he was laying his chips down, much like the lady in black. It didn't take a shrewd mind to figure out that both of these people were regular gamblers, and I decided to quietly watch them both for a while to see what I could learn.

The croupier would roll the ball counter to the spinning wheel and mutter something unintelligible in what I assumed must be Portuguese, though I didn't recognise the phrase. Presumably, it meant "last bets or no more bets" or something to that effect. Then shortly after he would reach out with his little rake and point to the number that had won, and then to either red or black for those who had chosen to bet simply on either colour. It all seemed easy enough, but as I continued to watch these people play, something strange began to happen.

After a period of watching the wheel spin round and round and the chips being pushed back and forth over the smooth green felt, I started to play a little game in my mind. I would gently close my eyes for a second or so as the wheel span and try to visualise the croupier's rake touching down to indicate a number and then a colour. And do you know, I was getting the colour right almost every time. Ten mostly successful attempts later, I decided it might be worth just changing £10 into chips and having a little dabble. An experiment, that's all.

Playing only on red and black, by the end of that first night I had amassed some £30 worth of chips. I lost a few spins but won more and felt pretty confident that I could have kept on going. It's worth remembering too that at that time a workman's wages were around £20 a week and the average mortgage maybe £8 to £12 a week. I had pocketed a week's worth of hard graft in just a few hours. We should all live through times like that.

Anyway, intrigued by the result of this little experiment, I returned to the casino for a second time the following night and settled in at the roulette table. I was placing small bets, easily under the table's stated 'minimum bet', though nobody said anything about it. I suppose I must have looked like small beer to the more hardened gamblers around me, throwing around their big wads of cash, but did I care? Not a jot. Within a few hours, I'd doubled my money again to sixty pounds.

Over at a nearby table, Barbara, Sally and Simon were having a whale of a time, giggling away as Simon exuberantly cast his bets left and right, sometimes winning and sometimes losing. I left them to their fun and kept on playing with 'the serious mob' as Barbara and Sally put it. I was pleased to be winning of course, but I wouldn't describe my small forays into the gambling world on those first two nights as anything particularly remarkable. Beginner's luck, right?

The third night, however, was different.

The money I had won so far was something of an anathema to me. I saw no fun in keeping it and certainly wouldn't dream of carrying on gambling to pay for little treats and goodies. This was dirty money, in my mind, not properly earned and not worth having. Still, the experience had been fun enough, so I resolved to get rid of my newfound wealth in the most appropriate fashion, by gambling it clean away again. That way the lesson would be reinforced that gambling never pays off in the end, and I could chalk the whole thing down to experience and move on.

Well, as I said, the first couple of nights I had found that if I closed my eyes and tried to visualise the colour that the croupier was going to point to each time, I would get it right more often than not, and that's how I would bet. But trying to predict the numbers, in the same way, was far hazier, and I wouldn't be tempted to try that. On the third night, however, having decided that I was going to lose the lot anyway, I decided I may as well have a go.

I spent about half an hour practising without laying any bets down whatsoever, closing my eyes and trying to see the end of the wooden rake pointing to a particular number, and finding as time passed that had I been betting on the numbers that I had seen, I would have been in credit. So the next time I saw one clear in my mind, right before the croupier called out for last bets (or whatever it was he was saying, I was still not sure), I placed half of my chips on the number eighteen and the lines all around it just to be safe. Sure enough, the little ball settled below the number eighteen and the croupier pushed a nice pile of chips my way. For the first time, some of them were large and rectangular, and satisfyingly chunky.

This same thing happened over and over again. I did lose a couple of bets but won far more, and the pile of chips in front of me kept growing and growing. Within half an hour or so I had become a high roller. I settled into a comfortable rhythm, difficult to describe and certainly strange to feel. I was in my own little world and didn't even notice that the space around me had become increasingly crowded as people were drawn away from other tables by the commotion surrounding ours. Some were just watching, but plenty more were betting too, laying their chips down on the increasingly chaotic board. Maybe they thought it was lucky or something, I don't know, all I remember is Barbara nudging me and saying that they were all here to watch me. I can be terribly switched off at times, especially when I'm concentrating on something else.

Well, the attention didn't perturb me at all, but it interrupted my focus enough that I let two or three spins go by without placing a bet, while I surveyed the jostling crowd. I noticed that the old lady in black was watching me intently, while the professional gentleman I had noticed on my first night seemed to be sweating a bit and looking generally uncomfortable. I guessed that he had gotten in over his head and was desperate for a big win now to save himself. I remember thinking it rather sad to see this poor man tortured by his addiction unless of course, it was something else that was causing his misery and losing money simply agitated the situation.

At this point, they changed over the croupier for a fresh one, and during the lull caused by the transition, the sweating man took the opportunity to note that I was doing very well and that he was pleased I was placing bets above the minimum as he'd noticed me doing on previous nights. Well, I didn't really understand the whole minimum thing anyway and he didn't elaborate on it, so that was that and we started up again with the new man behind the wheel.

I was winning regularly now, at least two out of every three bets, and there was a large pile of rectangular chips in front of me. Remembering that my goal tonight was to lose everything, or at least everything but my original ten-pound buy-in, I had the notion to put half of the pile on black all in one go. A whim, that's all it was, but I followed it and pushed the stack forth as the ball went tumbling around the wheel. Black it was.

"Hey, buddy," mumbled a voice next to me. The professional man, by now sweating unpleasantly, had slid around the table to pose his question. "What system are you working?"

"No system," I replied, confused.

"You must be working a system," he growled, his eyebrows furrowed, "you couldn't possibly be doing so well otherwise."

I shrugged. I didn't clearly understand what the man meant. Each number has the same chance of winning every time, that's the design of the game, simple and elegant. There's no system that could change your odds. That's the gambler's fallacy.

Ah, but that wasn't quite right though, was it. I was using a system of sorts. I was closing my eyes and trying to see what was about to happen on the table, and most of the time I was getting it right. This wasn't guessing, at least it didn't feel like guessing. It felt like somehow I was able to see a few seconds into the future each time. As another little experiment, I started placing a few bets about thirty seconds before the croupier called last bets, though sometimes I did this earlier. Since this was more than a few seconds before the outcome of the spin, I wasn't able to visualise the result of it, so these bets were made purely on a whim. To my surprise, most of these bets won too. But those wins felt different to the others simply by virtue of the fact that they were a surprise. When I closed my eyes and saw the rake point to a number, I felt sure I would be right. When I placed the bets early, I had no sense either way.

Again, I didn't really care at this point about winning or losing. The chips in front of me weren't real money. Not money I'd earned. Not money I deserved. So they were expendable to me as trivially as they had been acquired. I felt sorry for those gamblers, like the anxious man next to me, who fell into the thrall of this terrible vice to the point where it had control over their lives, over their happiness.

"You must have a fortune there…" said the man's voice again, enviously. It took me a moment to process what he had said, as I hadn't thought about the chunky plastic blocks as equivalent to real money. I suppose that's why casinos use them, makes it easier for people to let go.

The crowd played their part well, ooh-ing and ah-ing, gasping and groaning as the ball tumbled around the wheel. The professional man was now to my left and slightly behind me, and I could hear his reactions above the others each time. He had begun betting on the same numbers as me, but since I was leaving it late each time he was rebuked once or twice by the croupier for placing his chips even later. Obviously, he won when I won, but when we both lost it hurt him more because he wasn't keeping back a decent stash of chips in reserve. He was after a big win and thought I could help him get it.

The thing I remember perhaps most vividly of all was the sense of complete calm. I bet without fear, without a care for the outcome and felt neither particular joy nor disappointment as my stack of chips rose and fell.

Then I saw it in my mind's eye, the number seventeen.

"Last bets!" called the croupier in Portuguese, but I was still looking for my number. The wheel was spinning and the ball in motion as my eyes darted around the table looking for the right spot, but there were so many people playing by now and so many chips laid down that it was impossible to see most of the numbers. I asked the croupier quickly where seventeen was, and he pointed with his rake to a specific area of the table, where I placed some of my platinum chips, the most impressive, most expensive ones I had. It didn't seem to bother him that I was late in doing so.

The crowd waited with bated breath as the ball clinked and jumped before finally dropping into the slot under the number seventeen.

A gasp and then a cheer went up, and the croupier began to clear the table of chips that were covering most of its green surface, leaving mine and those under and around them. But something was wrong. My chips weren't on number seventeen at all, the croupier had pointed to the wrong spot. He moved to clear them away with the others when the professional man began arguing with him in Portuguese. He seemed pretty good at it, and I thought perhaps he might be a lawyer. Never did find that out. At any rate, the manager, who had obviously been keeping an eye on proceedings from afar, came over to see what all the uproar was about, and it was pointed out to him by more than one voice at once that the croupier had misled me to put my chips on the wrong number. The manager looked to the croupier, who grimaced his agreement and shrugged his shoulders as if to say that he didn't know what to do now.

"I'm terribly sorry," said the manager pleadingly, turning to me, "but we can only pay out on the winning number and it is up to the client to ensure he places his chips on the number he wants."

There was uproar. People were waving their arms and shouting at the manager, at the croupier, all kinds of words I didn't understand and some I did. The manager didn't seem to know what to do, and I began to be concerned about the possibility of the situation escalating. Quietly, I held up my hand and raising my voice a little, said simply that the manager was right. Immediately, the crowd quietened down.

"Let's just cash in the chips and go," Barbara said in my ear.

"No," I replied simply, "I'm going to play on."

"But you're just going to keep winning!" she said in exasperation.

"I don't think so," I replied, thinking for a moment before pushing a huge pile of chips, more than half of my stash, onto red. This is when I learn that the house has an upper limit, not just a lower one. The croupier looked to the manager, who in turn exchanged words with a man who I assume must have been his deputy, before nodding to the croupier to accept the bet.

It won. I hadn't expected that. One of the men around the table gave the manager a roasting, laughing at him and pointing out that now he'd have to pay out much more than if he'd just let me have my win on seventeen. They had to fetch out more chips just to give me my winnings, which were more than enough by now to have bought a house with. Or two. Or three.

To be honest, I was pretty uncomfortable about it all. I had been hoping to lose and get the whole thing over with as soon as possible, but luck, or whatever it was, had smiled on me once more. Clearly, a re-think was required. I looked from my vast pile of chips to the sweating man next to me, whose expression was hungry and desperate. Should I just take my £10 and leave the rest for him? He probably had a family who would have been very grateful indeed that I'd bailed him out. But no I decided to look away. Give it some more thought.

Once again I pushed half the chips forward onto red. Red had come up three times in a row, and I supposed it wasn't likely to come up again. Obviously, that isn't really how chance works, but it's how you think in a situation like that. Well, red it was. Oh dear.

"It's your lucky day," muttered the manager darkly, obviously unable to believe his eyes.

"If you leave it on red again, you'll lose," offered the sweating man, still far more carried away with the situation than I was.

"Yes, I know," I replied quietly.

I left the chips where they were as the wheel span again, the ball bouncing and turning, and falling… on black. The crowd groaned, and the manager shook his head with a too-knowing look of sadness which no doubt hid his relief and pleasure. 'Got you!' his hidden expression seemed to say. You could tell he'd seen this all before.

I looked down at my remaining pile. It was still huge, gold and platinum chips, still enough to buy virtually whatever one's heart desired. Again I glanced at the desperate man for a second or two as our eyes met and wondered whether I should just let him have what was left but something told me no, that wasn't the right thing to do, I am sure I saw the disappointment in this man's face as I turned away. Calmly, I set aside a few small chips, exactly £10 worth, then counted out six of the platinum chips, handing them to the croupier, thanking him for his services and pushed everything else onto black. The manager nodded his acceptance of the over-limit bid, and the crowd held their collective breath again as we waited for the ball to drop.

It was red. I had lost everything, thousands, tens of thousands, all but my original ten-pound stake. With a small smile, I walked casually over to the cashier, changed my few remaining chips, and made to leave. I caught sight of the sweaty man heading for the door too, gesticulating wildly with his arms and talking loudly about how crazy I was. As I reached the door, the manager and his deputy were waiting for me, and the manager opened it with a little bow.

"Thank you, sir," he said, "please come again." Then he paused for a moment before looking up at me earnestly. "Sir," he began hesitantly, "but, why?"

"Ask that man who just left," I replied, nodding after the sweating professional. "He knows, and so do you." And with that, I walked away from the casino for the last time. The experience had been fantastic, but it was time to leave it all behind now. Just a memory. That was the smart thing to do.

Barbara, of course, reacted as she usually does when I claim to have experienced something out of the ordinary, accepting the course of events without so much as a raised eyebrow. The only thing she said afterwards was how terribly bored she was while I was playing, and how pleased she was that it was all over. But I can't help feeling like I experienced something out of the ordinary at that table, some flicker of potential that we all have inside of us just waiting to be unleashed.

I suppose many people reading this will think me a lunatic, just as that man did at the casino. Maybe they're right. I threw away a pretty huge amount of money, knowingly, willingly, even voluntarily. But the thing is, in my mind those chips on the table represented dirty money, no different than if it had come about through drug dealing, or prostitution, or some other underhand way. Barbara and I pulled ourselves up from having £500 in all the world to a position where we now have everything we could possibly want, and we did it through the sweat of our brow, so to speak. I can go to bed at night knowing that I've done right, and done well, and without worrying about what tomorrow might bring, without obsessing about the pot of gold at the end of the rainbow, because I already found it. No, I already worked for it. The gambler has no such assurances.

I couldn't live like that sweating man around the roulette table, his future so painfully and publicly out of his hands, his happiness, perhaps his family's happiness resting on the bounce of a ball. I can scarcely imagine anything worse. Sometimes I wonder whether I should have given him all of my chips that night, solved his problems, at least in the immediate future. But then I think maybe he learnt a more valuable lesson by watching me lose it all and simply walk away with a shrug, no better or worse off than when I started. I hope he had a good think about it anyway.

Playing roulette was a fun enough experience, and certainly provided an interesting insight into human behaviour, including my own, and Barbara's, and all of the other characters around the table. Perhaps Barbara is right, and nothing remotely remarkable happened other than me experiencing a slice of what we all recognise colloquially as 'beginner's luck'. And yet, I cannot help but dwell on the process by which I was seemingly able to 'predict' the next numbers to come up. Not every time, mind you, but enough to win much more than I lost, which is very unusual for somebody spending three straight nights in a casino. They say that the house always wins for a reason.

More than the unlikelihood of the odds though, the process that I went through in order to see those numbers was the most striking thing. As I believe I have said many times by now, I am a staunch pragmatist. You needn't take my word for that, just ask anyone who knows me. I like to approach things in a calculated way, and I like proof, preferably visible proof. But unlike many people, I also like to keep an open mind, trust my instincts and call things as I see them rather than trusting to someone else's convenient interpretation of the facts. And the facts in this particular case are that I saw those croupiers' rakes point out each number seconds before they actually did so. I saw it distinctly. That's just a fact that I cannot argue with.

The second fact is that using this strange foresight, I was able to embark on a winning streak that whipped up the whole casino into a frenzy and caused our friend the sweating man, himself a seasoned gambler, to remark that the results I was getting were impossible. Now, maybe they were all just caught up in the moment, but there's no doubt that the size and frequency of my wins, in a game rigged in favour of the house, fall way outside the normal predicted range. We're talking lottery lucky. Well, maybe I was, but it is statistically unlikely enough so as to warrant investigation of alternative possibilities.

Now, one explanation would be that I was just very lucky. Beginner's luck. Coincidence. I just happened to make a lot of lucky guesses, and the numbers I saw before they actually came up were just a figment of my imagination or some adrenaline-fueled hallucination. Or maybe I convinced myself that the strangeness happened after the fact. I'm sure that would be Barbara's interpretation of events.

But there is another possibility, assuming I am not going completely ga-ga in my pre-dotage. Precognition. The ability to see things before they actually happen. Now just wait before you judge me a lunatic, because there are still more facts to consider.

The third fact, in this case, is that I knew I had to try to see the numbers as late as possible before the croupier called "no more bets", or I wouldn't be able to see anything clearly. Again you might say that this was all in my imagination, and all I can reasonably reply is that I know what I experienced and am not, so far as my doctor can tell at least, dangerously delusional. This suggests that if what happened was indeed some kind of foresight, it was very limited in scope. I couldn't zip forward to next year and find out who was going to win the Grand National. We're talking about a few seconds, thirty maybe at the most, at the outside. Such an ability, if it is indeed an ability, would seem to have quite a narrow range of uses in everyday life. But it would make for a cracking survival instinct, and nature is about nothing if not survival.

The fourth fact is that I didn't care one way or the other about winning or losing, and never intended to leave the casino with my winnings. I remained completely calm, and unemotional, and focused on what was happening (or about to be happening) in front of me. I often wonder, and this is just a hunch now, a feeling, whether that indifference played some part in what I was able to do. I remember looking into the tortured faces of the lady in black, and the sweating man, as they watched me win roll after roll, and seeing the desperation in them. The sickness. They had lost control of themselves and become subject to events rather than the other way around. Perhaps it's true that we need to master our emotions and seek a heightened level of self-awareness in order to access the remaining mysteries of our DNA. Or maybe we just need to believe that we are capable of things before we become so, like a sprinter knowing he can run a hundred metres in 9.6 seconds. Belief is a powerful thing.

Many people over the years have reported either experiencing or witnessing feats of precognition. I suspect many people reading this will have crossed paths with the phenomenon themselves once or twice, and perhaps dismissed it as simply déjà vu or some other handy pseudo-scientific explanation. Some badly designed wiring in our brains, perhaps, that delayed an electronic impulse somewhere in the chain of understanding long enough to cause us confusion, and the appearance that we have experienced something we could not possibly have done. But these are all just possibilities, untested, unproven, each as likely or unlikely as the next.

A couple of years later, feeling curious, I tried to replicate my gambling feat in the Hilton hotel in Istanbul. I couldn't do it. Something had changed and I couldn't put my finger on it. Maybe it was because, this time, I really wanted to win in order to prove something to myself. Maybe in setting foot inside a casino again I had become afflicted with the same sickness as the lady in black and the sweating man and lost control of myself. Maybe the greatest human vice of all, greed, has the power to curb our potential and blind us to our own possibilities.

Or maybe it was just beginner's luck after all.

Chapter Fourteen
Reflections of Past Events
1930–2000

My father didn't tell me how to live; he lived, and let me watch him do it.
~ Clarence Budington Kelland

Each and every one of us is a product of a particular and unique timeline connected to a myriad of circumstances throughout your life which combined to favour you with the here and now. I look back now at some of the family stories that might give a hint to what brought me to where I am and maybe that might give me a better understanding as to who and what we are.

***

Nan, my mother's mother, was married to a man who owned two restaurants in Paphos, Cyprus. Situated near the bus terminal, they did good trade and the family were considered well off by most standards, and there was the talk of a box of gold coins that had been accumulating nicely somewhere stashed away for a rainy day. Everything fell into disarray, however, when my grandfather died suddenly, leaving Nan on her own to deal with five children (three girls, two boys) as well as the family business.

She decided to sell up and leave for Nicosia, the capital of Cyprus, where some of her family were, and where she bought a fantastic house that I will always remember. It was built around an ancient Mulberry tree that stood majestically in an open courtyard, which provided wonderful shade from the fierce midday heat of the Mediterranean sun. There was a table and chairs out there, and it was always a pleasant place to sit and eat, and a fantastic spot to entertain guests. I remember vividly being a child there, held up by one of my cousins to grab ripe Mulberries from that tree. The fruit would turn from green to yellow, then red, then black, and that's when you'd pick them when they were at their most sweet and delicious.

Later on, when I moved to Camberwell in London, I found to my surprise and delight that there were many Mulberry trees growing around the place, probably a couple of hundred years old give or take, and every time I see one my mind goes back to those carefree days in Cyprus.

Nan's house still stands just the same as it ever did. I saw it a few years ago, its painted lime-green wooden shutters seemingly unweathered, and the great Mulberry tree as healthy as ever and still giving loads of fruit. Anyhow, sometime after moving back to Nicosia, it is said that the gold coins in Nan's box were diminishing fast, having married off her two sons and set them up in their own homes. But she still had three girls to feed and clothe, who were growing up themselves now and would soon be even more of a strain on the purse strings as it was the custom under normal circumstances for a girl's family to pay out a dowry on her wedding day.

The eldest girl was about seventeen years old, quite the beauty by all accounts, and suitors had already begun to come calling. But since Nan couldn't afford to pay out a dowry which would leave her penniless and unable to look after the rest of the family, what could a poor widow do? They were all turned away. Marriage to a poor man wasn't an option since it would burden her girls to a life of drudgery and that was a situation Nan would not accept.

However, there was a way for the charming and well-mannered young women of Cyprus to marry into unconditional wealth, and that was to make a match with a man from Beirut. Arabushak they were called, rich Arab suitors who came over specially to find themselves a wife.

I'm sure it all sounds very old-fashioned, barbaric even to young ears today. We no longer talk in our society of things such as dowries, of rich and poor, not in nearly the same sense at any rate. But you must remember that being poor back then was very different to how we use the word nowadays. Without a social safety net and all the perks of modern life and technology, being poor was a truly miserable existence. And on top of that, Nan's girls had had an affluent upbringing thus far, living in a big house with that fabulous Mulberry tree. They were certainly no street urchins and simply wished to continue living in the manner to which they had become accustomed.

Now, as I know from my own experience, making a match with a virtual stranger after family-arranged introductions was not uncommon, and in Cyprus, those introductions were sometimes facilitated through the local mayor or 'mouktar'. If you lived in a village, your mouktar would be mouktar to the whole village, but in a large city like Nicosia, mouktars would have their own constituency areas to look after. Considered to be wise elder statesman figures, they would know much of what was happening in and around the area and play a vital role in resolving problems between families, such as land ownership disputes and so forth.

But some mouktars also fancied themselves Cupid's assistants and would keep meticulous records of which young girls were both single and of marrying age. Any young man could ask to inspect the register to see if that nice girl he'd always fancied was 'on the market', as it were, and if the mouktar thought it a good match he would make arrangements for an introduction to take place. Of course, if the young man in question hadn't quite the best prospects the mouktar might suggest one of the other girls on the register whom he deemed more appropriate, or in some cases not even open his book at all!

Well, Nan's mouktar knew her well and been given very clear instructions that only those young men with good prospects should be considered for her girls. The dowry would still be a problem locally of course, but Nan knew of the

Arabushak and their fondness for Cypriot women, and she knew that her pretty, well-mannered girls would be just what they were looking for. And so it proved not long afterwards when a couple of Arabushak brothers came calling on the mouktar to see which beauties were available, as their father had done years before. Their father was very well off (a good start), and had set them both up in business in Beirut, the eldest, some twenty-one years old, as a tailor and his younger brother, a tender twenty years of age, as a shoe-maker.

As soon as these wealthy young Arab men arrived, the mouktar had Nan's girls in mind for them. But he wanted to find out if they were worthy as well as moneyed.

"Are you both healthy of mind and limb?" asked the mouktar.

"Yes, of course," came the reply.

"Do you drink?"

"Never."

"Do you gamble?"

"Never."

"Do you beat your women?"

"Never," replied one of the brothers. "Our mother was never beaten and we behave as we have been brought up."

"So you would never lay a hand on a woman in anger under any circumstances?" pressed the mouktar.

"Well," replied the eldest thoughtfully, "perhaps if she burnt the dinner…"

"A sense of humour!" laughed the mouktar. "I like that. I have just the girls for you…"

So it was that the two Arab brothers showed up at Nan's door to meet the girls. They decided that the seventeen-year-old girl should be married to the tailor, and the sixteen-year-old to the shoemaker, but that was the easy part. Arab customs were different, the men being expected to pay out a dowry to the family of the girls, and my grandmother was a tough woman to bargain with. She intended to extract every last penny she could from these two, and their resolve was tested to the limit. I'm sure they thought she was a money grabbing so and so, but Nan hadn't her own well-being in mind, she wanted to see how they behaved under difficult circumstances. She was pleased to see them polite at all times, they were good people she thought, and her girls were going to a safe home. At a little celebration after both girls were married off at the town hall, she gave each of them all of the money that the brothers had paid her, tucking it into their respective suitcases to do with as they wished. It was the dowry she could not afford.

When I was about thirteen years old, I went with my father to Beirut to visit the family. I had several cousins by then and one of them about my age, Mustafa, showed me around and took me to both of my aunts' houses so that they could see the son of their younger sister. They were magnificent houses and truly lovely people, so kind and happy, fussing over me and arguing about whose house I would stay in for the couple of days we planned to be there. In the end, a compromise was reached and I spent a day and a night in each one. They took me to my uncle's tailoring shop on the high street, where Dad was recognised before he'd even set foot in the door, and as soon as I was introduced people began measuring me up for a suit. Then my other uncle came in and insisted we visited his shop next, where he sized up my feet and showed me a variety of different animal skins that he had on hand for making shoes. I chose an alligator skin, which in no time at all became the softest, most comfortable pair of shoes you can imagine. They made me something of a trendsetter back at school, as I was the first person around our way to wear winkle-picker style shoes while everyone else's was blunt-toed. I had my leg pulled big time for that, but then three years later they were all wearing them, with The Beatles leading the way.

Some years after that trip, the Lebanese civil war all but destroyed Beirut, and Dad told me that the whole family packed up and left for Gaza, where they set their shops back up again. Well, it seems that the troubles in Gaza drew in one or two of my cousins, or maybe their children I'm not exactly sure, but I do know that one was assassinated by the Israelis for being a leader in Hamas. Dad knew what was going on out there, but he would seldom share that information. Occasionally, he would blurt something out mid-sentence like, "Your cousin Mustafa in Gaza has just been shot by the Israelis," before going back to talk about something else entirely. I suppose he thought that I should know those things. They were my family after all.

As for my mother, she was fifteen and of marrying age when Dad clapped eyes on her for the first time and became smitten. Nan thought she was too young to marry of course, but Dad had fallen in love and promptly became her suitor, whereupon he was equally promptly shooed away by her.

Now, Dad was a card, and he had all manner of tricks up his sleeve. Not about to be discouraged by Nan's withering dismissal of him, he would stop by from time to time and deliver gifts for the family, a sack of sugar or something equally luxurious. This was around 1942 with the Second World War raging in Europe and sugar was very hard to come by. Don't ask me where he got it from, maybe him being a cook in the British army had something to do with it, but the black market was something Dad knew all about and if there was a way to get what he wanted, he would find it.

Nan would share this sugary bounty with the neighbours. All manner of treats would spring forth from their stoves where previously there were none; jams and preserves, rum babas, baklava, all manner of sweet pastries and delicacies that people round those parts hadn't seen for some time, while World War Two raged in Europe and the Middle East not far from them. Apparently, it caused such a stir that there was a police investigation into black market activity, but the case was eventually dropped, no doubt after the officers were slipped a couple of jars of jam to take home with them.

If it wasn't sugar, it would be something else. Dad was determined to prove to Nan that he was a provider, and a good one, he made clear the usual dowry would not be required. But Nan insisted that her little girl Sherife (my mother), was too young to marry and indicated each time for Dad to clear off. Which obviously he wasn't about to do. Instead, seeking the appearance of respectability that he presumably thought might sway opinion his way, he joined the police force along with his brothers. Now don't ask me how the army let him out to join the police force in the middle of a war, can only think that there was a greater need for the men in blue at that time.

No sooner had Dad pulled on his uniform than word went round that the Deputy Commissioner of Police for Nicosia was looking for a driver. The successful applicant, in addition to possessing a driver's license, would be expected to speak and write good English, Turkish and Greek. Well, Dad couldn't drive, but he wasn't about to let that stop him snaffling this prime job opportunity, with all of the possibilities for forging high-profile connections that it entailed. He paid a local grocer a few coins to take him off around the streets for a few hours until he could say that he could drive. It was enough. There was no proper driving test as such in those days, just a form to be signed and of course, as usual, a small 'donation' could take care of that. Dad got the job.

So the weeks ticked by and Mum turned sixteen, which was acceptable as far as marrying went. Dad kept up his pursuit of her, stopping by the house regularly on some pretext or other to show off his nice smart policeman's uniform. He was a wily fox and knew that Nan would be worried about being left on her own after mum was finally married off, so he would promise to look after them both and insist that Nan must live with them after they married because they would never cope otherwise. It was sweet music to the ears of an ageing widow facing the prospect of a lonely existence, but still, she wasn't overly keen on Dad, and neither was mother apparently. He was too pushy, she thought, too arrogant and annoying. Instead, she asked Nan to find her a rich Arab so that she could go and live near her sisters. They were happy with their men and their lives now, so to follow in their footsteps seemed like the natural choice. Of course, neither Mum nor Nan realised at the time that Dad always got what he wanted when he set his mind to it.

Dad was always working on a new scheme or a new idea, and more often than not the people around him would find themselves caught up in a tangle of his making, which is how the deputy commissioner of police came to play a decisive role in my parents' courting. I'm not sure what the man's name was, Dad once told me it was Humphrey Wallis or something like that, never been good at remembering names but then Dad jokingly referred to him as 'Sir Humphrey', which got him rebuked a few times for showing a lack of respect, although Sir Humphrey seemed to be fine with it in private. And in turn, the commissioner referred to Dad as 'Enva', because he could never manage to roll his r's to say Enver. They both got along very well, and Sir Humphrey seemed to have a lot of time for Dad, despite his cheek. He was always a personable chap, to be fair, and people did like him. At first, anyway.

So one day, whilst driving Sir Humphrey about the city, Dad pointed out Nan's house and casually mentioned that he was engaged to a girl who lived there, and that she was very beautiful, and asked if the commissioner would like to meet the family someday. Sir Humphrey replied that of course, he would be delighted, so up they pulled outside the front door.

Dad couldn't resist making an entrance and having a little dig at Sir Humphrey at the same time, so he banged hard on the door three times just as he was taught at police school. It was the kind of knock that echoes around the street, announcing the importance of a visitor while also putting the fear of God into a person, even if they know they've done nothing wrong. So, it was understandable that Nan looked a little shaken when she opened the door, and even more so when she spotted a large Englishman in a police uniform climbing out of a big black car and heading straight for her. Poor Nan thought she was about to be arrested! It must be the sugar, passing around all those sweet baked goodies had finally caught up with her and she was about to pay the price for receiving black market goods from that rogue Enver Emin.

But that didn't seem to be what the commissioner was there for after all. A few pleasantries were exchanged before Nan, still not knowing what was going on, invited them both inside. They all sat down around the table and Nan just stared at the two men in uniform, wondering what was going to happen, before finally, Dad opened his mouth.

"This is the deputy commissioner of police for Nicosia," he said casually. "I have told him of my engagement to a beautiful girl and he wanted to come and congratulate us both, so perhaps some cay (Turkish tea) would be nice for our guest."

Nan was livid. How dare he scare the hell out of her, and then even worse presume upon her to make tea if you please… for this, this very important man. She was flustered too and didn't want to make a scene, so off she went to deal with the request, and to fetch out Sherife whom the commissioner had asked to meet.

Meanwhile, Dad took Sir Humphrey out into the courtyard to see the famous Mulberry tree. What Dad had to say about this tree had the commissioner laughing out loud, which can't have improved Nan's mood when she appeared again to call them back inside for their tea.

Turkish tea comes in what looks like a bulbous shot glass, usually on a tray or saucer with a lump of sugar, sometimes lemon, but never milk. Sir Humphrey stirred and sipped his tea, and made polite conversation with Nan by way of Dad since Nan couldn't speak a word of English and the commissioner had little Turkish.

"This is Sherife," said Dad in English, "my intended, whom I shall soon be marrying. Isn't she beautiful?"

Sir Humphrey agreed emphatically, and they made a little small talk, but soon enough it was time to go. The commissioner set down his tea, rose to his feet and took Sherife's hands, saying something to Nan in English that she did not understand.

"Just say yes," Dad whispered to her, which she did and nodded. Then the commissioner said something to Mum and Dad advised her likewise, so she too nodded and said 'yes'.

"You are a lucky man, Enver," said Sir Humphrey, "you have two charming women. I wish you all well."

"Yes, Commissioner," said Dad, nodding, and the two men took their leave to go.

Dad opened the car door for his boss, and then after it had closed after him with a satisfying thud, he turned to Nan and advised her quietly and casually that the commissioner had blessed the union of Sherife and Enver, and that he would be back later. Before Nan could react, Dad was in the driver's seat and the heavy black car was pulling smoothly away down the road.

"Enver, they didn't understand a word I said!" mused the commissioner.

"Not to worry, sir," replied Dad, "I interpreted everything for you."

"I see, I see," said Sir Humphrey thoughtfully. "So then what did you say to your prospective mother-in-law just as we were leaving? She had a face as if she were sucking lemons."

"Oh no, sir," replied Dad, quick as a flash, "she was very happy at what I had to say. That reaction you saw was one of surprise and delight."

"And what exactly did you say, Enver," pressed Sir Humphrey doubtfully, "to make her pull such a face?"

"Not much, sir," replied Dad, "just that you had married Sherife and me."

What Sir Humphrey said after that, Dad would never tell.

Well, that whole escapade turned around Mum's opinion of Dad. He was still pushy and a bit annoying, but at least he was inventive and she would doubtless have an exciting life with him if nothing else, so she asked Nan to agree to their union. Dad's persistence had paid off as usual.

Not that I'm complaining of course on this particular occasion.

***

Every boy should have a dad, ideally one that has a good grasp of life's fundamental truths. One that knows right from wrong. A conformist, if you like. Someone you can trust to teach you the ways of the world.

Well, my dad was none of those things. If you shook hands with my dad, you had to be certain to count your fingers afterwards. The man would rob Peter to pay Paul, except Paul would never actually get what was owed to him, rather just enough to placate him for a while and make things look vaguely right. Dad always thought he could handle people. "Leave it to me," was his constant refrain, "I'll sort it out."

He was never a thief though, not in the strictest definition of the word anyway. Sure, he would creep up to the precipice and take a peek over the edge, but he always stayed up there on just the right side of the law so that nobody could nail him down.

As for doing right by his wife and children, well it hardly occurred to him. The vows made on his wedding day lay in tatters on the ground in the wake of a spree of womanising, drinking and gambling. He enjoyed his vices did dear old Dad, and they all came as a package deal as far as he was concerned. After all, where was the fun in having a bet if you didn't have a whisky in one hand and a cigarette in the other and a girlfriend sitting on your knee? It was quite a blow when the doctors in 1961 had to slice off a chunk of his liver and ordered him to give up the booze and smokes. He did it, to his credit. But then after a lengthy recovery, he discovered that being fit, healthy and sober had given him something of his old sparkle back, so women were back on the agenda and how.

He was a Terry Thomas of his time, you might say. A charmer, well dressed and smart, with a razor-sharp mind and a little black book containing the phone numbers of literally scores of lady friends. Not that he needed it, as the old man had most of them memorised even up to a few days prior to his death.

Not just a hit with the ladies, mind you, dear old Dad. A master of lateral thinking and solving the unsolvable, he had people from all walks of life popping in and out of his office all day to ask his advice, usually on subjects completely unrelated to the buying and selling of houses. He would put up a good front for them, a respectable image, the homely family man who was always happy to lend a hand. Then once the workday was over Dr Jekyll became Mr Hyde, off in his flash car to see one woman or another.

So what did all of this teach me? How would I grow up in the shadow of this extraordinary person who was pretty much the antithesis of what we imagine a model father and role model to be? Well, to be honest, in one respect I was a lot like him as a young man always chasing the girls. A regular chip off the old block but then again, it was the swinging sixties.

I suppose the real legacy that my father bequeathed me was a certain way of thinking. Problems can usually be solved satisfactorily using a head-on approach, which is what most people will try first. The difficult problems remain unsolved because directness has failed, and you just end up running at it over and over, the same way, bouncing off unsuccessfully as if a towering chain-link fence were sitting in your way.

"So what do you do then?" Dad asked me, aged about thirteen years old. I shrugged. "Easy," he says with a smile, "you find a way to go around the fence."

In the same way that a fox will keep trying to find a different way into the hen house, Dad would keep coming at a problem from different angles, looking for a way around the fence, under it, over it, trying everything until he got what he was after. He demonstrated this to me many times over, and I was an attentive student. A man couldn't get a mortgage? Dad found a way. A building inspector wanted something pulled down because it did not conform to standards. Dad twisted, turned, and talked until the situation was resolved and the building remained standing. Police arrested a client. Dad popped over to the station and had them out of there in double quick time. How? Don't ask.

Because of this uncanny ability to fix things, he was almost universally liked by those who came into contact with him. He rubbed shoulders with the wealthy and important, built himself a reputation, even dabbled in high finance, which was a comical notion to those of us who knew him best, because Dad's attitude to money was cavalier, to say the least. I lost count of the number of times he would take a deposit on a house and then disappear with it as if it were his own personal pocket money. Maybe I would not have minded so much if the buyers did not keep coming to me demanding their cash back, and I had to find it for them while paying the salaries of twenty workers and keeping the business ticking over. Dad's attitude when confronted was simply to shrug his shoulders and wonder what all the fuss was about. He literally couldn't understand why people got so upset over little things like their life savings or the roof over their heads. Perhaps it was a form of sociopathy.

***

One particular story that I think sums up Dad, in a nutshell, is that of Bill the builder and his lovely wife Janet. Bill was self-employed and having trouble finding a mortgage as the banks wanted three years' worth of accounts to prove that he could pay them back. Bill had no accounts, but as the person he was buying the house from was my father, this was not to prove a problem. Dad did his thing, and within a few weeks, Bill and Janet had their mortgage and their nice new home. They could not thank Dad enough.

Under normal circumstances, that would have been the end of the matter, but you see Bill had another problem. He was a good-looking fellow, tall and thin but athletically built, with a head of natural blonde hair and a well-chiselled face. His wife Janet was likewise a fine specimen, and the two of them made a handsome couple. The trouble was that after ten happy years of marriage, they still had no children, and they both desperately wanted a family.

Well, the doctors said that the failure was on Bill's side of things, a detail which Janet confessed to Dad in a quiet moment when he popped round to their house for some reason or other. She loved her husband more than anything she said, but they did so want a child of their own, and, she wondered, would Dad mind lending a hand so to speak. That is the story as it was related to me anyway, but knowing Dad I expect he thought he could fix this little problem without much encouragement.

I had no knowledge of these events when, some twenty years later, I ran into Bill at a car auction and we got to talking about old times.

"Now don't act surprised," he said after a few minutes, lowering his voice, "and please don't say a word."

I frowned in puzzlement as he beckoned over a young man from a group nearby. As the man came closer I noted that he was lean and well groomed, with dusky skin and a familiar look about him.

"This is Paul," said Bill, before going on to tell Paul about how Dad and I had sold them their house many years ago. As he spoke, the realisation sank in that Paul was almost certainly my brother. Well, half-brother anyway. I remember thinking that it would have been nice to know him. I then remembered why we'd had to leave Cyprus in the first place, and started to wonder what the full implications of this new revelation might turn out to be.

After a few minutes of polite conversation, Paul returned to his group of friends, seemingly oblivious to the fact that his father and I were both well aware of.

"Er," I began awkwardly, "was that…"

"My son," said Bill, quick as a flash, "whom I am very proud of."

His tone of voice and the look on his face conveyed to me clearly that he knew what I was thinking. I nodded slowly.

"Sorry," I said after a moment. "Dad can be really bad."

Bill shook his head. He explained that he couldn't father a child and that Paul had been such a Godsend to him and his wife, who had passed away some ten years previously after losing a battle with cancer. She doted over the boy, who had then, in turn, sustained his father after their tragic loss.

"Paul is so thoughtful, and clever, and sharp," said Bill, smiling. "Just like your Dad," he added. "I have great hopes for him in the future."

It was a strange turn of events. On the one hand, there was an assumed moral question thrown up by Dad's involvement in the matter. But then here was a story of such joy and beauty, the happiness of a woman and her child, and a boy who carried a little piece of his mother with him and helped his father deal with the grief of losing her. How could anyone say in retrospect that what had transpired was wrong or bad?

"Just once," Dad would say when I asked him about this later, "that's all it took."

Well, at least Bill didn't come to the house with a gun intending to blow Dad's brains out, I suppose.

***

Dad never really grew up, in a sense. He was still chasing women and trying to cobble together audacious business deals right into his final days, which were spent largely in the company of a pretty, young, blonde, Russian companion.

"I'm twenty-six in there, Son," he would say, pointing to his head. "That's what's important, not what the body does."

He was helped to some extent by the fortunate Emin genes which enable us to look years younger than we really are, simply because we don't show wrinkles or grey hair until old age has a good, firm hold of us. I remember visiting a car-hire company in Cyprus which Dad had recommended to me, and asking as I was told for a certain Ms Emine would give me a forty percent discount. Well, it would be plain daft to pass up an offer like that, particularly as their cars were of an excellent standard and well serviced.

Ms Emine, a very smart lady of some forty-five years, was the boss of the enterprise, which was otherwise staffed by several younger girls behind a great marble counter, in a swish air-conditioned office off the high street in Kyrenia. She said nothing when I gave her my name, but she looked after us very well indeed and I got the impression by the knowing look she gave me that she had probably known Dad very well. Barbara said she had the distinct feeling Ms Emine might have blurted out at any moment that she was going to be my step-mother or some such, and I wasn't entirely convinced that this wasn't the case.

At any rate, having returned to the office towards the end of our trip to turn in the keys, I then made to leave, opening the door to be hit with a blast of exceptionally hot Mediterranean air, when Emine called me back. I returned somewhat gratefully to the counter where it was lovely and cool, and she watched me all the way with an odd smile playing on her lips. Clearly, she was puzzled by something and thought I might be able to clear it up for her, but evidently, she couldn't decide how best to phrase the enquiry, and so we just looked at each other for what felt like an awful long time.

"I don't suppose I could ask you a personal question?" she said finally.

"You could," I replied.

"I mean, you can't possibly be older than thirty-eight," mused Emine, sounding as though she were thinking aloud. Barbara laughed.

"You're kidding…" I said, shooting Barbara a mischievous look that begged her to say nothing. "I like what you're saying, do go on."

"I'm just trying to work out your age," said Emine furtively.

"You asked if you could ask me a question," I replied. "Why not simply ask my age?"

"He has a twinkle in his eye, just like his father," one of the other girls chimed in. "Don't you think so, Emine?"

"I give up," said Emine. "Do you mind telling us how old you are?"

"Fifty-five," I replied. Her jaw dropped, and the look on her face was absolutely priceless.

"But your father's fifty-five!" she exclaimed. "How could that be?"

Yep, that was Dad all over.

***

So the Emin genes have been passed down to me, which make me look younger than I have any right to. Not long after meeting Emine, I grew myself a beard, perhaps out of some subconscious desire to distance myself from Dad's roguish behaviour. I was still sporting a good head of dark hair at the time, and so I was surprised to see the beard emerge as salt and pepper. Clean-shaven Dad commented that it made me look old enough to be his brother. Job done.

Well, a beard was fine in England, but it comes with its own complications in a Muslim country, and I began to find that strangers in Cyprus would clasp their hands and direct a little bow my way when they passed me in the street. At first, I was confused, yet amused, and then one day I was picking up some photographs from the Cypriot equivalent of Pronto-Print when the man behind the counter did the same thing.

"Why are you greeting me that way?" I asked.

"But," the man replied, frowning slightly, "you're an Imam, are you not?"

Well, that would explain it. Muslims in that part of the world don't grow a beard unless they're holy men, and even then they trim theirs very neatly, just like mine. With my tanned skin, calm demeanour, quiet voice and well-groomed beard, I suppose I was easily mistaken for a man of the mosque.

It also explained an incident a few days previously when I'd been driving from Famagusta to Kyrenia when a police car pulled me over for speeding. I was wearing long white trousers and a white Russian smock that came down almost to my knees, and the police officer looked me over before giving me a polite warning about the dangers of that road, then a little bow with clasped hands, and off they went. At the time, it seemed quite bizarre. Now I knew that they'd just been cutting a holy man some slack. I shouldn't think many vicars would receive similar treatment back home.

***

As youthful as Dad looked, he always retained the capacity to act even younger. At the tender age of eighty years, he was thrown in jail on suspicion of being a spy. Eighty years old. How does anyone get their mind around that? The Turkish authorities locked him up in the clink overnight before hauling him up in front of an army court to explain why he should be granted bail. A few strategic calls to the presidential residence got him his bail, but Dad wasn't completely off the hook yet. He'd broken the rules and engaged in very suspicious behaviour under the noses of the military, who were not inclined to display a sense of humour about such matters.

You see, at that time the border between North and South Cyprus was closed, and everyone knew that it was a no-go area. If you wanted to cross, you needed to fill in a whole lot of forms and even then crossing from one side to the other was only usually allowed on compassionate grounds and with the permission of the army chiefs. You certainly couldn't just nip back and forth on a whim. Yet this was exactly what Dad was doing, assuming as usual that the rules which applied to everybody else didn't apply to him. He'd found a loophole, or so he thought, which would allow him to complete a quick little form intended for emergency crossings such as ambulance trips, and then claim if caught that he'd made an honest mistake or some such nonsense. Unfortunately for Dad, he ran into a jobsworth Turkish officer who was paranoid about Greek spies being all over Northern Cyprus and refused to be soaped up by Dad's elaborate yarn. His behaviour was extremely suspicious, he was told, and tantamount to spying.

"I'm eighty years of age!" protested Dad. "I'm not 007 of Her Majesty's Secret Service!"

Well, that only made the officer more suspicious, and he took the interrogation up to the next level.

"I'm no fool," he said, sitting well back in his chair and rolling up his sleeves, "so let's not waste time."

I think that line must have particularly tickled Dad, as he repeated it several times in recounting the story to me. Here was a glorified security guard pretending to be far more important than he was, or so Dad thought, and was about to say as much.

"I'm an old man, as you can see," Dad began, leaning across the desk casually. "I'm old enough to be your grandfather. Hell, I was your age when you shot out of your father's balls, so why don't you stop being a pretentious little erk and grow up!"

Dad laughed as he recalled the incident. Evidently, that strategy had worked for him before, but it wasn't going to this time. The officer went completely bananas, calling in two armed guards and shouting obscenities even Dad declined to repeat before ordering him thrown behind bars at a nearby army base.

It didn't help that he was also carrying papers detailing his business dealings with Cleftos Cleredies, a cousin of the President of Southern Cyprus and one of the most senior politicians in the land and who by the way was a leading Eoka terrorist in his time, or maybe you could call him a freedom fighter. By any name, Cleredies was not good news for Dad. It was a name that wasn't received too warmly in the North of the country, and Dad found himself with even more explaining to do.

Few people really understand power, where to find it, how to get it, how to use it. Dad was one of those people. He was always schmoozing the well-to-do and the influential, looking for ways that they could help him get a leg up one way or the other. I remember Mr Cleredies and his lovely wife having dinner under the Acacia tree in our garden in Sussex, and I know that Dad was also well acquainted with the president of the northern side of Cyprus, a Mr Denktash, as well as various African tribal leaders with whom he did a lot of business.

***

I can tell you this story now because Dad's old business partner, Ron, is long gone. Well, it seemed Ron came across a Nigerian gentleman who claimed that he could get him a ship full of oil at a discount price on the high seas. Nigerian crude was good merchandise and the ports in Holland would be happy to take it as usual at market price, so it seemed like a sure bet if everything was as it seemed, and Ron made quite a bit of money on that first deal. Enough at least to buy a large house, nice cars, paintings, and plenty more of life's finer things.

Naturally, when another such opportunity came along sometime later, Ron was ready to jump at it. The only problem was that he was about as close to financial ruin as it's possible to be, largely due to his young trophy wife who liked to spend his cash like it was going out of fashion. Ron needed a quarter of a million pounds in cash, which I should add at that time was a huge amount which he was only just able to scrape together by borrowing against his house, everything he owned, and then taking out an additional loan from the bank on top of all of that. It was make or break time in the truest sense of the phrase.

Nigeria being Nigeria, this money wasn't actually going to buy a tanker full of oil in any legitimate sense, but rather it was simply a massive backhander to a general in the Nigerian army who had the connections to assign the shipment. Ron landed in the country and was immediately picked up by an official car and taken to a hotel where a guard was placed on his door. For security, they said.

Everything seemed to be going to plan until sometime later there came a knock at the door. It was the general come to collect his slice of the action, which he did and left with everything Ron owned in the world in a suitcase. Not long afterwards, another group of visitors came to Ron's hotel room. They were dressed in smart suits and claimed to be the police of some description, they had come to search the place and take away any evidence. They cleared him of every last penny, even taking the cheap Russian watch he bought to replace the gold one he had sold to raise the funds for this expedition. Apparently, the general had reported Ron for attempting to bribe an official. Five thousand pounds cash was handed in as the evidence. Ron was told in no uncertain terms that he was lucky, that the bribe was no greater as that would attract a much more serious charge. Ron bit his lip and pleaded guilty to the bribe.

Behind bars now and facing some long months in what I'm sure you can imagine were pretty horrendous conditions. Ron was approached by the prison guards this time, who intimated that they would be able to send him home quicker if he could come up with yet another chunk of change for them. Unbelievable. Officialdom had a hold of him, to be truthful Ron should not have done what he did, however, the system had corrupt officials that made it more like institutionalised kidnap and extortion, yet there was nothing Ron or anyone else could do about it. This is why I will always avoid that country.

Well, they kept asking him for money and Ron kept trying to tell them that he was now completely flat broke and without a penny to his name, until finally, I suppose they just got bored of him, said that his sentence had been served after four months and booted him out of the country with a criminal record and banned from ever entering Nigeria again. Not that I'm sure he considered that a punishment by this point.

The man had lost his house, his land, cars, paintings, even his gold watch. On top of which, predictably, his pretty young wife flitted off to fields anew. Broke, and broken, poor Ron was at his lowest ebb. But he was about to have a change of fortune. Because he was about to run into Dad.

***

My father was never particularly one for helping people out of the goodness of his heart, yet while Ron didn't have any money or power to speak of, he did have a good brain and useful contacts in America and the Far East, and Dad saw potential in the friendship.

Ron knew all about high finance. High stakes. Multi, multi-million dollar transactions and loans and deals and who knows what. It was complicated but intoxicating, and dear old Dad in his naïvety couldn't resist. Before long the wheels were in motion on something big, a deal involving a substantial pile of cash borrowed from Arabs as it seemed. Though money-lending for profit is forbidden by Islam, so there must have been more to it than that. The go-between was a certain Colonel Saunders, an American chap, tall and striking with a strawberry-blonde head of hair, neatly trimmed beard and always turned out in the most expensive suits, accompanied by a man who he introduced as his lawyer. Saunders had a certain presence, to be sure.

I remember they all came round to my home once for a barbecue and had a good long chat about how the deal was to progress. Dad's job was to find a potential customer and pass their details on to the Colonel, who would carry out a background check before negotiating the lender's side of things with their agents. It all seemed above board anyway, and soon enough, Dad had found his clients in South Korea, Turkey and America, and begun to finalise the paperwork. It was a straightforward enough deal on the surface, an equal borrowing of the value of the assets and nothing more.

Sadly, Ron became very ill right around this time and passed away not long afterwards. Dad pressed on with the deal, however, in conjunction with the Korean interest, a fifty-something retired ship's captain by the name of Kim, who had turned his hand to finance and found several local factory owners in need of loans. Which Dad was of course more than happy to deliver. He made quite a few trips to and from Korea during that period, and on one occasion we feared we might have lost him for good when the Russians shot down a Korean plane near Moscow that had been bound for Seoul. In fact, Dad was to have been booked to be on that flight, having had meetings in New York, but changed his plans at the last minute. I had spoken to him on the phone, unaware it was to save his life and insisted that he came home immediately to deal with some pressing business that needed his attention. Many cross words later, he agreed. After Christos, that was the second time, by coincidence I'd saved Dad's skin. There was soon to be a third.

So, Dad had a whale of a time out in Korea, making tens of thousands of pounds and living the high life, rubbing shoulders with local dignitaries and rubbing other things with pretty local girls, as a result of which I have another half-sister. Honestly, I think we worked out that he must have left at least twenty offspring dotted all over the place by the time he shuffled off this mortal coil. Goodness knows what Darwin might have to say about that.

Anyway, all of this business success brought a number of interesting proposals his way, one of which came from an American named Cam Rogers if I remember right. His story was that he was something to do with a small airline in the US and wanted to buy another aircraft. Dad brought him around for a meal once and he spent a long weekend with us, during which we had some chats about engineering problems, a topic on which he spoke with some authority. I took him flying too and showed him the Kent countryside. Cam said he was involved somehow with a small airline back in the States that needed extra funding. He knew his way around a plane, so I let him take control. It was rather nice to have another competent flyer around, and all in all, we had a fun couple of days before Cam had to leave again on Monday.

A year or two later, Dad had a big meeting to attend in Belgium with Colonel Saunders and some other serious types, and he wanted to arrive in style and make an impression, so I agreed to drive him there in the Rolls Royce. Dad did not have much in the way of cash at that time having spent it on a lavish lifestyle, and any help I would offer was most welcome, so I left the business in the capable hands of a supervisor and off we went.

I dropped Dad off for his meeting and kept out of the way until it was over, then we returned to the hotel, a very pleasant country retreat just a few short miles outside of Brussels. In the morning, Dad took the car to go and attend to some business or other, while I opted for a swim in the indoor pool. I swam a length underwater, took a breath, swam another, and then as I surfaced I saw a man standing at the side of the pool looking down at me. Who the hell could that be? I wiped the water from my eyes to get a better view.

"Is that you, Cam?" I asked, surprised. It was. I climbed out of the water, dried off, and we sat down to talk over a couple of coffees. I told him that Dad had just popped into town, but he already knew that. Then I asked him if he was here looking for some funds, whereupon he lowered his voice and suggested that we go for a quiet word somewhere.

"What's up, Cam?" I asked when we got back to my room. "Is there a problem?"

"There is," he replied, before going on to explain that he was not exactly as he appeared and that I must believe he was a true friend to Barbara and I and potentially Dad's worst nightmare, but he was putting his job on the line now to help us. He was willing to consider Dad as simply a naïve participant in the proceedings, he said, rather than a malicious one.

"Cam, I have no idea what the hell this is all about," I said honestly.

"Just pack your bags," he replied, "and be ready to go as soon as your father gets back. Don't delay, don't call anybody or stop moving even for a second. Go straight back to the UK and forget about everything that happened here."

My face must have been a real picture, because Cam noted that I didn't seem convinced about what he was saying, and ventured to produce from his briefcase a bunch of papers, all stamped with official logos and seals, with photographs and detailed notes attached to them. I guessed Cam must be with the CIA, or Interpol perhaps.

"Do you recognise any of these people?" he asked. Of course, I did. One of the photographs showed Dad and me in the Rolls Royce on our way over there, clear as day, while another was a snapshot of Colonel Saunders and his sidekick. There were other people too that I didn't recognise, but apparently, they had all been at this same meeting as Dad and were due to resume that day. But unbeknownst to most of them, it was all a big set-up to catch Saunders who was apparently wanted for some serious fraud back in the US. Money laundering would be my guess.

"It's up to you," said Cam finally. "But if your father stays until this evening both you and he will be behind bars. I'm not making this offer to any of the others, they're all bad guys. You're not. I'm trusting you, but don't say another word about it to anyone or I'll be for the chop." And with that, he left.

Dad didn't return to the hotel until four pm, by which time I was starting to sweat a bit, wondering if we were nearing the time of the swoop now and whether we'd be too late.

"Cam was here earlier," I told him when he finally made an appearance, "with photographs of you and I taken in the last twenty-four hours. Whatever you're involved with is a sting, and the authorities will be taking them all into custody any time now."

I don't think I've ever seen Dad move so fast and so purposefully. We were out of the door, bill settled, in less than ten minutes.

***

Colonel Saunders was never to be heard from again, but Dad wasn't done with the money-lending business yet. He got wind of another opportunity, all above board this time, and Dad's role was to be in finding and preparing prospective clients, doing background checks and presenting his findings to the lenders.

Dad set up an office in Ankara with the help of a retired police officer by the name of Errol Barak, and soon enough turned up their first good prospect, a flour miller who wished to upgrade his factories as the old ones were unhygienic and cost a fortune to maintain. This man's sons had all attended college and gotten themselves a good education, and they recommended to their father that the whole lot be pulled down and replaced with modern silos and packaging facilities. At the time it was a hugely ambitious project, with a price tag of around $200,000,000. But the family owned a lot of land and other assorted factories all over Turkey, and they were confident that they would have no problem securing an adequate loan.

The process was simple enough, an independent valuation of the assets would be carried out and loans made up to that valuation, and not a penny more. Dad worked day and night getting the paperwork ready while these appraisals were taking place, and everything looked good for the deal to go ahead, with everyone due to take their little slice of the action; 1.5% split between Dad, his new Turkish partner, and another 0.5% for their local sub-agent.

The sub-agent was so confident in the outcome that he borrowed a decent chunk of change from some other lenders on the side to tide him over until things could be completed, enough at least to buy a nice new car and some other luxuries. I'm not sure if they have an equivalent saying in Turkey too, "don't count your chickens before they're hatched", but if they do it certainly never crossed this fellow's mind.

When the independent valuation came back, it was less than half of what would be required to redevelop the factories, only $85,000,000. In addition, the lenders had attached certain conditions to take into account some problems with the licensing and the land beneath some of the premises. The lenders' proposition was basically that every factory would be developed conservatively in a modular fashion, taking assessments of increased revenues and such into account as they went, rather than do the whole lot as one grand endeavour right off the bat.

Whilst sensible, this proposal was seen by the millers as a distinct lack of generosity and was not well received. But what really got their backs up was a further clause stipulating that the title deeds to the land and buildings would be kept by the lenders and not returned until every last cent had been repaid. Well, the family were livid with what they clearly saw as disrespect, and that was that. The deal was off.

Sometimes these things just don't work out, and there's nothing you can do but take what you've learnt from the experience, and try again elsewhere. Fees had been paid for the evaluations and paperwork and such, so nobody bar the miller and his family were out of pocket, but one party involved didn't quite see it that way.

The sub-agent who had originally brought the clients to Dad was a certain Mustapha Balik, Mr Fish in English, but this man was no fish. He was a wolf. A Grey Wolf, to be precise. Grey Wolves were well known in Turkey, a bit like the mafia in their ways and known by the authorities as terrorists, shady characters with whom one did not mess. I had experience of them myself from having employed a builder named Mr Iden to paint my house in Cyprus. Iden drove around in his big air-conditioned BMW, never even breaking into a sweat while his men did all the work for him. I say work, in fact, they did an appalling job before Mr Iden came and frightened my poor housekeeper into paying him in full before he left.

When on my return to Cyprus I confronted him a year later, Iden said he was disappointed that I was unhappy with the work, and naturally, he would return the money to me within the week. Well, a week passed, then another, and before long I was on a plane back to England. After two years of waiting, I just gave up. There was no sense in making more of a fuss about it, and the danger was that Iden might take it as an insult. You never insult a Grey Wolf, at least not unless you want your kneecaps shot off, which they would do without a second thought and not out of anger, but simply to satisfy some twisted sense of honour. That's how the Grey Wolves work.

Mr Fish was deeply unhappy that the deal with the millers had fallen through at the last hurdle. He had counted his chickens before they were hatched, and now, with debts to settle, the loss of his 0.5% share was a slap in the face. He reasoned that Dad had lied to him in saying over and over again that this was a done deal, which turned out to be untrue, and something that could not be tolerated. Someone would have to take the blame for it.

Meanwhile, I had problems at home that I couldn't deal with on my own, so once again I got on the phone to Dad and managed to drag him back to attend a court hearing he'd been putting off for a long time. He had barely been back a day when his office phone rang. Apparently, his partner Erol back at the Ankara office had just had his brains blasted across his desk by the Grey Wolf. Mustapha Balik had strolled into the office asking to see Dad, only to be told that Dad wasn't in the country, whereupon he pulled out a gun and pointed it at the retired police officer.

"Okay," he'd said casually, "you'll do," before shooting him in a manner so cold and calculated that the murderer then proceeded to pick up the office phone and call the police to come and arrest him. He served a few years, a court having decided that he was suffering some sort of mental problem and wasn't fully responsible for his actions. Turks can be guilty of excessive lenience when one man harms another in the name of honour. I remember hearing a story once about Turkish sailor, who came home unexpectedly early from a long voyage only to find his wife in bed with the local butcher. He shot them both on the spot, removed their heads and took them down to the local magistrate's house.

"They are still in my bed," he said dispassionately, "if you want to deal with it. I am too upset right now. I will go back to sea and return in three months."

Incredibly, the magistrate had no problem with this whatsoever. The crime scene was apparently cleaned up and the bodies put on ice until the man returned, whereupon he turned himself in and was taken to the local lock-up. Six months was the tariff for that double murder. Six months on account of the fact that his actions were entirely understandable under such traumatic circumstances. That's just the way honour works in that part of the world. Or did work, at least. I'm not sure you could get away with it so easily these days.

Actually, come to think about it, I don't believe any of my numerous half-brothers and sisters are born of a Turkish girl.

Now there's a thought.

Chapter Fifteen
A Thousand Strangled Cats on a Slow Train to Ankara
1965

Life is a long lesson in humility.

~ J. M. Barrie

Ankara hadn't produced the goods on that occasion, but it was a favourite hunting ground for Dad and not always in the area of high finance.

Back in the early sixties, as some of you may remember, the International Monetary Fund was called in to rescue Britain from the brink of bankruptcy. Our building firm had been doing well, but now that the economy had tanked it was virtually impossible for anyone to get a mortgage, and we were left sitting on a pile of cash without any obvious way to make it work for us.

Well, as I said before when the obvious route was blocked, Dad always looked for an unconventional way around, and his solution in this instance was that we should use the money to import copper pots and towels from Turkey. Goodness only knows what the old man's fascination was with these particular commodities, which as far as I could tell Britain was not exactly crying out for, but he was in charge and as usual I wasn't to have any say in the matter.

We drove to Turkey in his A60 estate, through Istanbul and on to Ankara, then to a place near the Russian border called Erzurum, from where you can just see Mount Ararat in the distance, where Noah's Ark is said to be if you believe in such things. The scenery was most welcome, as I was only really along for the ride anyway, lacking Dad's enthusiasm for the venture and just hoping we could get things done this time with a minimum of trouble.

I remember a big meeting at one of the factories that made the goods we were after. We were all sitting around a large boardroom-style table talking a bit of business when a break was called for refreshments. Turkish tea was offered, but Dad said that he preferred English tea served in the English style, which had pretty much replaced whisky by now on his long list of vices, and proceeded to produce a metal tray, and then a burner, and a kettle, which he filled with bottled water and put on to boil. The other men around the table were amazed and delighted with the performance, which was deliberate and calculated by clever old Dad, and good-natured laughter rang about the place as he went on to fish out some cups, a bag of his favourite Brook Bond PG Tips, and a thermos full of cold milk.

Tea was served, and the locals loved it. They dipped sweet Turkish biscuits as an Englishman might dip a digestive, and Dad even gave a quarter pound of the PG Tips to the managing director, whose wife had apparently spent some time in England and expressed a fascination for the strange way the English took their tea.

The performance was successful. Dad was always a good showman and had no trouble charming people into giving him what he wanted. For me, I was bored. I'd seen this all before, and I still wasn't enthused with the whole idea of the trip and what Dad planned to do with the money when we got home, so I told him I would be taking the early morning train from Erzurum back to Ankara, then wait for him. He was quite welcome to stay there by himself, keep making tea like a street performer and frittering away our savings on a business we knew nothing about.

When I arrived at the station around six-thirty next morning, I noticed many people buying fresh loaves, and cheese, and tomatoes, from a kiosk. Obviously, they all knew something I didn't, so I decided to follow their lead and purchase a few tomatoes, a small loaf, some little cucumbers, three tins of Pepsi and some beautiful, thin-sliced, cured beef, a bit like Parma ham. Standing there on the platform with my packed lunch in a brown paper bag, I had a feeling that the long journey home might be an interesting one.

I found an empty compartment on this old chuffer, got in and lay down. I hadn't had a good night's sleep, and maybe a little shut-eye would do me good. The train began to chug along for a short distance before I heard a rustling sound, then the compartment door opened and in tumbled a young man. He was about my age I guessed, early twenties, but whilst I greeted his arrival with mild curiosity, his reaction upon seeing me was downright hostile. He stared for a second or two, then almost growled as I made to move my little brown bag from the seat opposite. I think he had seen what looked from the doorway like an empty compartment, then to find me laying down in it was a bit of a disappointment to him. Nevertheless, I thought it was a little uncalled for.

The young man began to mutter as he made himself comfortable, complaint after complaint as far as I could tell. As we talked it seemed that he had problems back home and also with a friend at college, which is where he was now returning to after a few days off. I couldn't understand much of it, to be honest. Then after a while, he stopped rambling and looked at me.

"Are you an Arab?" he asked.

"No," I replied, "I have the same lion blood coursing through my veins as you do."

Sounds strange to say it that way, but that's how everyone talks over there, poetic and flowery always.

"Aren't you ashamed that you can't speak your mother tongue properly?" asked the man with a sarcastic sneer. I asked him what he meant, and with no small amount of glee, he undertook a critique of my language skills, pointing out how I used this word incorrectly or pronounced that one wrong. "Sometimes you are just talking complete rubbish," he finished nastily.

By now the train had stopped again and a couple of other people had joined us in our compartment. But this young man, whose name was Deniz, didn't let them bother him as he continued to mock me and preen himself, talking about how he was about to graduate as an engineer at Ankara University and would soon be rich and famous, unlike all of these piddling little peasants around him now. I was on the receiving end of this tirade of childish abuse and had no idea what was pressing his buttons. He surely had one hell of an attitude.

Feeling a little miserable, I sank into my corner of the little space and contemplated finding a different compartment at the next stop. But then I thought no, I couldn't let this little brat see me off with my tail between my legs. I would not overreact, or be bullied. It was a challenge, and I had plenty of time on my hands. We may as well see how smart Deniz really was.

"Deniz," I said, "some of these words that you said I've misused…" I gave him a few examples.

"They are not Turkish," he snapped back immediately.

"You're right," I replied, "they're Greek. I come from Cyprus and some of our words are Greek. And you know, our accent naturally is a little different but still understandable. My Turkish in Cyprus would sound perfectly normal."

He didn't have a comeback for that but just shrugged. I had regained a little face now and wanted to see if I could manage more than that. Though still being cautious as this boy may really be smart and make me look foolish again.

"So how many languages can you speak?" I asked casually.

"Turkish," replied Deniz flatly. "And I am starting to learn German too."

"I see," I nodded, "I see. But what about Indian? Chinese? Scottish? Welsh? Posh English? What about Yiddish?"

He scowled at me, confused.

"In England, they teach us all those languages," I went on, matter-of-factly. "They're compulsory. Even Texas American, which I don't like myself but you have to learn it if you want to enjoy a good cowboy film."

"I like those," said Deniz, still looking puzzled, "but they are always subtitled."

Hmm, I thought. Not as sophisticated as he made himself out to be. Perhaps it would do him good to learn a little lesson.

I made it clear that I was not very well educated at all, certainly not compared to him and his engineering degree, and surely, he must be by far my intellectual superior, but maintained that all of these languages I spoke were very common in England and that it was considered nothing special to speak them all fluently. This rattled his cage.

"Give me a demonstration," he demanded, looking suspicious.

"Alright," I said, "what would you like to hear?"

"American Texas," came the reply.

"Roll 'em, cowboy!" I drawled in my best John Wayne accent, "Where's ma gun? I'ma gona' to the OK Corral so git my horse, anna get my beans and brand this critter with a hot iron!"

"Yep," I concluded in a slow drawl.

It was utter nonsense, but I was counting on the fact that he didn't understand any English. He didn't, and my accent was good enough (or corny enough) to convince him that I really was speaking the local dialect of Texas. He seemed impressed, despite himself.

"What about Indian?" I asked. Deniz nodded, and off I went again. "Four onion bhajis and papadums and a balti curry with hot vindaloo," I said in my best Indian accent. I half expected to be shot down as a fool, but he seemed to like it and genuinely believed I was speaking another language.

"Ah," I continued while he was still suitably disarmed, "but what about Scottish? A truly poetic language. The language of Robert Burns, a great whisky drinker who never wore anything under his kilt."

His eyes widened as I went on to explain about the Scots, a romantic race of hard-drinkers who would charge into battle with their kilts up to the sound of a thousand cats being strangled, a tactic which scared the enemy to death and helped bring about many great victories. And woe betides any Scotsman who didn't show his enemy the old frighteners before lopping off his head.

"Thousand cats and frighteners?" asked Deniz, intrigued.

"Indeed," I replied, "the squealing bagpipes like a thousand cats being strangled, and all those kilts raised with everything swinging this way and that, coming towards you hell for leather. Would you not be frightened?"

"Are they circumcised?" he asked.

"No," I replied. "They are not like the Jews or the Turks." His face scrunched up.

"Sounds horrible," he said.

"Exactly," I replied. "I'd get up and run for my life with that chasing after me, wouldn't you?"

Denis nodded.

"I remember from history lessons," he ventured, "tales of the Scots with their bagpipes and their skirts like women. They were said to be fanatical warriors just like the Turks."

"Yes," I agreed, "but what about when the Scots caught the Turks? That's probably not in your history books is it, the Scots did terrible things, too shameful to even speak about. Have you heard about that?"

Again he nodded. A little bit of suggestion mingled with his own knowledge, such as it was, had this boy on the edge of his seat. As we talked, I was sure I noticed a lady in the corner of the compartment, who was reading a book, suppress a little giggle.

"So," I pressed on, "do you want to hear a bit of Scottish then?"

He did.

"Och, ya wee bairn with yer kilt up high and yer ginger beard!" I roared ridiculously. "Shag the enemy and shag their horses! Pickle the gooseberries in whisky and drink a wee dram, and eat haggis out of ma sporran!"

"Wow," said Deniz, taken aback, "you really know your stuff. All those languages and history too."

The lady in the corner must really have been enjoying her book now, as she raised it right up in front of her face and shook a little as she read.

"Did you say you can also speak Chinese and Yiddish?" asked Deniz.

"Yes, of course," I replied, "you can't order a Chinese meal back home if you can't speak the language. The English love their Chinese food. Many Chinese chefs go over there to make it for them, and in return, we honour them by learning some of their language."

"Go on then," he pressed.

"Hello, Mr Wung Lo!" I began, gesticulating wildly as I spoke, "Chicken chop suey, mandarin duck and flayed lice in wok!"

Well, this seemed to really hit the spot with him and he wanted more. I think I only managed to get away with it by keeping a completely straight face and really throwing myself into each stereotype with gusto, otherwise, he would surely have twigged. But I am my father's son and one thing Dad knew was how to put on a performance. I had this yob hook, line and sinker, and I was loving it.

"Come on, come on," he said excitedly, "what about Yiddish?"

"Ah, well," I replied, feigning contrition, "I'm afraid there I have misled you a little. I haven't actually begun learning modern Yiddish yet. But I did major in Gibberish, which is the old form of Yiddish. I do beg your pardon. I really hate to mislead people."

"What is this Gibberish?" asked Denis. "How is it different to Yiddish?"

"Gibberish is much harder," I explained seriously, "it's taken me half my life to master it, but now I'm so good that my father often says to me 'you're talking Gibberish, boy!'. But I just can't help but slip it in sometimes."

"So when would you use Gibberish and when Yiddish?" he asked, swallowing the lot.

"Well, it's just like old Turkish and new Turkish really," I replied.

"But that is only a difference in writing," Denis shot back.

"Yes exactly," I said. "Those Jews are very bright you see, they've sensibly modernised their language, simplifying it and shortening some words and suchlike, and that's the difference between the two."

"I see," he said, "so you speak the proper language from before it was adulterated?"

I nodded.

"I am sorry, sir," said Deniz, "for being so rude to you. You are a very clever man and you have put me in my place. My big mouth does get me into trouble sometimes. Can you forgive me?"

"But of course," I replied with a smile. The lady in the corner of the compartment, still hidden behind her book, made a strange rasping sound.

"Do you think she's alright?" I asked Deniz, nodding to her.

"Yes, yes, she's fine," he replied without really looking. "But please, I want to hear this Gibberish which is so hard to learn."

Well, I couldn't help myself at this point. I said that I would recite a certain verse I particularly liked, so keeping a straight face, began, I gave the awful rendition of complete and utter nonsense, such that anyone who understood anything about language would have realised that there was no sense to any of it. It wasn't just English with an accent, as all the others had been, but sheer rubbish, made up words and random sounds. As I brought the performance to a close, the lady in the corner of the compartment dropped her book into her lap to reveal a bright red face that was laughing hysterically.

"Please!" she gasped in perfect English. "No more!"

Deniz, alarmed, had to give her his bottle of water which she accepted, and then took a minute to compose herself.

"I am sorry," she said finally, turning to me, "that you have come across such an unsophisticated farm boy, but truly he deserved everything he got, as his behaviour when I first arrived was very bad. But honestly, I have not been so entertained since I went to the theatre in Ankara some years ago. You played your part so well, and how you managed to keep a straight face the whole time! I was almost dying of a heart attack trying to hold it in."

Apparently, she particularly loved the story of the Scots and their strangled cats and jangling bits and was very much looking forward to recounting it at her next dinner party. As for my gibberish, she said, "That nearly killed me off while I held my breath in fear of making a sound."

Deniz couldn't understand what we were saying in English as he looked from one to the other, before finally asking me what language this was now that I was speaking so fluently.

"He has made a complete fool of you!" the woman said sternly, getting up from her seat and giving him two good whacks with her book. He did not complain. The young man, to his credit, seemed to have learnt his lesson, and we settled in for what was still a long journey yet in this creaky old puffer that struggled to climb most gradients.

So slow was it that Deniz had time to jump off into a field of watermelons, pilfer one and bring it back on board with him. The woman, who turned out to be a school teacher, chastised him again.

"Stealing now?" she said with a look only a teacher can give. "What does that say of you? I'm sure that your father would not approve."

But I couldn't help but notice that she didn't refuse a slice of juicy melon when it was offered to her.

When we finally arrived in Ankara many hours later, I made my way to the hotel only to find Dad sitting in the dining room finishing his dinner.

Cars were much faster than trains in those days.

Chapter Sixteen
Heaven and Hell
2012

The mind is its own place and in itself, can make a Heaven of Hell, a Hell of Heaven.

~ John Milton

They say a little aspirin a day helps the heart work easier; it thins the blood and that in turn helps the red stuff to swish around the body. But wait. Not so fast, before you reach for the medicine cabinet, remember what we learnt earlier about listening to the experts.

It all started one morning whilst chopping kindling for our wood burner. I remember emerging from the warmth of the house in my shirt and jogging trousers and being plunged into a wall of snow. There I was, my head bobbing up and down with each stroke of the hand axe as I split logs one after the other, and after a short while, I began to feel faint and breathless. Something was definitely wrong.

I stood up with a wobble, feeling as though I might collapse at any moment, and managed to drag myself back to the house and threw myself on to the couch where I just lay taking deep breaths and wondering what the hell was going on. Then a few minutes later I felt fine again, got on with my day and thought nothing more of it. Unknown to me at that time, it would mark the first steps of a most remarkable journey.

Over the next few weeks, however, that feeling that there was something wrong returned sufficiently often that I was moved to visit the doctor. I had ascribed the headaches I was experiencing more and more to the pain I periodically put up with from the damaged disc in my neck and self-medicated with a couple of pain tablets. The doctors, on the other hand, thought it might be heart trouble and sent me to the hospital. Well, they seemed to be very thorough; checked my heart, then my breathing, a chest X-ray and a CT scan, then blood tests and goodness knows what else. In the end, though the experts could find nothing wrong with me and I was given a clean bill of health.

I must be fine, I thought. So why did I still feel a little shaky on my feet? Moreover, why, once in a while, would I stop driving and hand over the wheel to Barbara because I didn't feel able to safely continue? My eyes felt heavy at times, yet while I looked tired, I slept well enough.

"Something is going on that is making me feel ill," I would say from time to time. But rather than be accused of being a hypochondriac I kept my complaining to a minimum and muddled through my work as best I could. In retrospect, this was just asking for trouble.

Feeling helpful one day, I decided to sweep out Barbara's car. A few leaves and a little dust later, satisfied with my handy work, I stood up to admire the effect and clonked the back of my head hard on the inside of the door jam. Stars burst forth in front of my eyes and danced with me for a little while, but soon enough they were gone and, yet again, I thought nothing more of it. We all bang our heads from time to time and it's soon forgotten. Human beings aren't the most graceful of creatures, in spite of what we might like to believe.

The feeling of not being well, continued to grow. I was struggling to keep things together. Dealing with several problems at a time was normal for me, but suddenly it was becoming harder and harder to concentrate. Then one morning I slept in.

So what? you say. People sleep in all the time. And of course, you're right, but I don't. At least not on a Monday morning when there's work to be done. Eight o'clock came and went, and Barbara left me thinking that I had looked tired lately and the sleep would do me good. By ten-thirty she began to wonder if there was a problem and shook my shoulder gently, asking if I was going to actually get up or stay in bed all day. She would later explain that this was a joke meant to comfort her, as she had never in all our years known me to stay in bed this late.

"Are you ok?" she asked, finally.

"I'm feeling fine," I replied. She knew this was no help, as I would always answer the same way no matter how I was feeling, as the coming events would demonstrate.

"Do you want to see the doctor?" asked Barbara.

"I'm feeling fine," I repeated, hauling myself out of bed and pulling on my clothes.

"You haven't showered," said Barbara, looking worried. I simply stared at her blankly. Ordinarily, I shower each morning, but on this occasion somehow that was forgotten. Having been informed of this oversight, I'm told that I turned around, went into the dressing room and splashed water on my face before heading to the office and attempting, unsuccessfully, to turn on the computer at my desk. I say I'm told that's what happened because I have absolutely no memory of it, but evidently watching me fumble feebly for the power button on the computer for several minutes was what finally prompted Barbara to call the doctor and make an emergency appointment.

Having carried out a few tests, the doctor gave Barbara a note and suggested that we get over to Lewisham Hospital immediately. An ambulance was suggested but the boys were both waiting anxiously in the reception area and they could get me there quicker, and so with one son on each side of me, holding my arms to make certain I did not collapse, I was marched out of the surgery and into the car.

At the hospital, they conducted a CT scan of my head, and then sometime later, a doctor emerged to give my wife the news that I had a subdural hematoma and would be transferred to Kings College Hospital, which is a few miles away and has an excellent neurological unit, he said. They had people come in from all over the country to be treated for this sort of thing, so she shouldn't worry as I would be in the best possible hands. They would arrange for me to be transferred over there as soon as possible, as the bleed was substantial and he considered it to be an emergency.

"You're going to have an emergency operation" Barbara informed me. Under normal circumstances, words that are likely to produce a strong reaction, yet I simply stared into thin air as though lost in a daydream.

"You alright John?" asked Barbara, the worry in her voice unmistakable.

"I'm alright," I replied softly.

About an hour later, the doctor returned to relay his dealings with the powers that be at Kings' Neurological Unit.

"There's good news and bad news," he began. "The surgeon at Kings has seen the CT scan and believes the haematoma to be chronic. That means that it looks stable and has likely been there for some time." Was this the good news? Apparently so. The black blob, the size of an orange they had seen on the CT scan was congealed blood, in which case there was no active haemorrhage and no immediate rush to send me off for that emergency operation. They would find me that bed as soon as possible, and until then I would be moved from my present position atop a gurney behind a curtain in A&E to a side ward to make room for new patients.

"But, Doctor," Barbara protested, "he seems to be getting worse."

The doctor leant over, looked into my eyes and asked, "How do you feel, Mr Emin?"

"I'm alright," I replied as usual.

"I'm sure he's alright," the doctor said to Barbara. "If he gets worse, just call for somebody, but there's really nothing to worry about." And with that, he was gone again.

For the rest of that day, whenever a nurse asked how I felt I would answer the same way I always do, and they would say cheerfully, "He's responding well!" before moving on. That night, surrounded by concerned family visitors all asking how I felt, I am reliably told that I simply answered, "I'm fine," as though on an automatically recorded loop, staring back at whoever asked the question as though I didn't recognise them at all. My first cousin, with whom I grew up with, solemnly told the rest of the family that this bleed on the brain was not good news and that I would not be the same should I survive.

"He's gone," he whispered to Barbara before offering her a supportive hug.

Barbara offered me a sip of water and, when I failed to respond at all, called over a nurse.

"How are you, Mr Emin?" the nurse asked in a loud voice as if I were deaf.

"Fine," I replied automatically.

"See," said the nurse, "he's fine." Then she gave Barbara a smile and went about her business.

It was getting late now, we'd had no word from Kings and not a single doctor had approached me the rest of that day. As Barbara left my bedside to go home that night I was still sitting propped by the pillows, fully clothed.

Tuesday more family arrived to pay their respects in what everyone now seemed to believe were my final days, especially after Dell had told them point-blank that I would never recover. I had not moved for some time and my voice was impaired. Later in the evening, with my daughter and her husband John to my right and Barbara to my left, I began weakly to point my finger to the foot of my bed and jab the air as if I were seeing and talking to someone. My mouth was slowly moving though nothing came out. Amused by this theatre Barbara leant over me, blocking my view of whatever I was seeing. My arm tried to brush her away, resulting in a little laugh from those gathered around the bed.

"What was that all about?" asked my daughter Sarah, after I had finally closed my eyes and appeared to fall fast asleep.

"The only time he ever pointed like that," Barbara replied, "was at his father after he'd caught him doing something he shouldn't."

My condition apparently still worsening, Barbara again demanded to see a doctor. At first, the registrar was short with her. She didn't understand how the system worked, he said. The consultant at Kings had diagnosed me as not being in any immediate peril, and we would just have to wait for a bed there to become available. But then upon examining me himself, he quickly changed his opinion.

"He shouldn't have deteriorated like this," he said, peering at the CT scan. "A chronic condition wouldn't cause that."

He contacted Kings, who insisted that they knew best and requested a little more patience while they cleared their backlog and found some room for me. The registrar however, convinced there was something badly wrong, ordered another more detailed CT scan and, while he waited for it to be carried out, rang around a couple of other neurological units looking for a bed.

"Go home and get some sleep," he told Barbara as midnight came and went, "I'll call you if anything changes." Three-thirty am the phone rings. It was the doctor who told Barbara that I was being transferred as they spoke to St Georges at Tooting for an emergency operation. That second CT scan showed that there was indeed fresh blood at the site of the clot and that this was raising the pressure in my skull and squeezing my brain like a sponge.

Now here's the kicker. Had there not been a second bleed the problem would likely have resolved itself in time as the body has the ability to absorb bleeds in most cases. It was the continual aspirin I was taking for the benefit of my health that allowed that little bleed to continue, drop-by-drop, increasing the pressure within my skull and leading me right to the brink of death's door.

Experts, eh?

I am awake. I am calm. I look around me. I realise that I am lying in a hospital bed, flat on my back, not sure why. Am I in pain? No. Must stay calm. What could it be? A car accident maybe? Is something broken? I move my feet, legs and arms. All feel okay. I move my back and that seems fine. What on earth is going on? I touch my face, that too seems fine, except for the oxygen mask. An oxygen mask? And now what is this poking out the back of my head? Something metal sticking out to the left-hand side a few inches from my ear, a drain as it happens. There is a tube attached to it.

Oh well, at least I'm in the right place. I'm certain all will be made clear in time.

I might just close my eyes and relax. Why make a fuss?

Next thing I know, a jovial Nigerian ward sister is standing over me. "Nice to see you are with us at last, Mr Emin!" her happy voice echoes around the ward. Afterwards, I will smile whenever I think of her. "Are you happy, Mr Emin?" she asks. "You look happy. Come on, say you are happy!" she demands, laughing. I give her full marks for trying to raise my spirits, but she need not have worked so hard. I am always quick to see the funny side of most situations.

"What happened to me?" I ask. "Why am I here?"

"You'll have to ask the doctor when he comes around," she replied cheerfully, and then she was gone.

A short while later a male nurse came over. He introduced himself as Ian and asked if was ok to see my brother. *Bloody hell,* I thought, *do I have a brother? I don't remember that at all, my condition must be worse than I imagined.*

"I'd love to," I reply, not wanting to appear discourteous to the brother I didn't even realise I had. While I waited for him to arrive, I did a quick count of all the immediate family members I was sure I knew; Barbara, Denis, Sarah, Lawrence, named all of my grandchildren...Mum, Dad, my two sisters, but no brother. Who should come sauntering down this small ward but my cousin Dell? "Hi, John," he says. "How are you?"

"*Who* are you?" I ask

"Don't you remember me?" he replied.

"They tell me you're my brother," I say. "I just can't remember."

"Can you move?" he asks.

"Yes, of course," I say, I look up at him again. "What did you say your name was?" He seems too upset to reply at once.

"Bloody hell, Dell," I say cheerfully, raising my right arm to retrieve a box of tissues and offering him one, "you look as though you're about to burst into tears, what the hell is going on?"

"You sod!" he exclaims. "You do know who I am and you're having fun with me, I had to say I was your brother in case they didn't let me in. You scared the hell out of me! In fact, you frightened the hell out of all of us."

"Hello, Mr Emin," says the surgeon hovering over me now. "How do you feel?" There are more doctors clustered around the bed on both sides, and I wonder for one bemused moment what can be so special about my case to interest them all so. They didn't look like trainees. Well, one or two maybe, but the rest must have some years behind them.

"Well, Doctor," I reply, "I think I'm fine."

"What day is it?" he asks quickly, throwing me slightly off-guard.

"Well," I begin hesitantly, "yesterday was Sunday so naturally today must be Monday." It strikes me as funny that I actually had to work it out that way.

Not satisfied with that he then asked me some stock questions, my date of birth, the current month and year. Having answered him, he then asked, "Do you know where you are, Mr Emin?"

"To be honest, Doctor, apart from being flat on my back in a hospital bed, I have absolutely no idea where I am and how I got here. It seems an accident of some kind has befallen me, but no one has given me any details so I do hope you can enlighten me a little."

The doctors all exchange glances, then they smile and nod. Some sort of consensus, it seems, has been reached, but I am still none the wiser. He then went on to explain my condition and prognosis.

"By the way," said the surgeon, "it's Wednesday. But you're going to be just fine."

The doctors all disperse, leaving only a junior surgeon behind. He's the one who operated on me under supervision, as it turns out, drilling two burr holes in to my skull to drain the blood and relieve the pressure on my poor brain.

"Was I in danger?" I ask. "You were very lucky indeed, you came to us just in time. It was within this side or that side of the scalpel," he replies, cryptically.

"What do you mean?" I ask, and he explains by way of placing his hands on my knee to replicate the procedure, then mouthing the word 'whoosh' and pulling them both away suddenly to press his fingers over his face. Apparently, the pressure in my skull was so great that he had been caught off guard and got covered in blood and cranial fluid when the dam broke. He also explained that, so serious was my condition that they all expected to find a vegetable should I come around. Those nods and smiles now made some sense, at least.

The following morning, Thursday 5th April 2012, would mark the beginning of two days when I would be privileged to encounter Heaven and Hell in equal measure.

The breakfast trolley was doing its rounds and I heard that porridge was on the menu, along with tea and orange juice. Both drinks came in plastic cups with bent straws so that patients lying down can drink, but the porridge proved an altogether more problematic proposition. I still had fluid draining from my skull and had to lie virtually flat on my back. I could smell this porridge; it was sitting there waiting for me to eat it. But I also knew that, had I tried to eat it, dollops of milk and porridge would no doubt cover the bed. I needed help, but I could see the nurses were very busy dealing with other patients and some of them were gravely ill so I chose to drink my tea through the straw and relax. Porridge could wait another day.

"You didn't eat your porridge, Mr Emin," remarked nurse Janet, when they came round to collect the breakfast trays. "Didn't you feel like it today?"

"Maybe tomorrow," I replied as the cold porridge was taken away. There was no point in making a fuss. I was lucky to be alive and no doubt getting better by the minute. So I was a little hungry, so what? *Rest and think nice things, and you'll be out of here before you know it.* I can do that, no problem.

Then it began.

It was a bright day outside, and the sun streaming in through the windows gave a warm, orange tint to the blindness of having my eyes closed, which was soothing and comfortable. Then in a flash, the colours began to come. First, it was very much like seeing a multicoloured canvas.

Shocked at what I had just seen, I opened my eyes and the vision stopped. Was I hallucinating? I looked around the ward to get a good dose of reality and then closed my eyes to see if it happened again. It did. However, this time there were also trees, grass, walls, and a street scene. Was I dreaming? The colours were brilliant, like a Walt Disney film, and there were people as well. One drove by in a fantastic looking car, looked at me and waved as if he knew me.

"Good morning, Mr Emin. How are you today?"

A voice beside me made my eyes snap open. The doctor and several others had assembled around my bed, and I had been so engrossed by the colours and everything I was seeing that I had not sensed them approach.

"Yes, sir," I replied, smiling, "I feel fine."

"Did we disturb you from an agreeable dream, Mr Emin?" he asked, to some laughter. "You seemed to be in a happy place."

"Not a dream doctor," I replied, "but I've just had the most amazing hallucination while I was wide awake. Is that normal?"

"Probably the drugs," he replied, with a knowing smile, "not to worry. A day or two should sort that out." And again they were gone.

Well, yes, common sense dictates that the drugs they must have given me in the operating theatre must be pretty potent things. Hallucination or not, what I was seeing was amazing, so I resolved to simply relax and enjoy it for as long as it lasted. It was infinitely better than high definition television, that's for sure. The colours were brilliant, the grass the most beautiful I had ever seen, there were a multitude of meadow flowers, the whole picture was beautiful beyond anything I have ever previously experienced.

Yet there was a little problem. People in the dream were seeing me too as if I were actually there with them. They were acknowledging me with a smile and a wave. I seem to be the new guy on the block and everyone wanted to welcome me to the neighbourhood. Maybe I was as much a ghost to them as Pop was to me years ago when I saw him by the side of my bed. Was my soul travelling to this place, just as those that have actually died, their hearts stopped and their souls depart in a moment to reach that Heaven they claim they have seen? Was my soul giving me a tour of some of the strangeness that surrounds us all though we seldom see it for what it really is?

Every time I closed my eyes, a completely different scene would appear. I had no control as to what the next one might be. There was one breathtaking moment when I closed my eyes to see what would be next and I found myself on the ground, then in a flash seemed to travel backwards at tremendous speed to find myself looking down on earth, which appeared the size of a football. My eyes sprang open in sheer surprise. In another scene, I found myself at a gathering in some sort of walled garden with lots of flowers and trees, a most beautiful place. I stood at the periphery of this gathering with a total sense of calm, wondering how this was possible. Everything seemed so real, so clear, as though it were in high definition. To test myself I brought my hands together and scratched my left-hand palm, there was pain. I stretched my arms wide and strained the muscles as you might do first thing in the morning. I was clearly awake whilst I was viewing all before me. How could I make up images such as these I thought? I felt connected to everything and everyone. These were all strangers to me, yet I seemed to know them. One by one the nearest to me stopped talking, looked at me and gave me a knowing nod and a smile.

I must say that this acceptance by these kindly and smiling people left me a little uncertain. I was constantly trying to reason this new reality. If I was a director of a film and planning filming a scene such as this, there is no way my mind could have imagined all the intricate little things that I saw. I seemed to be aware of everything in the smallest detail.

Then looking around and further into the midst of those gathered, there were people that I instinctively knew though I could not recognise them for some odd reason. Strangely, all these people in this colourful and beautiful place were rather dull, more like grey, devoid of colour which struck me as being very odd.

I concentrated on one or two faces. I looked hard then saw the side of my father's face which lit up in brilliant colour for a second or two. *That is my father*, I thought and chuckled to myself.

Then, on recognising my father there was a definite change, first one then another of those near me looked up from what they were doing, smiled, and shook their heads slowly to indicate a 'no'. The message was clear. I was to go no further. Yet, I wanted to walk into this gathering anyway and reach my father, and speak to him if I could. For some reason I had an urge to look down at my feet, I remember giving a little laughing snort through my nose as there were no feet or for that matter no legs arms or anything at all. How weird.

I decided that I would move towards him. As I did so there was this overwhelming realisation that I should not go further. I felt as if I were a gate-crashing guest to a party, there seem to be unwritten rules that I instinctively knew and I was about to break. This was too much. I flicked my eyes open.

"Mr Emin?" came a voice from the side of my bed, it was the nurse who had come to take my blood pressure.

Drat, I thought. It might have been fun to talk to Dad, hallucination or not.

Blood pressure and temperature taken, I tried to get back into my adventure. I lay there and relaxed as before, though this time, in an attempt to control where I went by keeping my eyes open for a while and thinking of my father before I closed them. Nothing happened. I saw nothing but the light through my eyelids. Maybe I was trying too hard. However, the ability to hallucinate at will had left me. Oh well. It was fun while it lasted, but now it was time to move on.

Friday morning went just as the day before; bed bath, sheets changed, new bedclothes and Janet the nurse actually helped feed me my porridge that day, which was a pleasant surprise. The gaggle of doctors came and went with a "well that sounds good, very well, Mr Emin," after I had told them that the hallucinations had stopped late Thursday afternoon. Not much happened that day until the afternoon when it was nap time. All was quiet, with everyone apparently either dozing or asleep. I have never been able to sit still for long. Time has always been my enemy. For me, there is never enough time to do all that I wish to do in any given day. Yet, here I lay virtually fixed in one spot where I could not even fidget if I had a mind to.

I closed my eyes to try to sleep. *Wham.* Black triangular shapes; small, large, all moving around in some sort of pattern. Shocked, I opened my eyes once again and wondered what the hell that was all about. Determined to get to the bottom of this, I relaxed once again and closed my eyes to be immediately met with the most remarkable vision I had ever seen in my life. It was breathtaking by its grandeur.

A huge, slow-turning whirlpool of what looked like black tar. It must have been at least the size of a football field. There before me, I could see a cast bronze elephant standing astride long ways along the edge on the other side of this pool, its front and rear legs stretched far apart to form an arch. It must have been fifty feet tall. I wondered at the enormity of the casting process of such a large piece of bronze. Nothing on earth could make such a thing, material, furnaces, labour the questions just mounted in my mind. Everything was once again in high definition and every little part was one shade of black or another. I could not do justice to the picture I was seeing. There was an extreme beauty in the scene that simply took my breath away.

There were palm trees, once again different shades of black and white. On the far end to me there were people walking to the side and hesitating and then slipping down the edge of the rim feet first, some simply diving in headfirst and sticking in half way. There were dogs and horses, and helpers that stayed at the edge that were black from head to toe' their faces hidden by the drooping hoods they all wore. In this very slow whirling mass of black tar, there were little bits of colour that would slowly vanish as they sank. That chap that dived in headfirst was wearing a brilliantly coloured white and blue striped jumper, he was swirling around in slow motion with his elbow and twitching right leg not quite engulfed yet by the black mass. A beautiful chestnut horse, its head under the tar, kicking as it sank very, very slowly.

Completely mesmerised by all this, I also knew instinctively that this was a dangerous and forbidden place for me. I should not be there, I knew that. Yet, the splendour of form in all that I saw was hard to turn away from. I did not wish to leave immediately, as for me this experience was once in a lifetime.

This was Hell or at least what the mind would make of it. I have always said that we make our own Hell or Heaven on this earth ourselves, yet what I was witnessing was far too complicated for me to even begin to believe I could put together all that I had seen in my poor tired mind.

I began to experiment and had several visions if I can call them that. As I said, all I had to do was close my eyes and it would begin, then merely open them to stop what I was seeing. The dark theme was the same each time, another page of the same book.

In one, I was sitting on a low wall which made up the edge of a walkway, with another similar wall on the other side of a eight-foot wide path and every so often square oak posts rising a couple of feet above peoples heads forming a pergola design. There were no roses or any form of growth that I could see, this was a bleak scene and this time the sharpness and clarity of the picture was diminished to the grade of an old black and white film; not exactly grainy though nevertheless notably different to the clearer pictures I had encountered earlier.

It was winter, overcast and drab, and people had heavy coats on. They could be seen walking across the park, no one waved as before. I was watching the passing people scurrying this way and that. Then on the outside of this path on the other side of the wall, four men appeared arm in arm, framed by two of the oak posts. They were smiling and looking at me. This was becoming very personal now. For the first time, there were people that came towards me. We were uncomfortably close. They could hop over that wall in an instant.

I kept my nerve and pinched the skin above my elbow to ensure I was still fully awake. Whatever was happening in my mind also raised my apprehension to a high level. These were glimpses of Hell, which my always-enquiring mind would seek to understand. Opportunities like this are seldom offered so reasoned to hold tight and face this new reality. I said it again to myself, what possible harm could come to me, though I knew I was playing with something I had absolutely no previous experience of. Yet somehow I felt there was a truth in what was happening and that I ought to be cautious, lest my very soul was put in jeopardy.

The figure to my far left, who had a free arm, pointed it at me and they all chuckled. This was so very different to the brilliant scenes I had seen before. These men seemed ageless and all had black overcoats, the one to the far left had large black buttons running down. These people were acknowledging my presence. As far as they were concerned, I was there with them, yet my body was still safely on that hospital bed. As hard as I tried to reason all this in my mind I just could not get over the complex nature of what I saw.

My eyes still closed I wondered if I should open them and cut this one short. Then I thought these people whoever they are, are smiling at me constantly and seemingly friendly. I kept looking and wondered who they might be and from where they had come from. As if to answer that question, the far left person turned and had a few words with the others, they all smiled, as if in agreement, then the free arm began to point once again in different directions. First, to the east, then the west the south and north, the sky then the earth and they laughed and chuckled and then he pointed his arm outstretched at me with clenched hand and one finger pointing accusingly. Why point at me? I thought, *what possible connection did I have with these people?*

His face started to change, as did the one next to him and the others all followed suit. Within seconds, that first chap had turned into the ugliest demon you could imagine. That was it for me, I was out of there, eyes opened and it all stopped.

I was genuinely frightened by what I had seen and I am certain others in the ward must have heard me gasp as I extricated myself from that encounter. It took a little while for me to calm down but I was not going to give up so easily.

My thoughts were to gently apply this ability if you can call it that, and pull away if it becomes even slightly scary. As before, I closed my eyes and immediately there was a moving picture. This time it was hard to make out two females stooping over a table with a black pot upon it. One person handed the other a wad of bank notes. There were actual words that I could hear.

"Sorry not this time," said the figure receiving the cash.

"There will be another time," replied the other. Then it hit me. That's my half-sister Tracey. What the hell is she doing in my delusion, fantasy, hallucination? Call it what you like, what the hell?

Was there a lesson to learn? Is this where my poor lonely little sister's soul resides while she goes about her business, could it be true that the living and dead are not so far apart? Could it be that Hitler's soul resided in Hell while he killed millions? What a thought.

My eyes shunted open and I stared at the ceiling for a few seconds trying to piece together that last encounter. I could not immediately make sense of what I had seen. Gone was this brilliant definition, gone were the intricate little things within the scenes, gone was my ability to interact or be seen this last time, but now there were words as clear as if I was standing at the end of that table.

Following that last encounter, no matter how hard I tried, there was nothing further. Months have passed and still nothing. Reason suggests that what I experienced were hallucinations brought on by the chemicals used in the operating theatre, though if that were so why did they not start on the Wednesday after the operation? Why the gap? Also, more to the point, why on two different days, for an hour or so?

This is where I raise my head above the parapet a little and try to reason what actually happened. Given that I have now a propensity to believe in ghosts, where I have questioned where they reside in the overall scheme of things. Then the strange events following that epic dowsing session on the Cyprus mountainside, where members of my family twice swear to have seen my spirit as solid as you and I appear to them and then after a while disappear, although I was actually two thousand miles away. Yes, that spirit of mine was doing things that I was not aware of, though I was most certainly awake each time.

For someone such as I who has virtually always expected proof before entertaining some strange notion, this last encounter with the extraordinary has left me with more questions than answers, yet my mind is saying you were very privileged to have been shown these places. Maybe I need help, but then who cares? I have witnessed something that very few have. Yes, me the hard-nosed pragmatist, that would have said we do not have a spirit, that we are merely lumps of meat, a mechanism to make things. Clever monkeys, that's all. Clever monkeys we may be, though I have now come to the conclusion that we do not recognise a fraction of who we are and our potential.

Strange as it might sound, whilst the description I gave of these encounters was accurate to the best of my knowledge in both cases there was also a definite feeling that as colourful and beautiful as I found the first session, somehow I felt very strongly that this was not the final place we go, but rather more of a waiting room. There were two very different aspects, just as real as each other. My father was in some form of Heaven, where it was beautiful, bright and colourful, conversely, my little half-sister was in some kind of Hell where it was black and white which devoured colour with an atmosphere of fear and gloom. The problem for me is that there were man-made things all around me. There were cars, houses, walls along with streets and street furniture. These were all things I could relate to. Could I trust what I saw or was it a figment of my imagination, conjured up to give meaning to what would otherwise be something that mankind could not even begin to understand, or was what I saw another dimension? I could not interfere with what was happening there. I could not walk up and chat with my father. It was as if I were a temporary guest. What seems very real to me is that whatever I saw along with those that have given their own version of what is nowadays called a near-death experience is a reality of some form, as all have a very similar story to tell.

What was the purpose? Already I have alluded to the thought that we all are two things. Firstly the throwaway lump of skin and bone we see in the mirror that eventually turns to the dust we all came from. The clever people think that is all there is of us. Others believe that there is something greater that moves on to a higher place. The one uniting thought in those and virtually all other religions is that we have a spirit, a soul that moves on. Many millions, possibly billions, believe in the soul moving to some kind of Heaven.

Those people that have related their near-death experiences to us have, no doubt in my mind, experienced their spirit moving to another place that their minds could make sense of.

Some say they have visited Hell and that Christ held out his hand and pulled them out and back to the living for them to tell the story and no doubt mend their ways from there on.

So with that thought in mind, I would suggest that NDE stories are in the main real, though they only represent what we expect to see and that would make some kind of sense to us. I hasten to add again, the real picture may very well not be understood.

Maybe I am completely wrong but, I am beginning to believe that dead or alive our essence dwells in another place and that place reflects the person you are today. So it isn't a matter of going to Heaven or Hell when we die, as your essence is already there, all we need to do is understand the truth of who and what we are right now. Are you a kind charitable person that sees beauty in most things? Or, are you mean and consider no one but yourself.

Is the world a dark and foreboding place for you? All this might tell you where your soul resides while you go about the arduous business of living in what can be a difficult world. Our Heaven or Hell is here and now, we make choices that place us in one camp or another. Don't know if there is any merit in all that, though it feels right, following my experiences. Why do I think that? I return to the thought that without my conscious knowledge my spirit went off and did its own thing thousands of miles away, time and distance having no meaning. We seem to be two distinct entities. One able to do things that we can only marvel at.

I firmly now believe that the spirit can travel and leave the body. We human beings have absolutely no idea yet what we are and what we are destined for. We are made up of two components, what we see in the real world and an essence that is not of this world at all but another place which for convenience I will suggest is another dimension that we have yet to get to grips with. For me, at least, this all adds to the strangeness of life that we so often shrug off as just one of those things.

Chapter Seventeen
Meat on a Stick

Mad inventors? You have to be a bit mad sometimes to dream up new ideas, as pure logic rarely unfolds new concepts.

~ John Emin

You may have come to the conclusion from reading this book that I am as mad as a hatter. If so, I shall choose to take it as a compliment. A great many of mankind's spectacular achievements have been conceived by people thought by their contemporaries to be stark raving bonkers.

Not that I am comparing myself with Socrates of course, or Einstein, or Sir Isaac Newton, who rendered himself clinically insane once by boiling up several pounds of mercury in his study just out of curiosity. Still, there is always the chance that all the pieces of the perpetual energy machine in my garage will fall into place someday and I might make that leap in the collective consciousness from mad inventor to genius. I say leap, but it's really the finest of fine lines and every true inventor knows it.

I have written this book for two reasons. Well, three really I suppose. The first was that it helped me pass the time after the car accident when I couldn't sleep. The second was to share some of the stranger and (hopefully) more interesting events of my life. And the third, most important reason, was to try to inspire others to re-examine the unusual events of their own lives with fresh eyes and thereby, help kindle a new spirit of discovery and wonder in a world that has grown increasingly stagnant in the realm of dreams and ideas.

To that end then, this final chapter is not really about me at all, but about you. I hope that you will recognise elements of yourself and your own life in the conclusions drawn and questions posed here, and consider what your experiences might be able to tell us about the future of mankind and what we are really all about.

It begins with an approach. I hesitate to call it the Emin Approach for fear of appearing vain, but then again when one writes a book about one's self, perhaps it is already too late for that. I can say at least that it is an approach, my father would well have recognised, being that it involves stepping back from the invisible fence blocking a particular train of thought and attempting to find creative, alternative solutions. It also involves trusting your instincts, something the old man always believed in even when his instincts nearly got him killed on several occasions.

Perhaps then we might call it the way of the open-minded pragmatist, one who demands a degree of proof before entertaining a particular notion, but then once entertained does not let contemporary conventional wisdom cloud out what they have seen with their own two eyes.

For example, I have seen a ghost in our house, several times throughout the years. For me, that's just a matter of fact. I saw Pop clearly with my own eyes, as did my son and his wife who saw him two feet away as solid as you and me for several seconds before he faded away, and then there were my other two children. He was our uninvited guest for over thirty years and was almost part of the family. My son also claims to have seen me as a doppelganger in my office when I was actually thousands of miles away, and Dad almost had a heart attack when I appeared in front of him under similar circumstances. Now, there are a hundred and one possible explanations for such occurrences and I'm sure they have all been examined at some point or another. But the truth is, the thought processes we have all been taught since we were little precluded us from entertaining any of those explanations that do not tally with current scientific thinking – what we know we know, to borrow a famous phrase.

This is a problem for me because nothing that could be described as hard scientific fact can adequately describe what I experienced for myself on several occasions, which is fine, because actually, logically you would not expect it to. If everything were explainable with science, it would mean that we had reached the end of human discovery and knew everything we were ever going to know. Moreover, despite various pronouncements of so-called thinkers in recent time, most sane people would agree that that is extremely unlikely to be the case. Therefore, we are left turning to the unknown for solutions, which the establishment frowns upon.

Well, all right, so current science cannot explain the existence of ghosts. But quantum physicists are seriously venturing the notion of alternative realities, built upon string theory and other such strangeness, such as the reports by people, after having a near-death experience. Have we not wondered why these reports fall into a narrow band of afterlife activities? Why are the stories so predictable? Why are we not surprised any longer at what we hear? Does this add strength to the notion that these people experienced something very real? If there are indeed many other worlds all sharing the same physical space as ours, why could they not cross over with each other?

To look at the problem from the perspective of the open-minded pragmatist then, we should start with what we (in this case I) know to be true. I saw a ghost (or at least a phenomenon that I will describe as a ghost). It appeared and disappeared before my very eyes. These are the facts, so what are the possibilities? A) I am completely mad. Unlikely, despite what my wife might tell you. And besides, many other people with no history of mental health problems have reported seeing ghosts too, so let's go ahead and rule that one out. B) Pop was really there. Your brain is having a problem now because you are not supposed to accept something so ridiculous in the context of conventional wisdom. Yet, it seems here to be the most likely to be true. How about that?

Assuming Pop was real then, where did he come from? Why was he not there all the time? How was this, seemingly solid then transparent figure of him able to exist without his physical body? All of these questions too have many possible answers, but I believe that some are vastly more likely than others, based on what I know, what I have experienced, and what my instincts tell me.

When I first saw him by the side of my bed, Pop was just nodding thoughtfully as if to say, "okay I know this is my bedroom, but someone else is in it now…" I had the distinct impression that he was following the likely events through in his mind, but without fear or agitation, just completely calm and accepting of what was going on. Wherever he had come from, and whichever plane of existence he was currently occupying at that moment, he obviously was not in any pain. He had no need to eat or drink, or sleep, no worries at all by the look of him, but was simply a little puzzled to find these strange people in his house.

On that occasion, the figure I saw did not interact with us in any physical way, but there was at least one other occasion when I was lying in bed trying to get to sleep and felt a very definite tickle just under my arm. Not a brush or something that may have been caused by the fabric of the sheets or whatnot, but the recognisable touch of several forceful fingers. My arm shot down like a triggered trap and I looked around quickly to find Barbara fast asleep, so it could not possibly have been her. Then I did just as we are trained to do when these strange things happen, I lay down again and decided to just forget about it. Then an afterthought popped into my head.

"Pack it in, Pop," I said sleepily, "it's not funny."

That happened to me just the once, but it definitely was not a dream as I was awake and fully conscious the whole time. Somehow, I just knew it was him.

So that experience suggests to me that these ghosts, or spirits, or whatever you want to call them, have at least a limited power to exert influence on our world. If Pop could touch me, presumably he could touch other objects too if he wanted. But wait, I don't expect you to take this all on faith in the light of my experience. Go ahead and ask your family and friends if they have ever seen a ghost, or witnessed some such occurrence that could not be explained. I think you will be surprised at the answers you get.

My carpet layer Richard was brought up by his grandmother, who each morning, when he was a lad, would give three knocks on his door, and then another single one, in order to wake him up for school. The same definite and recognisable pattern every morning, three and then one, always. Well, the lad grew up and became a man, and got himself a job, and Gran would keep waking him up, I suppose partly out of habit and partly just because that's what grandmothers do. The thing is, she didn't stop when she finally passed away to the consternation of his wife, but would return periodically to help her grandson get up in the mornings, with three knocks on his door and then another, just the same as always. This man told me that story without embarrassment or any indication that it was particularly out of the ordinary. Just one of those things that we all accept as truth without dwelling upon it.

Come to think of it, that story reminds me of another, related to me by my son Lawrence soon after returning home from a holiday in Spain with his wife Donna. Lawrence had called during the trip to let us know how much fun they were having, partying to the early hours and sleeping in till noon, and I remember worrying that they might miss their early flight home due to overdoing things on their last night there. They were both heavy sleepers as well, this being before they had children of their own to snap them out of that luxury habit.

Well, apparently, I must have been worrying more than I realised because I woke up a couple of times during that night to mumble, "I only hope he gets up in time" or some such before rolling over and dozing off again. It was not a good night's sleep, I can tell you that much.

"Lawrence, wake up or you'll be late!" I called out not long after dawn. This woke Barbara, who asked me if I was okay.

"You shouted loud enough," she said dryly. "I'm sure Lawrence heard you all the way over in Spain. Go back to sleep and stop worrying."

"Did you hear that? Did you hear it?" said a voice nearly a thousand miles away. Lawrence was shaking Donna to get up and get dressed quickly as they only had a few minutes before they had to be out of there and on their way to the airport. Their alarm clock had not gone off, but he had had a weird dream that I had shouted in his ear as though I were right next to him. Strangely, the words I'd used were exactly as Barbara heard me utter that very morning. This leads me to believe that we are all connected in some way, distance not being an obstacle.

There have been countless reports of inexplicable things happening where energy has clearly been expended to produce a solid form, move solid objects, or otherwise interact with our world in a way that we are unable to explain. I mention energy because I believe that it is the key to this particular puzzle. The energy that we expend ourselves, that flows about us every day in movement and sound and heat, powering our various electrical devices, that energy is all accounted for. It has to come from somewhere and it has to go somewhere. The first Law of Thermodynamics. Everyone knows that.

But the energy that causes these spirits to appear and all manner of other strange phenomena, that energy seems to come from somewhere else. It is not of this world if you follow my line of thinking.

Take the phenomena of Spontaneous Human Combustion (SHC). Experts who have studied SHC claim that it is an entirely explainable effect and will pour scorn upon anyone who dares suggest otherwise. The facts of the matter are far less clear-cut than they would have us believe. The burn is very precise, limited in physical terms in a way that combustion simply isn't anywhere else. Fire is a wild and unpredictable thing, capable of swallowing up a whole building in minutes given half the chance. Nevertheless, the burn in incidents of SHC seems to be controlled, without a visible controlling influence. Moreover, it burns ludicrously hot, much hotter than the furnaces they use at a crematorium. What could cause such a strange and violent, yet seemingly targeted reaction? Where does the energy for it come from?

I believe it may be a mixture of real physical energy, the energy that we know, and understand here in our world, and a dimensional energy (for lack of a better name) that is able to alter our world in a way that no scientist today understands. Spontaneous human combustion is more than just an oddity; it is rare, and cannot be replicated convincingly, using our current knowledge. This energy I talk of may pass between worlds, probably at the behest of some entity on the other side. The combination I would venture might catalyse a reaction in our world that caused the water in our bodies to break down into its component parts and burn at a molecular level, a controlled fire of an oxygen and hydrogen-fuelled burn would create the kind of temperatures necessary to vaporise a person, this could be a hint of where we might find limitless energy. Some witnesses to the phenomenon of spontaneous human combustion have soon after the event remarked that it was like a steam bath in the room which is to be expected if you burn hydrogen and oxygen as described. Now maybe I'm completely wrong, but this theory would go some way to explaining what it was that they found. Though I hasten to say again, something very strange must have happened in the process. The open-minded pragmatist would be forced to at least entertain it as a possibility, given what has been witnessed and experienced yet so far not adequately explained by conventional wisdom.

What if the spirit, or soul, is a real entity that exists in the same space and time as our bodies but on another plane, in another world as postulated by some quantum scientists? If it were distinct and separate, yet still tied to us, that would explain why Pop's 'ghost' was able to appear before me in his old house long after he died, and how my son could have seen me sitting in my office chair nodding away at him when I was actually far away. Time and distance seem capable of being manipulated from what I have seen and experienced, though hasten to add, some things we have learnt, things that we believe are fact, may not be so where time and distance are concerned.

For all intents and purposes, contrary to accepted wisdom, the crux of the matter might break down like this: time, distance and energy in the physical world are constant. But time, distance and energy in the alternative dimension are not constant. In some cases, the same ghost is reported over hundreds of years, so time might be of no consequence, nor distance as it seems I travelled two thousand miles in the blink of an eye to sit in my office chair to be seen as a solid person. As for the energy to do all this, maybe it is huge beyond common understanding. There seems to me to be no reason at all why the laws of physics might not be completely different in another plane of existence. And of course, the really exciting thing about this, if true, is that it might open a way for us to somehow combine the two dimensions to realise an infinite energy supply and possibly travel vast distances in a short while, and more importantly, 'in real time'. It sounds crazy, but then all of the great leaps in human understanding of the world sounded crazy the first time they were ventured. My point is if we can make ourselves collectively more open to the possibilities, and less inhibited by the chains of old knowledge, then logically we should be able to accelerate the process of discovery.

The soul is a concept that crops up over and over throughout history in civilisations that had no way of ever communicating with or knowing about each other. It is something that seems hard-wired into the human consciousness, and I for one do not believe such a thing could be merely a coincidence. If our very genes incline us towards something, there must be a reason. There must be. Now whether that reason is that we were created to believe in such things by a god, or some other form of creator, or some other reason entirely, I do not know. But there will be an answer, and one day human beings will know it, of that I am quite sure. I now question, does our soul reside within each of us or does it reside elsewhere whilst attached to us? Time and distance do not seem to matter from my experience of these things. I saw my deceased father in a place I would call a waiting place in Heaven and my half sister who is alive in Hell, is that where her soul resides, while she goes about her business? If my unusual NDE experience was a truth rather than a hallucination which showed me aspects of another reality then it seems to me that our souls reside either in the light or in the dark while we are either dead or alive. How strange. But from my viewpoint, it begins to make sense.

Have you ever seen a ghost? Which is a good starting point, if you have, you are certainly not alone. If so, what did you ascribe the experience to at the time? Tiredness perhaps, a trick of the light, daydreaming, actual dreaming, a moment of temporary insanity. These are all explanations that we tend to prefer even when we know deep down that they are not true. Nevertheless, we are afraid of the unknown, so when we experience it our minds at top speed assign a convenient name to the happening and before we know it, it is as good as, forgotten about. Filed away in the part of our brain, that we only access in the moments right before sleep, when for some reason our mental inhibitions seem to desert us fleetingly.

If not a ghost, then, perhaps you have experienced some other strange phenomena? Déjà vu maybe? Most of us experience that quite frequently, so much so in fact that we are barely even surprised when it happens. Nevertheless, it is legitimately an unexplained phenomenon. Some people will tell you that it is just a flaw in the human brain, an anomaly of memory and really nothing extraordinary at all. When pressed those same people will be forced to accept that this is only, to their minds, the most likely explanation. Maybe they are right. But then again maybe I am right when I suggest that déjà vu is a variation on what I experienced in that Portuguese casino. A form of precognition, the ability to see a few seconds into the future. How and for what purpose? Again, I couldn't say. Though it would be perfectly in keeping with nature's great catalogue of quite extraordinary survival instincts. It is widely believed by very reputable scientists that migratory birds possess a special form of sight that allows them to 'see' the Earth's magnetic fields, and that's why they don't get lost travelling vast distances. How is it that we accept that notion with barely a raised eyebrow and a couple of seconds before moving on to something else entirely in our minds, but we refuse to believe that human beings could possess similarly amazing abilities either as yet undiscovered or perhaps lain dormant for millennia?

In addition to the question of how such a thing as precognition might be possible, there is also, of course, the question of why it might be possible. Science is loathed to ascribe motive and purpose to a world that is supposed to be born of chaos and subject only to the power of chance. We do ourselves a disservice not to consider the possibility that there may be a method to the madness. Could it be that something, or someone, enabled me to put on such an impressive display in that casino in order to affect some desired result? Maybe it was a test of my resolve, to see if I would fall prey to the same sickness as the addicts around the table. To see if I could make that conscious choice between good and bad, or maybe the display was not for my benefit at all, but for theirs, for those people like the sweating man to see their choices for what they really were.

The idea of oracles predicting the future is as old as time, and again something that crops up in various civilisations completely unrelated to one another. Around the year 1558, Nostradamus wrote of a great war in which men who looked like monkeys would fly through the air spitting fire and communicating across great distances. Hundreds of years later the skies were full of aeroplane fighter pilots, with their strange rubber face masks and radios, raining down death upon the world. For me, the truly interesting question isn't so much if and how men like Nostradamus really could see the future, but rather why? For what purpose?

Experts can tell us many things, but cannot tell us infinitely more. A significant percentage of our DNA, up to 80% in fact, is known as non-coding DNA, or 'junk' DNA. This means that either it seems to fulfil no function whatsoever, or it does fulfil a function but we don't yet know what. If this fact alone does not knock your socks off, it is surely proof that we have as a species become desensitised to the wonders of our own bodies.

Why are we carrying around so much inactive or unexplained genetic material? Some people would say it is just a byproduct of evolution, perhaps a remnant from a time when our genetic ancestors had different needs and functions. Nobody really knows, but the open-minded pragmatist in me has a few suggestions.

My contention is simply that mankind is very advanced in evolutionary terms, I believe that we must have had an intervention at some time in the past, call it God or little green men or whatever you like, but some kind of intricate involvement with our DNA that produced modern human beings in our various forms, with a shared level of intellect. As far as I can tell, the theory of evolution does not even give us time, as a species and based on the timeline of the fossil record, to evolve into our many different races with distinct physical differences. Maybe we were all brought here from different places and implanted with the DNA of still higher beings, curtailed and 'switched off' in places so as to prevent us from running too fast, too soon. Who knows maybe we will learn to unlock those codes as we progress. Though I have the uncomfortable feeling that opening that door will be the tipping point for humanity.

Scientists have recently claimed to have discovered hitherto mysterious segments of DNA that control our life cycles, and put forth the possibility that manipulating this part of our genetic code may allow us to live longer, others have gone further, postulating that this 'junk' DNA may in fact control all manner of abilities we could scarcely dream of, such as self-healing and hyper-intelligence. But then, why do we have it the way it is now? It makes no sense. Unless this junk DNA is left over from whatever creature, or a God whose image we were created in. Or else given to us as part of a master plan and yet to be activated. What if the eureka effect is caused by a person's ability to temporarily, perhaps accidentally or perhaps by design, activate a tiny fragment of this junk DNA and thereby gain access to knowledge previously known only to our creator, yet present in each and every one of us if only we knew how to get to it at will.

Once you start thinking about mankind in these terms, it becomes reasonable to apply the junk DNA theory to other human phenomena besides the eureka effect. For example, during times of great stress, panic, fear etc., human beings have been known and observed to be capable of feats of superhuman strength, acts they could not otherwise have carried out such as lifting a bus off of a trapped child. People have seen these things happen, yet we have no satisfactory explanation for them. What if, in those moments of great stress, or fear, we unknowingly activate a portion of our junk DNA that grants us temporary access to these otherwise unexplainable powers?

Perhaps our bodies are merely vessels taking part in some great inter-dimensional experiment, created by some other life form to house the soul, which truly belongs in a different world to our own. Like a parasite, the soul needs a body to survive and so it hops from one to the next, a form of reincarnation if you like, driving humanity ever onwards to the fulfilment of our destiny when the souls have achieved their purpose. The idea of it is deeply troubling, no doubt, repulsive even. But if the body and soul are indeed linked but separate entities, as we must on the evidence contemplate seriously they may be, then we must also entertain the notion that the soul may have its own purpose and destiny somewhere that is not here. As for me the proof that we are all two separate entities, the lump of meat we see in the mirror each morning and the not so apparent other thing that seems to me to have a mind of its own. Without my knowledge, or in any way me being aware, people have witnessed me as a solid person interacting with them in England when on both occasions I was in Cyprus and fully awake. As a staunch pragmatist virtually all my life, I find it hard to say, my beliefs have changed, and now following that sort of proof feel that the inner person is for real and importantly has a mind of its own.

Have you ever looked into the eyes of a complete stranger and got the distinct impression that they are wise well beyond their years? Or held a newborn child and had the strangest feeling that this tiny person might not be quite so new to the world after all? If the soul is perpetual then its attachment to each individual person might be akin to the seasons of an apple tree which comes to life every spring, blossoms and brings forth flowers and fruit and then fades away again before the dark winter comes upon it. Some years will produce a bumper crop while others are lean and hard work, but this depends on the conditions and the care given to the tree.

The tree in this analogy is the soul, and each new season represents a new human being to which it belongs to for that brief period. The choices we make would have a lasting effect on the development of this intangible essence that carried through to future generations. Perhaps this would go some way to explaining what we perceive as the human development of our species, the idea that we collectively become more refined, more civilised (for lack of a better word) as time goes on. Human nature cannot rapidly evolve, according to Darwinian doctrine. Yet we as a species do seem to be evolving technologically, at least in many ways and at a rapid pace.

Reincarnation is a popular theme in the history of humanity, and I do not believe that this is an accident or coincidence. Clearly, others have seen and experienced things that led them to similar conclusions, and people in their droves have come to find something comforting and familiar in the idea of reincarnation, even if they do not clearly understand why.

When I met my wife, in a split second I knew that she was going to be the mother of my children. The realisation came to me like a shock of electricity, and even now I remember the moment clear as day, as being something deeply strange and inexplicable. But it turned out that I wasn't the only one puzzled by our feelings, as when Barbara, [18 years old and very shy] on our very first date, asked if I wanted to marry her, she said it was, "because I know you." She felt the same way, even if she too didn't understand what was going on. What if it was just our souls recognising people they had known before many lifetimes ago, and the physical shock I felt was caused by energy pulsing through from the alternate dimension where the soul resides?

Again, this all seems to me to make sense as a theory on the basis of what I have seen first-hand and heard from others whom I do not believe to be either liars or lunatics. It is not the only possible explanation of course, nor even necessarily the most likely. Perhaps you have ideas of your own on the subject. If not, why not? Have some ideas for goodness sakes; contemplate these things, which are at the very heart of what it is to be human. I am talking about experiences that ordinary people like you and I have from time to time, that we just gloss over and leave unexamined. Why do we do that? Let us examine them! The next time you have a déjà vu or witness something strange and unexplained, don't just wave it away with a convenient 'coincidence' or another such cop-out. Go back and replay the moment over, maybe there's more there than you first realised.

The funny thing is, you know, that many of the 'strange' ideas I am putting forward here are not really mine at all. They're not even new. In fact, a substantial portion of the six and a half billion people of the world's population, perhaps even a majority, already acknowledges them. A religious text from as far back as history goes mention phenomena akin to the spirit or soul, albeit under a variety of different names. Many people believe that they have one. However, tell these same people that you have seen a ghost and they would probably laugh at you. We are nothing if not a species of contradiction.

Similarly, the Bible, for example, says that man was created in the image of God. Nobody can really decide what that means, even in the higher reaches of whatever church you prefer. But it would make a lot of sense combined with the idea that our so-called 'junk' DNA contains a vast amount of unexplained and un-tapped knowledge and abilities. What if God, or an entity we have come to know as God, really did create us in his own image, but with a substantial portion of our potential deactivated, perhaps to prevent us from wreaking havoc on the universe?

Again, I am not saying this is the truth, only that it would make sense. It seems to me that as science progresses, more and more it appears to validate old ideas and concepts from religious texts, the origins of which are unclear. I have never been much of a religious man, despite many years ago winning the fourth year prize for religious instruction, but I have read my Bible and my Koran, and it is striking how often they seem to predict things that people of those times couldn't possibly have known about.

Is this an endorsement of religion? Well, yes and no. There are for sure a lot of good things to say about those kinds of books and the positive messages they contain for people who care to actually read them rather than taking somebody else's word for it or else cherry-picking the parts they like and discarding those they don't without applying common sense, which surely renders the whole notion of faith pointless. If we all lived our lives according to the teachings of Jesus Christ, or a gentle interpretation of the Koran, the world would be a veritable utopia, and God would be proud of all that he surveys. Do we behave kindly to one another? We do not, or perhaps cannot live that way. Self-described God-fearing people turn out to be the meanest of the mean, whilst true goodness can be found in places one might least expect. It makes no sense. So I suppose the real lesson to take from this is that religion can tell us a lot about ourselves, but it cannot make us what we are not. Or, not yet, at least.

***

Many religious texts, including the Koran and the Bible, contain some variation on an end-of-days scenario when a select group will be granted some great glory and will finally be allowed to understand what this world is all about. A striking notion, no doubt, but what does it mean? Is there a creator lurking in the wings, waiting for the story of mankind to play out before he collects the battle-scarred souls of the righteous? Could be. Maybe it just means that someday a small section of humanity will evolve to a point where they alone are able to realise the potential of their full genetic code, and therefore exercise superiority over all other things.

What's more, these same texts suggest that such a process might involve an element of selection. If we do have a creator, an architect, perhaps they will be looking only for the well-nurtured souls that dwell in the light as opposed to the dark, when the time finally comes to collect. The notion of good and evil is deeply ingrained in the human psyche, and many scientific studies have demonstrated that we have an innate inclination to and understanding of morality. Therefore surely our choices are singularly our own responsibility. If 'bad' people have no excuse for their wrongdoings, it stands to reason that they and their children may at some point have to answer for their poor choices, and the detrimental effect that they have had upon the souls in their possession.

Have you made a positive contribution to the world? The answer may have more resting on it than you imagined.

We can read these little hints and possibilities all kinds of different ways. But the point is, for our immediate purposes at least, to simply think about them. Turn them over in our minds, mix and match different ideas, events, experiences to find which potentially fit together and then see what our instincts tell us about them. Unashamedly I will repeat again "I have seen the same ghost, many times over several decades." This is the very first part of the puzzle for me, which I acknowledge.

I strongly believe that the future of mankind rests in the hands of the innovators, and freethinkers, along with the dreamers, which each and every one of us can be if we so wish. Why? Because history proves that it has been ever thus.

I believe that man is far more than we yet realise, and that only by opening our eyes and believing in ourselves, can our potential, truly be realised. That we will someday collectively look back on the times in which we now live, and wonder why on earth we didn't reach higher, move faster, and face headlong up to the challenge of discovery, unencumbered by the shackles of past mistakes.

We must not be afraid to be bold, and creative, and unafraid of the mocking jeers of closed minds and mean mouths.

I believe that we are all of us special and ought to be open to change for the better and that one day, perhaps even one day soon, we will truly understand why, we are not quite there yet, and in the meantime, there is much work to be done. Whilst mindful of, we need to look past the things we perceive as important; our homes, cars, jobs, bills, whatever 'top story' is being peddled by the newsreaders on any particular day. None of it is important in the great scheme of things. In realistic terms, human beings will be extinct at some point, like all of the species of animals that came before us and all those that will come after. But even if the heavens fell right now and all life on Earth was snuffed out like a candle, what I have seen and experienced leads me to believe that there would still be something left clinging to the fabric of our reality that contained the essence of our best efforts. This is what makes us special.

Or maybe I'm wrong, and we really are 'meat on a stick'.